Greville G. Corbett (Ed.)
The Expression of Gender

The Expression of Cognitive Categories

Editors
Wolfgang Klein
Stephen Levinson

Volume 6

The Expression of Gender

Edited by
Greville G. Corbett

ISBN: 978-3-11-035414-0
e-ISBN: 978-3-11-030733-7

Library of Congress Cataloging-in-Publication Data
A CIP catalog record for this book has been applied for at the Library of Congress.

Bibliographic information published by the Deutsche Nationalbibliothek
The Deutsche Nationalbibliothek lists this publication in the Deutsche Nationalbibliografie;
detailed bibliographic data are available on the Internet at http://dnb.dnb.de.

© 2015 Walter de Gruyter GmbH, Berlin/Munich/Boston
Cover design: Frank Benno Junghanns, Berlin
Typesetting: PTP-Berlin Protago-T$_E$X-Production GmbH, Berlin
Printing: CPI books GmbH, Leck
♾ Printed on acid-free paper
Printed in Germany

www.degruyter.com

Contents

Greville G. Corbett
Introduction —— 1

Sally McConnell-Ginet
Gender and its relation to sex: The myth of 'natural' gender —— 3

Michael Dunn
Gender determined dialect variation —— 39

Peter Hegarty
Ladies and gentlemen: Word order and gender in English —— 69

Greville G. Corbett
Gender typology —— 87

Marianne Mithun
Gender and culture —— 131

Niels O. Schiller
Psycholinguistic approaches to the investigation of grammatical gender —— 161

Mulugeta T. Tsegaye, Maarten Mous and Niels O. Schiller
Plural as a value of Cushitic gender: Evidence from gender congruency effect experiments in Konso (Cushitic) —— 191

Author index —— 215
Language index —— 219
Subject index —— 221

Greville G. Corbett
Introduction

Gender is an endlessly fascinating category. It has obvious links to the real world, first in the connection between many grammatical gender systems and biological sex, and second in other types of categorization such as size, which underpin particular gender systems and also have external correlates. While in some languages the way in which gender is assigned to nouns is semantically transparent, for example, in Dravidian languages such as Tamil, others are rather opaque: though their systems still have a semantic core, there is much more to be said about gender in familiar languages like French or German. Of course, there are other grammatical categories with links to the real world, but compared with these gender is surprising in that it appears to be an "optional extra". That is, many of the world's languages have gender, but many (probably somewhat over half) do not. The differences continue: in some languages gender is a relatively superficial matter, while in others it is central, being found through the noun phrase and on the verb by agreement, and interacting in morphology with other features, typically number, case and person. Thus the description of some languages requires constant detailed reference to gender, and for others it is absent.

Given its links to the real world, gender is a feature that speakers are partly aware of. There is discussion of the appropriate use of gendered pronouns; learners comment on the difficulty of acquiring gender in some languages; the gender of borrowings may arouse the curiosity of first language speakers. But gender is like an iceberg since most of its interest is not apparent to normal speakers.

The authors of the volume take seven complementary perspectives on gender. Sally McConnell-Ginet tackles one of the most approachable and yet most difficult issues: 'Gender and its relation to sex: The myth of "natural" gender', and asks what meaning can be attached to gender. It also seems evident that in some respects women and men speak differently. In some languages, such as Chukchi, the differences are dramatic, as documented and analysed by Michael Dunn in his chapter 'Gender determined dialect variation'. In interesting contrast, Peter Hegarty homes in on the way in which gender affects an apparently small linguistic choice, the order of conjoined noun phrases, in his chapter 'Ladies and gentlemen: word order and gender in English'. The core linguistic types of variation between gender systems are laid out in 'Typology of gender' by Greville G. Corbett. One way of understanding complex systems is to examine their behaviour over time. This is the approach of Marianne Mithun in 'Gender and culture', where she examines subtle gender distinctions and the ways they came about within the Iroquoian family, particularly in Mohawk. The variety found in gender has naturally attracted psycholinguists, and Niels Schiller reviews this field and presents recent research findings in 'Psycholinguistic approaches to the investigation of grammatical gender'. Finally these psycholinguistic techniques are applied to Konso, a language with a challenging gender/number system in 'Plural as value of Cushitic gender: Evidence from gender congruency effect experiments in Konso (Cushitic)' by Mulugeta Tarekegne Tsegaye, Maarten Mous and Niels Schiller.

Some of the most exciting gender systems are found in languages whose survival is uncertain; the proceeds from this volume are therefore going to the Foundation for Endangered Languages.

We thank the Max Planck Institute for Psycholinguistics (Nijmegen) for funding and hosting a workshop on gender, which made it possible for authors to discuss each other's presentations and so to shape the different contributions into a single volume, as well as to gain from the helpful comments of the audience. We are also grateful to Lisa Mack and Penny Everson for their help in preparing the typescript and to Wolfgang Konwitschny for seeing the volume through to publication.

Sally McConnell-Ginet
Gender and its relation to sex: The myth of 'natural' gender

1 'Grammatical' vs 'natural' gender systems: First pass

In McConnell-Ginet ([1988], 2011), I included the following:

> The word *gender* in the title of this chapter refers to the complex of social, cultural, and psychological phenomena attached to sex, a usage common in the behavioral and social sciences. The word *gender* also, however, has a well-established technical sense in linguistic discussions. Gender in this technical sense is a grammatically significant classification of nouns that has implications for various agreement phenomena.

The title of the present chapter also includes the word *gender*: my thesis is that something like sociocultural gender as delineated in the first sentence of the extract above mediates connections between sex and pronoun choice in English (often said to be based on 'natural' gender, discussed below) and also, though less straightforwardly, between sex and the technical notion of 'grammatical' gender in linguistics.

The word *sex* includes the division of humans and many other animals into female and male classes, based on reproductive potential; it also includes matters of sexuality, not just sexual identity but also sexual desire and activity. Sociocultural gender is not a matter of the sexual division of people into female and male as such, what people typically mean by 'natural' gender, but of the significance attached to that division, the institutions and ideologies, the prescribed and claimed identities, and the array of social practices that sustain those institutions, ideologies, and identities. What we have in English, I argue, is not a 'natural' gender system but what Terttu Nevalainen and Helena Raumolin-Brunberg (1994) call a 'notional' gender system: concepts and ideas about biological sex matter at least as much as sex itself to the choice of English third-person pronouns. (In principle there could be 'notional' gender systems involving first- or second-person pronouns – Japanese might illustrate – or even agreement beyond pronouns, but this chapter just contrasts the English notional gender system with grammatical gender systems in earlier stages of English and in various Indo-European languages.)

As a technical linguistic notion, gender is about agreement. Nouns are assigned to classes such that which class a noun belongs to determines or 'controls' formal properties of other expressions linked to the phrase it heads, what Corbett 1991 calls 'agreement targets'. Agreement targets include articles and attributive adjectives, often also adjectival and verbal expressions predicated of that phrase, numerals, and relative pronouns and, importantly for my purposes, anaphoric pronouns for which a phrase headed by the noun in question serves as antecedent. The technical issue of most direct relevance to this chapter involves what Corbett (this volume) dubs the assignment problem.

How nouns get assigned a gender is, as Corbett's chapter documents in detail, a very complex matter, and it varies considerably cross-linguistically. For some languages, the main principles for assignment are formal; for others, they are semantic in the sense of involving features of a noun's referents; for many, both semantic and formal features play a role in assignment. Not surprisingly, assignment principles may shift over time, and at any given time there may be some lexical items whose gender cannot be determined by the general principles then operative in the language more broadly (and there may be variation in gender assignment). Mithun's illuminating discussion in this volume of gender in Iroquoian languages, especially Mohawk, shows this very clearly. Nonlinguists do not always realize that gender semantic assignment principles need not connect to sex at all: animacy, shape, and many other features figure in grammatical gender systems crosslinguistically. Still, as Corbett's chapter points out, sex is far and away the most common feature to figure semantically in gender assignment.

What is of interest in this chapter are languages where sex and, crucially, ideas about it play some sort of role in either a full-blown grammatical gender system such as is found in many Indo-European languages (e.g., German, French, Russian, Hindi) or in a limited system like that of English where only pronouns show gender agreement. In languages with grammatical gender linked to sex, it is often the case that inanimates for which sex is irrelevant can be assigned to the same gender classes as sexed humans (or, for that matter, that nouns designating sexed humans can on occasion be assigned to the 'wrong' gender class). For non-native speakers acquiring such languages, such mismatches can seem very odd. Mark Twain's 1880 essay "The Awful German Language" seizes on such clashes to underscore the difficulties many speakers of languages like English have in learning a grammatical gender language like German, where they are tempted to assimilate the German feminine gendered pronoun *sie* (and other marks of feminine gender agreement) to something like what English *she* conveys, masculine *er* to *he*, and inanimate *es* to *it*. Native speakers of German, in spite of what Twain suggests, are not thinking of the referents of 'wife' (*das Weib*) or 'girl' (*das Mädchen*), both neuter gender nouns with female referents, as unsexed beings.

Seeming to make the connection of grammatical gender to sex even looser, there are also many cases where, e.g., one language assigns feminine gender to a word designating referents that are designated by masculine gender words in another language. Why, asks many a naive language learner, do nouns designating 'table' and 'moon' get assigned feminine gender in French (*la table, la lune*) and masculine in German (*der Tisch, der Mond*)? We can even find words designating the same referent that are assigned different genders in a single language. In German 'head' (in the sense of the thing on the top of the neck where we find eyes, nose, ears, and mouth) these days is usually *der Kopf* (masculine) but was earlier and poetically *das Haupt* (neuter), still used in some contexts.

Such cases establish clearly a strong conventional, 'non-natural', component to gender class assignment. (In some cases, as Corbett suggests in his chapter in this volume, there are formal principles at work.) In contrast, English is said to be a language with 'natural' gender. What this is supposed to mean is that sex of a noun's referent is what determines gender agreement – in English, amounting just to the form of a referentially linked pronoun. A little reflection shows some of the problems here. What about epicene nouns, which refer to humans of either sex? When, for example, we speak of a specific child (say, *Lee's youngest child*), the pronoun chosen will depend on the gender ascribed to its referent. But if we talk about *any child* and have a linked pronoun, the gender of that pronoun cannot be determined on the 'natural' basis of sex, given that children are sometimes female, sometimes male. In this case, the 'rules' of prescriptive grammar say to use *he*, but other choices, discussed later, are common. Even if prescriptive rules always held sway, thus fully conventionalizing the decision in cases where sex is for some reason not determinate, more is going on than 'natural' agreement with biological sex. English has gendered pronouns used in other contexts where the antecedent either does not provide a definite referent and allows for either sex or where referents provided are of mixed sex or not sex-differentiable. As we will see later, these 'indeterminate' cases are just immediately obvious instances of the non-naturalness of gender in English. English pronoun selection is not a matter of 'natural' but, as I have already indicated, 'notional' gender.

What I will also argue is that even conventionalized grammatical gender systems often connect to sex in non-arbitrary but non-natural ways, drawing on notional gender though doing so in different ways than languages like English. Research by psychologist Lera Boroditsky and her colleagues (e.g., Boroditsky, Schmidt, and Phillips 2003) strongly suggests that speakers do treat grammatical gender classifications even of nouns outside the conceptual core (e.g., those designating inanimates in Indo-European languages) as notionally relevant. Even though French speakers don't think of moons or tables as female beings and German speakers don't take them to be male beings, associating feminine and masculine characteristics with feminine and masculine gendered nouns does occur more than chance would predict. The fascinating phenomenon of feminine (and, to a lesser extent, masculine) pronouns for inanimates in English gives considerable support for treating gender in contemporary English as 'notional' rather than 'natural', but I can only point to it in this chapter; Curzan (2003) has an excellent discussion of historical data, and Curzan (1999) is also relevant.

My focus will be on how gender systems notionally connected to sex classifications deal with human referents, the 'home turf' of gender for Indo-European languages and the primary arena in which contemporary English pronoun usage is said to depend on 'natural' gender. Sex is, of course, an important classificatory principle in many languages. My thesis, however, is that it seldom stands alone. So-called 'natural' gender almost always gives way to 'notional' gender, both in languages like English where it dominates the show, and in grammatical gender languages, where it is also plays a role, more limited (and varying across languages) but important.

As I will argue below, grammatical gender systems involve matters of sex and sociocultural gender more than is sometimes thought. My evidence comes from work others have done involving a variety of languages with grammatical gender. From surveying some of the relevant recent research, I conclude that even for languages with conventionalized grammatical gender, ideas about sex and sexuality can interact in somewhat surprising ways with the gender system. Indeed, I suspect that most grammatical gender systems in which sex plays some role have at least an attenuated 'notional' (or 'natural') gender system as a part. This point was essentially made for English in Moore 1921, quoted in Baron 1971: "natural [notional] gender did not *replace* grammatical gender in Middle English but survived it."

My own research, especially McConnell-Ginet ([1979], 2011), shows that gender in English, while not 'grammatical' in the fullest sense because pronouns are the only agreement targets, is not really 'natural' either. English-like languages have what I now call notional gender systems: pronominal usage cannot be understood without considering sociocultural gender and the ideas about sex and sexuality current at a given time. And it is such gender 'notions' that can be embedded in and affect agreement phenomena, especially but not only pronouns, even in languages where grammatical gender predominates.

Notional gender systems like that in English have long been called 'natural' because linguistic form seems to link to sex quite directly: there's no need to learn what can look from the outside like arbitrary nominal classes in order to choose the correct pronoun. The choice of an English pronoun is apparently determined by the sex that the speaker attributes to the referent of its nominal antecedent or of the individual designated deictically (cases where something like a demonstration establishes reference rather than an antecedent noun phrase). If someone is referred to using words like *woman, wife, girl,* or *daughter,* words that semantically indicate femaleness of those so denoted, then a pronoun for subsequent reference to the same individual is standardly the feminine *she*. Similarly, *man, husband, boy,* or *son* are semantically male and can head antecedent nominals for the masculine *he* whereas *turnip, fish scale, shoe,* and *stapler*, none of which designate sexed or even animate referents, all select the neuter pronoun *it*, which designates nonsexed referents, including all inanimates.

Of course, what I have just said 'usually' holds. Even my introductory linguistics texts admitted that there were some exceptions in English to this 'natural' arrangement in which sex and gender supposedly coincide. For example, inanimates like boats and cars, which have no sex, are (still) often referred to with feminine pronouns, and there are also cases in informal speech where inanimates are referred to using masculine pronouns. And the choice of pronouns with nonhuman animals is quite a mixed bag: some, e.g., always use masculine forms for dogs and feminine for cats, a practice that pet-owners invested in their female dogs or male cats often deplore. Although such practices do indeed shed some light on gender ideologies, they lie outside the scope of this chapter. Actual English pronominal usage even just for human referents is both more interesting and complex than is evident from the usual stories told of its supposedly 'natural' gender system.

We have often felt comfortable calling gender in English 'natural' (and sometimes using that term also for certain phenomena in languages whose gender systems are primarily grammatical) because choice of English gendered pronouns is seldom surprising in light of familiar cultural ideas about sex and sexuality. Gender ideologies have overwhelmingly viewed gender beliefs and arrangements as 'natural', as dictated by biological imperatives, generally not realizing that sociocultural gender is far from static and unchanging but varies historically and crossculturally. Curzan (2003, 30) agrees that *notional gender*

> may better capture the psychological and social aspects of gender assignment in the language. It is possible, however, and I think pragmatically preferable to retain the description *natural gender* with the understanding that its definition rests not purely on biological sex but instead on social concepts of sex and gender [i.e., on sociocultural gender]. ... [G]iven the clear correlation between linguistic and social gender, and the growing understanding of what the latter involves, the description *natural gender* could *naturally* [italic added] come to encompass and appropriately refer to both biological sex and the social constructions engendered by it.

> Corbett (1991: 32) ... notes that semantic gender categories reflect the world view of speakers ... it is possible to predict variation to some extent given knowledge of extralinguistic factors. Instances of gendered anaphoric pronouns that cross biological lines are not exceptions to an underlying "real" or "unmarked" system of natural gender; they are part of a natural gender system which is natural *because* [italic in original] it corresponds to speakers' ideas about and constructions of gender in the world about which they speak.

What Curzan has done here is provide an excellent account of why calling such gender systems natural has persisted even among those who know well that biological sex is by no means the only factor in pronominal choice. But I fear that there is still far less understanding of sociocultural gender than is needed, particularly of its contingent and historical character. Perhaps most important, *natural* is still too readily understood as encoded in our genetic make-up, the inevitable outcome of human biology; linguists may better understand sociocultural gender than they once did, but even among that group the term *natural* can mislead. For linguists, a shift to 'notional' gender positions us better not only for understanding languages like English in the early 21st century but also for exploring changes not only in English-like languages but also in those with grammatical gender systems.

2 Grammatical gender

2.1 Referential pressures and (dis)agreement

Many (perhaps most) words apparently referring semantically to female humans are assigned to a single gender class (called feminine in Indo-European languages) and many (perhaps most) referring semantically to male humans are assigned to a different single gender class (called masculine in Indo-European languages). Furthermore, languages generally use the same personal pronouns for anaphora (i.e., where there is an antecedent for the pronoun) and for designating an individual indicated deictically or through a proper name (which might or might not be gender-marked).

Specifically demonstrative pronouns do occur in a number of languages but in English their use to refer to human beings is limited to identificational contexts such as *who is that*? or *this is my sister* but not **this is married to Lee* or **I haven't been introduced to that*. Even in languages where demonstrative pronouns can readily be used for human referents, anaphoric pronouns can, so far as I know, also be used deictically, and they are often a primary resource for deictic reference. Not surprisingly, then, in grammatical gender languages deictic references to human beings to whom the speaker attributes female sex typically use feminine pronouns, whereas masculine pronouns are standardly used for deictic references to human beings to whom the speaker attributes male sex. I qualify this claim because of the expressive uses discussed below, but what the claim amounts to is that so far as deictic pronouns go, grammatical gender languages often look very English-like, which is to say that sociocultural gender is what is relevant for pronominal form. Ivan Sag (pc) points out that this fits well with the analysis of agreement that he and Carl Pollard have developed (see Pollard and Sag 1994, chapter 2), which takes agreement in gender (as well as person and number) to arise from co-indexing. English, they propose, has a pragmatic constraint that *she* can only be anchored by an entity presented as female, *he* by an entity presented as male, *it* by an entity presented as inanimate (or at least as not sex-differentiable).

Notice that deictic pronominal references to inanimates in languages like French that have only masculine and feminine gender must choose a gendered pronoun without any direct linguistic controller. How this happens might seem mysterious, but Corbett 1991 plausibly hypothesizes that what Rosch 1978 calls a basic level expression comes into play and its gender is what determines the pronoun chosen. Pollard and Sag 1994 agree that an expression is involved but note that there may not always be a single 'basic level' expression to do the job. They cite (p. 78) Mark Johnson's 1984 unpublished discussion of grammatical gender and pronoun reference, which notes cases where alternative forms might be available. Johnson observes that certain small structures could be designated in German by either *das Haus* 'the house', neuter, or *die Hütte* 'the hut', feminine, the latter suggesting something small and rundown. Interestingly, the same suggestion could be conveyed by using the feminine deictic pronoun *sie* to refer to the structure rather than the neuter *es*. The pragmatic constraint operative in grammatical gender languages, according to Pollard and Sag, is that an entity can 'anchor' a pronoun's index only if the features of the index, which include gender, match those of some common noun "that effectively classifies that entity at *a level of granularity appropriate to the context*" (78, italics added), which allows for competing expressions in some settings.

Deictic usage is important because when there is some kind of conflict in grammatical gender languages between gender of a controlling noun and attributed sex of the individual designated by a target pronoun, the pronominal form appropriate for target sex is often chosen, and this is more frequent the greater the distance of the pronoun from its controller. Corbett 1991 speaks of 'hybrid nouns', those that permit variable gender agreement where that variability is sensitive to the kind of target involved. He posits an agreement hierarchy in which attributive modifiers (in a very 'close' syntactic relation to the controller) outrank predicates, which in turn outrank relative pronouns, with personal pronouns least likely to agree with the gender of the controller. So if someone speaks of the masculine *le professeur* and is referring to Julia Kristeva, a distinguished woman, then subsequent pronominal references are highly likely to use *elle* rather than the *il* that my French teacher in high school insisted upon. There seems to be considerable room for referential leakage from deictic practice, leading to what looks like gender disagreement between antecedent and anaphoric pronoun when attributed sex of the referent does not match grammatical gender of the supposedly controlling antecedent. Such gender disagreement under deictic pressures is reported for a wide range of grammatical gender languages (including, as documented in Curzan 2003, Old English). Details vary significantly, however. Formal agreement pressures appear much stronger in some languages than others (in, e.g., Czech, Polish, and Greek as compared to German and French, according to descriptions of these languages in Hellinger and Bussmann 2003). (Such differences may be linked to the same kind of grammatical differences that affect the gender congruency effects in language processing that Schiller reports in this volume.) Yet disagreement, although probably more common in informal language usage than in 'careful' writing, is always lurking as potentiality, presumably because deictic practices strengthen the salience of attributed referent sex in pronominal selection.

To bring home my point that it is sociocultural or notional gender that is at stake in gender (dis)agreement, let's consider again the German *Das Mädchen* 'girl', another 'hybrid noun' in Corbett's terminology, one that requires (at least in formal Standard German) neuter agreement for attributives and relative pronouns but allows feminine personal pronouns (providing evidence for the agreement hierarchy). The -*chen* suffix is a diminutive, and Corbett notes that diminutives are often assigned to neuter rather than feminine or masculine genders, a phenomenon related to the frequent assignment in IndoEuropean languages of the young of 'sex-differentiable' categories to neuter gender. What struck me particularly in Corbett's discussion of *Mädchen* is his mention of a suggestion from semanticist Manfred Krifka that the older a girl, the more likely the feminine personal pronoun *sie* will be used (conversely, the younger the more likely she will be referred to using the neuter *es*). Now age does not make someone who is straightforwardly a biological female on all counts (genetic or chromosomal, hormonal, genital) any more a female. As a girl matures and moves towards menarche and potential fertility, however, the sociocultural significance of her female sex certainly does increase. Sex as such is not what matters here but sociocultural gender considerations are coming into play in (variably) conditioning the form of the personal pronoun. Grammatical gender is not, of course, irrelevant. It might well be that it is more likely that someone will be referred to using *es* if *Mädchen* antecedes the personal pronoun than if that same individual is referred to deictically (by the same speaker in a similar context) – i.e., with no anteceding nominal. Nonetheless, sociocultural gender often puts pressures on grammatical gender systems, with the precise details dependent on many specific linguistic and other factors but with pronominal reference a particularly vulnerable point, probably in large measure because of deictic usage. It is tempting to speculate that a notional pronominal gender system lies embedded in any grammatical gender system, its impact and pervasiveness depending at any given time both on language structure and history (long established conventions take on lives of their own) and on language and gender ideologies.

2.2 Feminist-inspired change in languages with grammatical gender

In languages with feminine and masculine grammatical genders, nouns denoting male humans exclusively are overwhelmingly masculine gender, and nouns denoting female humans exclusively are overwhelmingly feminine gender. Epicene nouns, those which can readily denote humans of either sex, can often be assigned to either grammatical gender class (assignment may depend on phonological factors in such cases). So long as there is a sharp sexual division of labor, however, the range of genuinely epicene nouns is limited, and occupational terminology and social titles will be gendered. In such circumstances, women and men occupy very different positions and do very different things so that speakers are likely to find the gender assignment easy, 'natural' in some sense; of course, it's *le maçon* 'mason' and *le médecin* 'doctor' in the masculine and *la dentellière* 'lace maker' and *la sage-femme* 'midwife' since it is men who are masons and doctors, women who make lace and practice midwifery. Yet when gender arrangements are changing, especially when women are moving into positions and jobs once reserved for men (movement in the other direction, though it does happen occasionally, is less common and typically less prestigious), grammatical gender often strains at the seams, perhaps in part because of deictically driven disagreement.

Burr 2003 offers a very interesting account of linguistic politics in France. In France the major thrust in attempted language reform has been the feminization strategy that tries to make women visible as they enter into public life in positions previously reserved exclusively for men. It was in 1997 that six of the eight woman nominated by the new prime minister, Lionel Jospin, put forth a circular demanding that they be addressed as *Madame la Ministre* and had stationery drawn up with feminine job titles and signs changed on their office doors to feminine forms. And, importantly, Jospin made sure that indeed feminized designators would be used for top women in his government, issuing a circular to that effect in early 1998 and drawing strong condemnation from the *Académie Française* and others rushing to defend the French language from this latest assault.

The start of the Jospin government was by no means the first time that the topic of making women linguistically more visible was raised in France but this particular moment had far more effect than earlier efforts. Burr explains (120)

> [C]hange could only come from the very top of the hierarchy. ... [R]eluctance to use feminine denominations has always been strongest with respect to high-level professions, functions, grades and titles traditionally reserved for men, and women who had themselves reached the top of the hierarchy were among the fiercest opponents of this use. ... [Nothing could] effect a real change so long as this hostile attitude towards feminisation prevailed among almost all high-level women.

Indeed a terminological commission had been formed in 1984 by Yvette Roudy, who was charged with developing policies to promote women's rights. That group, which included a number of linguists, proposed femininizing via allowing hitherto masculine forms optionally to take feminine agreement – i.e., making previously masculine forms double-gender (allowing, e.g., *la professeur* alongside *le professeur*) – and also in some cases through creating new feminine nouns (*la maçonne* alongside *le maçon*). With new feminine forms there were also new feminine plurals (e.g., *les maçonnes* in addition to *les maçons*) whereas the double gender strategy resulted in a single plural form (e.g., *les professeurs*). The commission also proposed masculine forms to partner with feminines as in *sage-homme* for any male midwives who might present themselves. The rules published in 1986, however, dealt only with feminization, prescribing its use in official documents and providing rules for producing feminine forms, specifying the double gender strategy with forms ending in *e muet* 'silent e' and some others. There are potential hazards even with specific rules. In some cases existing feminine forms paired with masculine agentives are, as Connors 1971 had noted earlier, already in service for other purposes. Adriaen and King 1991 (32) offer examples like these: *un trompette* 'a male trumpet player' vs *une trompette* 'a female trumpet player' or 'a trumpet' and *un manoeuvre* 'male laborer' vs *une manoeuvre* 'female laborer' or 'a maneuver'.

These rules were slightly modified in 1999 in guidelines from the *Institut National de la Langue Française*. At the same time, the 1999 document took account of developments in Canada (see King 1991), Switzerland, and Belgium, offering more lexical options than the 1986 document and also showing more appreciation of why such issues might matter, something that did not happen during the discussion of the 1980s. The first female prime minister of France, Edith Cresson, was virtually always referred to using masculine gender forms, *le premier minister* 'prime minister' or *le chef du gouvernement* 'head of government'. It's probably no accident that focus on this issue required some male leadership as well as female: the first women in high-level positions have special pressures to show that they are doing exactly the same job (or perhaps even better) as their male predecessors and having a different job title might seem to suggest otherwise. We'll return to this potential pitfall of feminization in our later discussion of English, but it is important to acknowledge that the strategy has apparently enjoyed some success not only in France but also in a number of other countries where grammatical gender languages are used.

Of course, actual usage continues to be very mixed and generally is guided by social and political rather than linguistic gender ideologies. Burr concludes (132):

> That the way women are addressed and talked about does matter in French society can be seen by the fact that every time the question of feminine personal nouns arises there is loud protest from [some/many] men, from patriarchal institutions like the French Academy, and from women who either accept the structures and values men have created or who are afraid of losing their face, being ridiculed or attacked. ... [T]he specific linguistic means ... are ... secondary in nature in comparison with the fundamental question of the social function of change.

Not surprisingly, when reference might be to sexually mixed groups or to individuals of unknown sex or generic and not really to individuals at all, the various groups put in charge of directing linguistic change in French in pursuit of social gender equity have all opted for masculine gender. Burr comments that even many feminists perceive plural masculine forms as generic, not really masculine. In contrast in some other countries using languages with grammatical gender (including other French-speaking countries), issues of masculine generics and of principles dictating masculine plurals for groups of mixed or indefinite sex have received considerable public discussion. I will discuss the issues of the supposed 'unmarkedness' of masculine gender only when I turn to English, where the push has generally been for neutralization rather than for the feminization of occupational terminology and other personal nouns that has predominated feminist-inspired interventions in European languages with grammatical gender.

2.3 Expressive uses of grammatical gender: Beyond sex

Deixis is not relevant only for choice of third-person pronominals. A language can have sex-invariant first- and second-person pronouns but show feminine or masculine agreement on predicates depending on whether the speaker or addressee is being ascribed feminine or masculine gender. In English and other languages where gender is a matter of third-person singular pronominal form (and of some semantically feminine or masculine nominals), saying something about the speaker or the addressee need carry no gender messages. In contrast, the French speaker uttering *je suis heureuse* 'I'm happy' is self-attributing feminine gender whereas one uttering *je suis heureux* 'I'm happy' self-attributes masculine gender. And second-person forms that predicate adjectives of the subject (whether expressed explicitly or, as in imperatives, evoked implicitly) take gendered forms that depend in the most straightforward cases on the sex attributed to the addressee. What matters for our present purposes is that languages with sex-linked grammatical gender provide rich resources for challenging gender binaries and for policing gender boundaries not only in speaking of third person individuals but also in speaking of the self or of an addressee.

2.3.1 Gendering minority identities in French literature

Anna Livia (2001) focuses on literary uses of linguistic gender and includes a chapter devoted to what she calls 'liminal identity'. There she includes a detailed account of the exploitation of the French gender system in *Appelez-moi Gina*, the autobiography of Dr. Georgine Noël, born Georges in Belgium and assigned male sex at birth and reared as a boy but from a young age identifying as female and finally at age 39 undergoing sex reassignment surgery. Of particular interest are the switches in gender Noël uses in speaking of the self, which proceed far less straightforwardly than might be thought. As Livia puts it (168),

> Noël uses the binary opposition of the French linguistic gender system throughout her autobiography to express or underscore many of her changes of mood, attitude, and identification, an expressivity that goes far beyond the simple polar opposites of "binary thinking." *Appelez-moi Gina* demonstrates how a structural binary may be subverted into expressing more than one simple opposition.

Importantly, her initial announcement of her birth evades gender by using the passé simple (*je naquis*), which though not very colloquial does not mark gender, rather than the more frequent passé composé (*je suis né*, m, or *je suis née*, f). She apparently wants to resist, at least in this narrative, sex assignment of that baby from whom she has become an adult. Before beginning a basically chronological narrative of her life, Noël does speak, using conditional verb forms, of what might have been had she undergone sex reassignment surgery at age 15 (Livia 2001, 169).

(1)   Heureuse d'être femme et épouse, j'aurais aimé adopter les enfants.
        Happy to be a woman and a wife, I would have liked to adopt children.

This is a hypothetical femininity, but in recounting her early childhood she uses masculine forms (170–171, italic added).

(2) a. J'étais un enfant *souffreteux*.
        I was a *sickly*$_m$ child.

    b. J'étais *bon* élève.
        I was a *good*$_m$ pupil.

    c. *Engoncé* dans mon costume trois pièces
        Stuffed$_m$ into my three-piece suit

Again and again she speaks of herself as *seul* 'alone$_m$', noting how out-of-place she felt with male classmates, but then she says

(3) La fille cherchait à naître *isolée* au milieu de tant de garçons
     The girl was struggling to be born, *isolated*$_f$ among so many boys

It is only after she decides to keep a diary in code, not trusting her parents, that her account includes recurrent uses of first person feminine without the protection of the conditional form. Particularly telling is her account of following the male friend Edgard for whom she saw her affection as a heterosexual attraction:

(4) Je suis *revenue* dans la cour avec Edgard.
     I came *back*$_f$ into the playground with Edgard.

She tells of her parents' discovery of her diary and their speaking of her in the masculine while she listens from the next room, speaking of herself in the feminine. But in an expression of disgust at her body she resumes the masculine

(5) *Sûr* que ce n' était pas à moi ce machin-là
     Sure$_m$ that it wasn't mine that thinggummy-jig there

Yet when she learns of the possible availability of surgery and hormone treatment that would make her body conform to her self-perception she returns to feminine self-description, punctuated with occasional masculine renderings of frustration at her actual constrained situation, too young and too poor to embark on medical sex reassignment. Eventually she leaves home, going first to medical school and then to Africa. Although she wears women's clothes only in the privacy of her own quarters, her self-descriptions are consistently in feminine form. The one striking exception, Livia notes, occurs when Noël is speaking disparagingly of the African men being treated for AIDS after having in a careless drunken moment shown a feminine side to European colleagues by appearing in women's clothes. Such slippage, Noël notes, must be avoided in the future.

(6) Né homme, je devais continuer à manifester ma supériorité sociale et sexuelle.
Born$_m$ a man, I had to continue to show my social and sexual superiority.

The masculine past participle *né* contrasts sharply with the nongendered inflected verb form *naquis* used when the birth is first mentioned. A final example comes from Noël's discussion of her surgery. Although Noël has identified as a woman for more than 25 years, masculine forms describe the self awaiting surgery (*reveillé* tôt le matin 'waked up$_m$ early in the morning') and feminine for the one recovering (*couchée* sur le dos 'lying$_f$ on my back'). Noël sums up that event (168):

(7) Avant j'étais un transsexuel; maintenant j'étais une femme.
Before I was a transsexual$_m$; now I was a woman.

Yet the use of gender as she narrates her past does not show such a sharp bifurcation; the preoperative self is presented sometimes as masculine but often as feminine, and gender choice expresses Noël's and the larger social views of sex class. That is, deictically anchored gender agreement in French does not just fall out from sex of an individual. For first-person discourse it may express the speaker's sometimes conflicted views of their own relation to sociocultural gender systems.

Noël's autobiography is just one sample of the works Livia examined in this general category of transsexuals. What is so striking is that transsexuals in speaking of themselves do not just switch gender marking at some point but there is considerable vacillation, especially in speaking of themselves prior to reassignment of sex. And the same thing holds when others speak of them in the third person but it is first-person discourse where grammatical gender languages offer gender-related possibilities and also constraints not present in languages like English, where gender-marking is a third-person phenomenon.

Livia also examined writings of and about people who challenge gender binaries in other ways, e.g., people who fall in the small group of those for whom assignment to either of the standard two sex categories is problematic, often called *intersexual* or *intersex*. Anne Fausto-Sterling (2000) estimates that for some 1.5 to 2% of babies, standard criteria give mixed results for sex assignment due to chromosomal configurations other than the standard XX or XY, hormonal conditions of various kinds, or non-canonical genitalia. In spite of the absence of definitive critieria, however, the practice has long been to assign female or male sex to the child, often also prescribing various medical procedures to try to make recalcitrant bodies conform to the binary imperative. As Fausto-Sterling (2000, 3) explains:

labeling someone a man or a woman is a social decision. We may use scientific knowledge to help us make the decision, but only our beliefs about gender – not science – can define our sex.

Not surprisingly, like transsexuals, some people forced in infancy into a sex class in order not to rock the binary boat do not fully identify with the sex to which they were assigned and may eventually embrace the other sex identification. Such was the case of Herculine Barbin, reared female but eventually embracing a male identity. Michel Foucault edited Barbin's memoirs and it is very interesting to read them with a focus on Barbin's use of gender to express shifting and conflicting gender identifications through childhood and adolescence.

Livia also considers writings of and about people who put themselves in the same sex category as that to which they were assigned at birth – as she puts it (185–186), their sexual anatomy and gender identification are not conflicted – yet for whom same-sex desire leads them to reject the 'compulsory heterosexuality' so firmly embedded in gender ideologies in many sociocultural and historical settings (though not all – see, e.g. Cameron and Kulick 2003, 22, of ancient Roman sexualities). She speaks of "cross-expressing" of gay men and lesbians, noting that "[a]t a time when ... gender distinctions in nouns and adjectives in French are tending to disappear, many gay men [sometimes] use feminine terms to address or refer to others in the community [sic], including their lovers and themselves" (188) and citing a 1994 sociolinguistic survey reported in Pastre 1997. Livia observes that "this linguistic strategy is intended not to reflect a feminine persona so much as to dissociate the speaker, addressee, and any third party described in the feminine from heterosexual alliance and to create a homosexual alliance ... [These men] are proudly designating themselves as well as the referents as traitors to heterosexual masculinity." (188)

Although Livia's analysis of the significance of particular gender choices may sometimes be open to debate, her larger point clearly holds. "Grammaticalized gender ... provides linguistic devices for expressing gender fluidity." (192) It is not that there is some particular gender identity that gender choices index but that gender choices offer a way to position oneself outside socioculturally enforced gender binarisms.

2.3.2 Gendering the *hijra* minority identity in Hindi

Another kind of liminal identity is involved in cases where alternatives to female and male identities are institutionalized. Kira Hall with various colleagues has written extensively on the hijras, an Indian group who early in life are treated as members of a third 'sex' – or at least as not either (fully) female or male. Some (by no means all) were born intersex, most of them are raised male, many but not all undergo voluntary penectomies on entry into the hijra community, and they adopt female attire and many other aspects of female appearance and behavior, including speech – at least to some extent and in some respects (e.g., there is frequent commentary on their 'masculine-sounding' voices and on the ways they use obscenities). Most hijras, however, describe themselves as *na mard na aurat* 'neither man nor woman'. Hijras typically live communally, often with a guru heading a family-like unit, and there are also much larger networks and a relatively recent political awareness and organization to assert rights such as being able to vote 'as women' or even hold political offices reserved for women. Hijras often go in groups to weddings or to households where a son has been born and dance and sing, sometimes on invitation but more often not. Families pay them to get hijra blessings bringing the promise of many sons and general prosperity (or, depending on perspective, to avoid the hijra curses, believed by many to bring infertility and other misfortunes). The word *hijra* literally means 'impotent', but the belief in hijra powers, though still widely held, is waning in many Indian communities. Many hijras do sex work (though some activists claim ascetic spirituality), some threaten curses or obscene behavior like showing their genitals to claim alms from passers-by. Most hijras lead economically precarious lives and experience considerable social ostracism from outsiders: they find support and affection within the hijra community.

There are hijras across India from many different language groups, but Hall and O'Donovan 1996 and Hall 2003 focus on the speech of several Hindi-speaking hijras in Banaras. In particular, Hall 2003, which I only read well after I had begun writing this chapter (having mistakenly assumed that it mostly repeated Hall and O'Donovan 1996), makes quite explicit a major point of this chapter: that 'natural' gender is a myth.

She sets out to

> challenge the very assumption implicit in the term "natural gender", i.e., that gender is a fixed phenomenon, rooted in biology and therefore free of ideological influences. What happens to a language's classification system in instances when the referent's gender can no longer be assumed as either male or female? And what might these instances of "unnatural gender" tell us about the relationship between gender in language and gender in society? (137–138)

I'm challenging the term 'natural gender' on other grounds as well, but Hall's formulations and her linguistic data are very relevant. Hall 2003 includes considerable background on the linguistic varieties grouped under the label 'Hindi' and some discussion of prior sociolinguistic work on Hindi so it is a rich resource for present purposes and helps expand conceptions of the varied ways 'notional gender' can affect usage in a language with grammatical gender.

Except for some pidginized or 'contact' forms of Hindi, all varieties of Hindi have feminine and masculine grammatical gender. Details of the gender system vary across varieties, however. In some dialects feminine gender is now reserved for nouns designating female referents and has been lost for inanimate nouns. And many varieties show far less extensive gender concord than might be found in 'standard' Hindi, where the system of concord extends even to postpositions (like the word translating English 'of', which is *ka* when modifying a singular masculine, *ke* with plural masculine, and *ki* for both singular and plural feminine). Furthermore standard Hindi requires not only gender concord between subject and predicate adjectives but also gender-marked endings for verb forms in all three persons and both singular and plural, requiring first-person utterances to identify the speaker as masculine or feminine and second-person to assign gender to the addressee. In Banaras, where Hall worked, however, the local Banarsi Bhojpuri variety, used alongside standard Hindi, makes much less use of gender concord, and extensive use of gender-marking is often heard as 'foreign' or 'over-educated'. And Hall reports a study with evidence that such attitudes toward the strict gender-marking of standard Hindi are most prevalent among poorly educated women.

Hijras in Banaras, however, generally come from elsewhere and are said to speak Hijra Boli, which is in many ways is like a lingua franca or pidginized variety. Where Hijra Boli differs strikingly from pidginized forms of Hindi reported for the streets of Bombay or Calcutta, where grammatical gender is essentially absent, and also from Banarsi Bhojpuri, where grammatical gender is on the decline, is in its strong emphasis on grammatical gender. Hijras adopt, e.g., the verbal morphology that marks their first-person statements (usually) feminine or (less often and for special effect) masculine. As Hall puts it

> [T]he variety of Hindi adopted by the hijras tends to overemphasize gender, using masculine and feminine gender in places where it normally would not appear ... or treating nouns that are masculine in standard Hindi as feminine and vice versa. To give one illuminating example: The word *hijra* is grammatically masculine in standard Hindi, but the hijras frequently treat the noun as feminine through verbal agreement when it acts as subject of the sentence. As I argue here, this usage reflects a kind of gender overcompensation or even hypercorrection. Upon entering the community, Benaras hijras work to distance themselves from masculine representations. ... The fact that the word *hijra* is grammatically masculine sometimes gets in the way of this communal distancing, so hijras will mark the noun as feminine as part of "doing gender." ... [G]rammatical gender is most often overemphasized, not underemphasized, in the hijras' construction of a "more feminine" self. (139–140)

Non-hijras in Benaras were often shocked in helping Hall transcribe tapes to hear a hijra use morphological resources to mark herself or another hijra as feminine for they thought of the hijras as male, even if imperfectly male, and these usages seemed highly 'unnatural'. Not surprisingly, gender marking in first person is part of what hijras count as *zanana boli* 'feminine language', something they adopt along with saris and female names. Of course eschewing *mardana boli* 'masculine language' is significantly harder than putting on a sari rather than a lungi (cloth wrap worn by men in northern India). The hijras themselves spoke of *zanana boli* as less direct and more intimate than *mardana boli*, which of course would involve much more than gender agreement in first-person utterances.

Those who have been within hijra communities for at least six months generally do indeed adopt the feminine gender markings for themselves and other hijras that are viewed as shocking by outsiders: more informative in many ways are instances of hijras marking themselves or other hijras as masculine. Least surprising, perhaps, are uses of masculine gender for reference to the pre-hijra self, which are not infrequent. And hijras occasionally live in non-hijra households where they find it more comfortable to present themselves 'as men', wearing male clothes and masculinizing their first-person utterances as they did in boyhood. There are also frequent masculine references to new initiates, those who are still acclimatizing themselves to feminine ways of doing things. But, perhaps more surprising, there are also sometimes masculine references to other hijras of whom the speaker disapproves, a distancing maneuver. Yet masculine reference can also be used positively – e.g., of a hijra guru much respected by the speaker or in self-reference in order to strengthen a statement. First-person masculine references also occur in angry speech. Hall suggests that hijras draw on cultural ideologies of femininity and masculinity at the same time they also challenge them, using grammatical gender as a powerful resource.

3 English and 'natural' gender

Anne Curzan (2003) opens her very interesting book on the history of gender in English with an account of the American Dialect Society's choice in 2000 of *she* as the word of the millennium then closing. *She*, first cited in 1154, represents, as Curzan puts it, "change at the very core of the English vocabulary." Phonological shifts had by then been conspiring to render inaudible the distinction once carried by the contrast between *heo* 'she' and *he* 'he' (inanimate *hit* 'it' stayed quite distinct). Somehow *she*, whose origins are still debated but probably lie in one of the Scandinavian languages that Anglo-Saxons heard around them, was pressed into service, and English was spared the gender-impoverished fate of those languages with a single pronoun for all animate beings.

It was none too soon, as the system of grammatical gender found in the Germanic ancestors of English and in Old English was under serious threat by the time *she* entered the language. Grammatical gender persisted for several centuries, however, in some regional varieties though Chaucer's English did not show evidence of the grammatical gender system of its ancestors. No matter where it is spoken, contemporary English is a notional rather than grammatical gender language, with pronominal selection depending not simply on sex but on sociocultural gender, ideologies and ideas about sex. Gendered pronouns for inanimate referents and gendered pronouns that don't take account of sex for non-human animals might seem the most striking 'non-natural' aspects of contemporary English gender, but, as I noted earlier, even restricting attention to human referents shows us that what matters is less sex as such than attitudes linked to sex and sexuality.

What I was told in English classes many years ago was that we use *he* for individual male humans, *she* for individual female humans, and *they* for groups of whatever sexual composition. Well, that was basically the story given for deictic uses. Where there was a linguistic antecedent, choice of pronoun was said to depend on the semantics of that NP. A singular NP semantically denoting female humans (*girl, sister, daughter, wife, woman*, compounds with *–woman*, and a few other forms) takes *she*. Singular NPs semantically denoting male humans (*boy, brother, son, husband*, and some others) select *he*. But, as noted earlier, that leaves unanswered what happens in other cases: an epicene antecedent where the referent's sex is unknown to the speaker (e.g., *Lee's new tenant*), a disjunctive ("split") antecedent with a feminine and a masculine disjunct (e.g., *my mother or my father*), a 'notionally' plural but grammatically singular antecedent (e.g., *everyone*), or, of course, a singular generic (*the careful shopper* or *an intelligent child,* where these are used to say something about careful shoppers or intelligent children generally). Some said that, although *she* is marked feminine, *he* is simply unmarked for gender and this is why we get so-called masculine generics. But that view cannot be maintained, as we will see.

3.1 Referential practices: Enforced gendering

By and large, pronominal reference in English to a single specific human being, whether involving a linguistic antecedent and its linked pronominal or a deictically anchored pronoun, involves a forced choice between the feminine pronoun *she* or the masculine *he*, which in such uses is most definitely not neutral.

(8) a. (pointing) What is she/he doing?

b. Someone called, but she/he didn't leave her/his name.

The choice of *she* is marked feminine and attributes female sex (or at least notional feminine status) to the person at whom I am pointing. And, contrary to the view that *he* is simply unmarked, in such contexts *he* is marked masculine and attributes male sex (or at least notional masculine status). It simply cannot be used as gender-neutral or unmarked in references like these to a specific person, whether deictic as in (9a) or controlled by a pronominal antecedent as in (9b). Now it is possible to avoid gender attribution in such references but not easy.

(9) a. What is that person/are they doing?

b. Someone called but they didn't leave their name.

To my ear the notionally singular *they* sounds better in the second case, but it is certainly possible in the first – especially if the person in question is not readily assigned masculine or feminine gender (perhaps too far away to see clearly or, rarer, someone whose external appearance is sex-neutral). Still, *they* seems virtually impossible in certain contexts – e.g., when the antecedent is a proper name or a notionally gendered noun.

(10) a. ?#Chris could tie their own shoes when they were three.

b. ?#Joan's dad has Alzheimer's and apparently forgets their own birthday.

Notionally singular *they* has certainly extended its reach since I first began thinking about the meaning of English pronouns, but it is still not available for every occasion when an epicene pronoun might be wanted.

Those who advocate gender-neutral policies for reference as essential for gender equity (see, e.g., Beardsley 1973–74) almost universally fail to consider how difficult it is to avoid gender-marking in third-person singular references to specific people. The difficulty is especially acute in extended discourse about the same person when repetition of a name (these too are very often gendered) or description sounds very odd, sometimes seeming to suggest that a different person is being discussed. In the current state of English, gendered pronouns seem more or less inevitable. Of course, to speak of some other human, I choose between *she* or *he*. How could it be otherwise? That's 'natural'. Or so it seemed to me for a long time. But many languages do not in fact require such a choice, and the potential pitfalls presented are beginning to be felt by substantial numbers of English speakers. This is not to say that speakers of languages that make gender-neutral reference easy do not consider the division of people into men and women of great importance. It is just that their languages do not require them to attend constantly when talking of others to the distinction between women and girls, on the one hand, and men and boys, on the other.

English speakers have never had a straightforward gender-neutral pronominal choice for referring to another person. The neuter OE pronoun *hit*, still heard in the North Carolina mountains where I lived during my early adolescence, was pretty much reserved for inanimates by the time grammatical gender was on the wane. There are some instances of *hit* in earlier OE sources controlled by a nominal with human reference that was assigned neuter gender; e.g., Curzan (2003, 62) reports the neutral *wifman* 'woman' anteceding the neuter pronoun in two instances as compared to 16 feminine agreement patterns in one OE corpus. But these most emphatically were not notionally gender-neutral uses – they simply represented grammatical gender agreement, which in the particular case happened to conflict with notional gender.

Nowadays *it* is occasionally heard in reference to very young humans, and it does sometimes serve generically with antecedents like *baby* or *child*. Here's an example:

(11)   [T]he child comes to believe that its power to command ... reflects its superior value, and this is what awakens and flatters its amour-propre. (*Philosophical Review* 119.2, April 2010, 184)

But *it* tends to sound dehumanizing if used in speaking about a particular human, even a very young one. When told a baby has been born people often respond with *what is it?*, to which the answer is supposed to be *it's a girl* or *it's a boy*, and from then on they're supposed to speak of *she* or *he*. Doctors are advised when talking to parents of intersex babies to use something like *your baby* rather than *it*.

Using *it* of a human being past infancy is almost always an act of derision, a refusal to attribute fully human status and often an expression of disapproval of that individual's apparent attitudes towards sex and sexuality.

(12)   Where did it come from?

With accented *it*, I have heard this and similar utterances used by people who disapproved of the long-haired man or flannel-shirt wearing woman whom they indicated. The pronoun *it* is simply not available as a neutral way to refer to adult humans. Its imputation of non-humanity, however, is certainly consistent with the widespread view that true personhood cannot be gender-neutral, which leaves intersex people in something of a limbo (and makes speaking of them challenging).

Being either *she* or *he* is not only considered essential to one's humanness. Sex is also considered a permanent personal characteristic, which indeed it is for most people. But not for all and in particular not for transsexuals. Though a first-person transsexual memoir written in English would not yield data like that from *Appelez moi Gina*, trans men and women do often encounter problems in getting long-term friends and family to refer to them as *he* or *she*, to speak of them as they would of other men and women. Some professionals who work with people undergoing sex reassignment use *they* to speak of them during the period of transition. Even speakers who are trans-friendly encounter difficulties when speaking of the person at times prior to sex reassignment: does one use the pronoun that was then appropriate or the one that now fits? Nonetheless, first-person reminiscences in English would avoid this difficulty.

It is no accident that the wonderfully comic crime fiction novels by Sarah Caudwell featuring Oxford don of jurisprudence, Hilary Tamar, are first-person narratives. In English, in contrast to many languages with grammatical gender, one readily speaks of oneself in gender-neutral terms. Others speak to Hilary or use the name – one never knows for sure whether Hilary is woman or man. Caudwell manages this so skillfully that people reading the novels do not always notice the absence of definitive gendering of Hilary: they sometimes mentally provide *she* or *he* on the basis of whichever familiar gender assumptions happen to attract their attention. But the novels are full of little hints that Hilary and friends do not lead gender-conventional lives. Sarah Caudwell, sadly, died in her (his? – the author used a *nom de plume*) early 60s, leaving open the question of Hilary's sex.

Many possible epicene or gender-neutral third-person pronoun choices for referring to humans have been devised for English over the years, not with much success. Baron 1986 surveys neologisms proposed for this purpose before the 1980s, and Livia 2001 devotes a chapter to neologistic epicene forms in English-language fiction. Such innovations have not had a very good track record, as linguists often point out, but they do sometimes find considerable support from various groups of nonlinguists. Because enforced gendering of standard singular pronouns is particularly problematic for transgender people, especially in others' accounts of their lives (as we noted above, there is an issue for others of which pronoun to use for the person in their pre-transition life), they have been particularly interested in finding new alternatives.

Gender-neutral options are attractive for other reasons, especially for those who would like to challenge strict gender binaries. One fairly popular set of pronouns in recent years is *ze* (*ze* is here), *zir* (we see *zir), zir* (is that *zir* coat?), *zirs* (is that *zirs*?), and *zirself* (Chris has learned to get dressed by *zirself*); another set includes *E/e* or *Ey/ey* for the nominative, *em, eir, eirs*, and *eirself* for the other cases. These are called Spivak pronouns because mathematician Michael Spivak introduced them; they have achieved some currency online and are easy to remember because of their strong similarity to *they*, one reason they might become more widely embraced. Whether some one of these gender-neutral neologisms actually becomes widespread depends on factors that are difficult to foresee. The history of English shows that personal pronouns can change: speakers added *she* when the inherited female and male forms were losing their distinctiveness and abandoned singular *thee/thou* in favor of plural *you* for singular addressee reference. If gender-neutral reference to specific individuals does become widespread, my guess is that it will come through widening uses of *they* to include usages like those in (10) but some neologism might indeed beat out *they*.

English speakers have been interested in what is happening in Swedish, where the gender-neutral singular third-person pronoun *hen* introduced in the 1960s got a boost in the spring of 2012. Not only was it added to the Swedish online National Encyclopedia as an alternative to *han* 'he' and *hon* 'she', but it was also used in a children's book about Kivi, "who wanted a dog for *hen*'s birthday" (http://www.slate.com/articles/double_x/doublex/2012/04/hen_sweden_s_new_gender_neutral_pronoun_causes_controversy_.html; site accessed 11 June 2012). What distinguishes the Swedish case from most attempts to add a gender-neutral option in English is that influential figures in government and education seem to be urging that gendered pronouns be used no longer (or at least this is how matters are interpreted by many observers). Such apparent gender-neutral prescriptivism has enraged some Swedes and perhaps even more non-Swedes. Many websites include comments both for and against *hen*, sometimes but by no means always well-informed on linguistics or social gender. This buzz in the blogosphere vividly illustrates the 'passion' associated with gender in language of which Corbett, this volume, reminds us, with a quote from Ranko Matasović.

It is often difficult, especially for those accustomed to think of enforced gendering as 'natural', virtually inevitable, to imagine alternatives between the constraints of enforced gendering and those of coerced gender-neutralization. In principle, English discourses might eventually have some/many occurrences of gendered pronouns alongside some/many occurrences of gender neutral pronouns for individual human referents. Such changes could not happen overnight, however.

3.1.1 Expressive uses

There are uses of *she* to refer to people who are attributed and claim male sex. Rudes and Healy 1979 give many examples collected in their ethnolinguistic investigation among gay males in Buffalo, NY. Rudes and Healy found what they saw as both positive (youth, glamour) and negative uses (excess, disorganization, lack of 'naturalness', nastiness or a more global rejection). We are of course dealing with notional gender, where that includes ideologies operative among these gay men about self-presentation and other characteristics as well as their playing with gender stereotypes others might embrace. Such uses do not show anything like gender-inversion among gay men – they are not ascribing 'feminine' identities to one another but disavowing prominent styles of presumptively heterosexual masculinity. Nor can research like that of Rudes and Healy be taken as evidence of broader practices in some supposed 'gay community'. Indeed, most discussions of this phenomenon are decades old, and it is not clear that the practice continues much nowadays. As Barrett 1997 makes clear, there are multiple communities within which gay men and others rejecting heterosexual norms engage in social, including linguistic, practice. Pronoun switching is one available resource and certainly has been used in a variety of ways among some groups of gay men.

Reports of analogous practices among English-speaking lesbians don't seem to exist, and linguist Robin Queen (personal communication) speculates that the rather different histories of gay men and lesbians may account for this gap. Of course this does not mean that *he* might not be used by some lesbians for referring to one another on occasion. What it does mean is that the use of pronoun-inversion to signal ingroup status and to comment on (and perhaps thereby to 'police') self-presentation by others in the group seems confined to gay men and perhaps mainly to past generations of gay men, far more of whom were closeted and not generally 'out' than is now the case. (Pastre 1997 surveyed French-speaking gay men and lesbians on the topic of using masculine forms to refer to one another; she not only got a much lower rate of response from the lesbians than from the gay men but some expressed hostility and only a couple reported using masculine forms, which they reserved not for reference but for address in intimate, romantic settings.)

In general there are few reports of uses of masculine pronouns to refer to those who claim and are attributed female identities. Mathiot and Roberts 1979 report what seemed to be instances of 'elevating' the referent, highlighting competence or other attributes of someone claiming and attributed female sex by referring to that person using *he*. I have not directly observed such uses nor are they reported elsewhere in the literature so it is not clear how widespread this phenomenon might be.

There are also dismissive uses of feminine pronouns heard in presumptively heterosexual communities of practice, often accompanied by other feminine forms like *girl*. Coaches (male) of male athletic teams sometimes engage in this kind of disparagement. Like pronoun-inversion among gay men, this practice is probably on the decline.

3.1.2 Presumptive leaps

Back in the early 1970s some feminists told a story along these lines.

> A young boy was rushed to the hospital from the scene of an accident in which his father was killed and prepped for emergency surgery. The surgeon walked in, took one look, and said "I can't operate on him – that's my son."

Many people hearing the story would say things like

(13)   How could the boy be his son? The boy's father was killed.

They were assuming that the surgeon was male and overlooking the possibility that the surgeon was the boy's mother. (They were also assuming only one father, though that would not have affected pronoun choice.) Though recognizing the existence of a stereotype that surgeons are male (perhaps less robust now than when the story was first told but by no means completely moribund), semanticists tended to cringe when people took the story to illustrate that *surgeon* is semantically 'male'. After all, it is not contradictory to utter sentences like

(14)   She/my mother/Jennifer is a surgeon

What McConnell-Ginet (2008) proposed is that words have cognitively associated with them not only information about their linguistic properties, including their conventional meaning, but also what I call conceptual baggage. Although conceptual baggage is not part of what the words conventionally mean, it can be essential for understanding how what is said using those words contributes to the inferences interlocutors draw, often with neither speaker nor hearer consciously accessing the conceptual baggage on which those inferences rely. There are many cases:

(15)   A: I've got to drive the babysitter home.

        B: How far away does she live?

(16)   A: The police have identified the burglar who took Kim's silver.

          B: Was he local?

Babysitters and burglars can be male and female respectively, but the pronouns used by the questioners reveal their feminine and masculine notional gender. People make such presumptive leaps often and not only on the basis of single words like *surgeon*, *babysitter*, or *burglar*. An example like one I've used from my own experience illustrates.

(17)   Sally: I've got a student who does very well on homework and in class but freaks out taking exams.
          Sally's colleague: Give her some old exams so she can practice working problems under time pressure.

In so far as referent sex matches pronoun choice, such gender assumptions are generally not noticed by either party. It's the mismatches we catch. The student whom exams tripped up happened to be male; my correction embarrassed the colleague who would never have said that exam anxiety was a distinctively feminine phenomenon. And when my friend told me she'd taken her sick cat to the vet and I inquired "What does he think is wrong?", I was the one corrected, to my chagrin. In fact I know that these days more women than men enter veterinary practice, I even know some women who are vets, and I have given considerable thought to gender-stereotyping. Nonetheless, my tongue betrayed me. These are not cases where *he* is gender-neutral: any reference to a specific individual by *he* attributes masculinity, perhaps only figurative as with the inversion uses but not neutral.

And of course pronoun selection can evince presumptions of heterosexuality.

(18)   A: I heard from my former student Carolyn that she's getting married this summer.
          B: Is he a linguist too?
          A: I think *she* is an anthropologist.

We have seen that uses of *he* and of *she* that are either deictically anchored or anaphorically dependent on a noun phrase referring to a specific individual person are equally gendered. There is no neutral ground for *he* in this arena: notionally singular *they* is used in some contexts (e.g., if sex is unknown or the speaker would prefer not mentioning it) but still avoided even by non-purists in others.

A special case of 'unknown' sex occurs when the apparent antecedent for a pronoun is an overt or implied disjunction that makes the possibility of either male or female referent very salient.

(19) a. If Mary or John calls, tell *him/?her or him/them I'll be back in an hour.

b. If my mother or father/one of my parents calls, tell *him/?him or her/them I'll be back in an hour.

Of course *him* would be fine if I'm someone whose parents are both men. There is, however, no possibility of using masculine pronouns in cases like these without implying a masculine caller. Notionally singular *they* is a common choice in such cases of sex-indeterminate reference to a single individual (who is, of course, the one who calls).

3.2 From specific to general

3.2.1 Shakespeare and company: Generalizing quantifiers

The grammatically plural *they* has a long history of being used with notionally plural but grammatically singular antecedents, a usage proscribed from the 18th century on but nonetheless encountered widely from William Shakespeare to Jane Austen to Virginia Woolf. The so-called pronominal forms *anyone* and *everyone* or NPs where *any* or *every* are the determiners are a primary arena where English speakers of my generation were drilled on using *he* generically. But even here *he* is sometimes problematic.

(20) a. Everyone should be sure that ?he understands the assignment.

b. Everyone got Chris's e-mail, didn't *he? (cp. didn't they?)

The (b) sentence is especially odd and this oddness is only slightly ameliorated if the addressees are all male. With *anyone*, the masculine form may work a bit better but not much.

(21) a. Anyone turning in work that is not ?his own will be subject to disciplinary action.

> b. Anyone who solves the bonus problems gets an A, doesn't ?*he? (cp. don't they?)

Without the valiant efforts of generations of teachers and editors, *they* would prevail in such contexts, its plurality fitting well with the notional plurality of the antecedents.

In the prose of my youth, however, it was not just *everyone* and *anyone* controlling masculine anaphoric pronouns (avoiding cases where the target pronoun was in one of those pesky tag questions). We also frequently encountered *every* and *any* as universal quantifying determiners with what would seem to be epicene content nouns. Sentences like those in (22) were common, even in contexts where it was clear that there might be female humans to whom the generalization was supposed to apply.

(22) a. Every student must bring his own writing materials to class.

      b. Any politician who talks regularly to his constituents knows that he will sometimes disappoint some of them, perhaps most eventually.

Yet such usages were mainly encountered in written material, with *they* very frequent in speech. Matossian 1997 and Newman 1997, two interesting studies done well after my youth, found *they* with grammatically singular antecedents very common indeed. Strikingly, Matossian found women in her Philadelphia and Minneapolis groups less likely to use the putatively generic *he* and more likely to use *they* with singular 'general' antecedents than the men; among these same populations, women's use of other 'incorrect forms' (e.g., double negatives) is usually somewhat smaller than that of men. (Notice that such frequential differences in usage among women and men in the same communities are not evidence for "gender dialects" as that label is used in Dunn's contribution to this volume.) Other research (e.g., Khosroshashi 1989) shows clearly that both interpretation and production of so-called masculine generics is tied to gender ideologies as well as to language ideologies. Women who are committed to pushing for greater gender equity are less likely to produce sentences with masculines serving generically but more likely to interpret such sentences as applicable to females as well as males.

Grammatically plural *they* with a notionally plural antecedent is increasingly seen in print and heard on the airwaves as well as being produced often online (not surprising, given the relative informality of much online usage). An example from the February 28, 2011 issue of *Newsweek*, not exactly a 'radical' publication:

(23)   No one's just a "peace activist" anymore – they have a specialty. (p 18)

Notice that *he* would be quite bizarre here. This might be because the pronominal reference (what semanticists sometimes call E-type) in this case is actually linked to the unexpressed but evoked *everyone* (in the contextually given domain of young actors), but that too would be grammatically singular though notionally plural.

In the semantics literature sentences of the sort we have looked at in this section are analyzed as universally quantified. The term *generic* is often reserved for sentences that generalize but (1) lack overt quantifiers in the plural and (2) seem to permit exceptions. Bare plural subject generics (e.g., *women love babies, men can't cook,* etc.) have received considerable attention (see McConnell-Ginet 2012 for some discussion), but of course gender is neutralized in the plural so I will focus my discussion on singular generics, beginning with feminine generics.

3.2.2 Singular feminine generics

I will begin with some examples I used in McConnell-Ginet ([1979], 2011). Some of them aren't strictly speaking generic but they are all cases where there could be male referents, and where the choice of *he* as an anaphoric pronoun is taken as reference to a particular male whereas *she* is compatible with the referent's being male.

(24)   a.   When the nurse comes, he'll take your blood pressure.
        b.   When the nurse comes, she'll take your blood pressure.

Sentence (24a) makes reference only to a male nurse whereas (24b) could be used quite correctly in a context where the nurse in question might be of either sex but the speaker was simply making a general statement applicable to whatever nurse happened to come. In professions like nursing, still predominantly populated by women, feminine pronouns are the norm. A sentence like (25) is distinctly odd.

(25)   ?*The careful nurse will be sure he takes the right medicines to the right patients.

And *teacher* also often still takes a generic or indefinite *she*. I was struck when one of my kids brought home something written by the male head of a junior high school department with roughly equal number of women and men teachers involved in the self-instruction program, including himself, reported:

(26)   Students have to check with the teacher regularly so she knows how they're progressing.

Generic feminines of this kind have been in use for some time, and they show clearly that English gender is notional.

But feminine generics do not require predominance of women as possible referents. Sometimes the choice seems clearly to reflect anticipation of a largely female audience as in (27), which occurred in a mass-circulation women's magazine.

(27)   Behaviorists believe that what a person does is determined by the situation in which she finds herself.

And, as with the presumptive leaps in choosing pronouns for specific reference, a speaker's gender stereotype can lead to a feminine generic. Two more examples from my 1970s collection:

(28)   Physicians fear – with some reason – that a patient who discovers she can lose weight quickly, without hunger pangs, may fast unwisely on her own.

(29)   When I walk down to them and point my fingers and say "you," why that person even forgets her own name in the excitement. [interview with emcee of quiz show that did use contestants of both sexes]

I've often extended the benefit of the doubt to speakers using what seemed to be generic *he*. It is noteworthy when such a person switches pronouns. I listened to a lecture on teaching with *professor, student*, and so on controlling *he*. So the following offered strong evidence of gender stereotyping, almost certainly operating below the level of conscious attention.

(30)   When a student finally says something after sitting silently half the semester, don't intimidate her.

Even a noun like *parent*, wearing its sex-neutrality on its sleeve in its primary use to provide a sex-indefinite alternative to *mother* and *father*, can control an indefinite or generic *she*.

(31)   When a parent hears her baby cry, she rouses quickly.

A lecture by a distinguished psychologist for whom *speaker, child*, and *subject* all were anaphorically linked to *he* contained such a generic feminine occurrence of *parent*. Three decades later such a switch would be far less likely, as more and more speakers move away from masculine generics.

Generic *she* was once more or less restricted to cases where women were especially salient. Sometimes there was their predominance in some occupation, other times their role as audience, and other times the operation of strong stereotypes. Nowadays, however, we also find generic *she*, sometimes alternating with generic *he*, in writing or planned talk when there is no special contextual prominence of women. These uses are self-conscious expressions of certain gender ideology: their use signals the user's disavowal of default masculine generics and usually recognition that many such generics were not interpreted as truly inclusive or even fully meant as inclusive. Here's an example of this kind of generic feminine from a recent article in one of the leading philosophy journals:

(32)   [A] policy is legitimate only if it is *generally acceptable* – only if there's an adequate case for enforcing the policy coercively such that, for every member of the society, and for every *qualified* belief that she holds, she can accept that case consistently with her holding that belief.
      (*Philosophical Review* 119.2, April 2010, 256)

At least in certain circles, the generic *she* has emerged as a more forceful way to reject generic *he* than rephrasing with the plural to eliminate gendering or opting for the disjoined *he or she* (or *she or he*). Some of my students have reported English teachers allowing generic *she* but rejecting *he or she* as much too clumsy (which it can be if there is a long string of linked forms, perhaps possessives or reflexives). Generic *she* may seem downright 'unnatural' and it still carries a little 'shock' value, which is part of the point, but its increasing usage is changing the generic landscape and, with it, the relation of sex and gender in English.

3.2.3 Other generics

Treichler and Frank 1989 remains the most thorough discussion of generic usage and possible alternatives to the then still very common singular *he* with intended general force. It was the existence of generic *he* that led me first to question the view of gender in English as 'natural'. Leonard Bloomfield described gender in English this way:

"The distinction, then, between the pronoun-forms *he* and *she*, creates a classification of our personal nouns into *male* (defined as those for which the definite substitute is *he*) and *female* (similarly defined by the use of the substitute *she*). Semantically, this classification agrees fairly well with the zoological division into sexes." (1933, 253) This formulation seems to overlook generic *he* in such instances as (33a,b) from the same book.

(33)   a.   Suppose, for instance, that day after day the child is given *his* doll (and says *da, da, da*) immediately after *his* bath (p.30).

           b.   Even if we know a great deal about a speaker and about the immediate stimuli which are acting upon *him*, we usually cannot predict whether *he* will speak or what *he* will say (p.32).

How could a system that treats words like *child* and *speaker* as male be thought to "correspond fairly well" with zoological sex? Presumably, because Bloomfield and many others were accustomed to thinking of maleness as the 'natural' condition for humans, with femaleness only a distinctive condition. It is certainly possible to have a default rule that has singular epicene controllers serve as antecedents for singular masculine pronouns. What is not possible – at least not for many contemporary English users – is to view such an arrangement as one where sex as such is the principle for pronoun assignment, a 'natural' gender system.

It does continue to be the case that male human beings are far more visible in most contexts than female. And it also continues to be easy for many people, especially but probably not only men, to think and also speak of prototypical humans as male. It is conflating male humanity with humanity generally that permits what Black and Coward 1981 dub "false generics," where there is no pronoun but the clear implication is that what would seem to be a clear case of an epicene noun is being used as if its referents were all (adult) males. Here's an example, adapted from an anthropological essay.

(34)   The villagers all left, leaving us behind with the women and children.

Variants of this example have been widely discussed, and there are many similar cases where even though the language used looks gender-neutral, the message conveyed is not.

And even when the context begins with reference to a particular person of a specified sex, if one party is focused on that individual not as such but as exemplary of a category there can be gender confusion. An advice column in the real estate section of my local paper on the 16th of February, 2011 began with a reader's question about selling their house to a tenant living in the house. The tenant is referred to several times in the course of the rather involved question as *she* as in *she gave me a down payment*. The 'expert' begins the response by speaking of "your tenant", " your buyer", "the buyer," "your borrower," etc., with no pronouns. And then after several paragraphs I was astonished to read

> [I]f you have not sold the house to this person and he is merely renting the house from you until he can finance the $50,000 to complete the purchase, then the payments he or she is making to you ... [A]n accountant can help you determine whether the buyer/tenant is paying you rent or interest on the loan you gave him to purchase the house.

The advice-giver seems to simply forget the sex of the tenant/buyer and speak of a presumptively male generic tenant/buyer, though recalling at one point that the actual individual in question could be female.

The point is simple: it is not only linguistic practices like the so-called generic masculine that tend to render women less visible than men even though these practices certainly are consequential.

4 'Grammatical' vs 'natural/notional' gender systems: Reform strategies

I will close by briefly considering the rather different linguistic strategies that have been taken by English-speaking feminist activists and most of those in languages with grammatical gender. In languages with grammatical gender, gender marking is far more pervasive than it is in English-like languages, where it is primarily limited to personal pronouns. There are, of course, some feminizing affixes (*-ess, -woman, -ette*), and at certain points in history they were relatively widely used. In the 19th century, for example, it was proposed that the women faculty members at Vassar College be called *professoresses*, and for a long time women chairing organizations were called *chairwomen*. In the case of, say, *chairman* vs *chairwoman*, the two forms are morphologically parallel, but in many other cases the feminine forms have been viewed as suggesting the women and men are doing different things in their positions. Speaking of a *poetess*, many felt, implied less significance that the plain term *poet*. In the case of acting, one might want to say that what males and females do is indeed different as casting in the modern era typically matches the sex of character and the person acting the role. Typically but not always, and even in acting many women now call themselves actors. A woman I met in the 1970s had recently managed to land a good job in the traditionally masculine field of drafting: "I am a draftsman and that's what I should be called," she said, "because I do just as good a job as any of the men holding that title."

There's been debate over how masculine the -*man* suffix 'really' is – too bad, I've often thought, the spelling didn't become -*mun* to reflect that the suffix is pronounced differently from the independent word *man*, which did actually begin life as a neutral form, only later specializing to contrast with *woman*. Sometimes the -*man* suffix is replaced by -*person*, but there is a tendency for chairpersons and the like to be overwhelmingly female, with males continuing as chairmen. Nonetheless, in spite of Bloomfield, there are many words in English that strike users as gender-neutral, and there has been a concerted and moderately successful push in many locales to replace gender-marked occupational labels like *fireman* and *stewardess* by gender-neutral labels like *fire fighter* and *flight attendant*. The occupations too have changed; many more women are now rushing off in fire engines and many more men are urging passengers to buckle their seat belts.

The push in the US at least has generally been to remove gendered references, to promote gender-neutral ways of speaking of people, including the use of *they, he or she*, and alternating pronouns for generic antecedents. But the push in many countries with grammatical gender has been towards providing feminine alternatives to designate women in positions previously open only to men and designated by a masculine noun. Sometimes there is a new word, sometimes the old word becomes double-gendered, able to control feminine as well as masculine targets. When every noun is gendered (and in a number of languages, either masculine or feminine), then feminization probably seems the more 'natural' strategy and it does have the advantage of increasing women's visibility, especially if it is embraced by high-ranking women.

In a talk at the September 2010 IGALA meetings, Malka Muchnik detailed the problems she sees for Israeli women who are trying to change Hebrew so that it will better serve their interests. Feminization, she argued, did not work because it was not embraced by powerful women; neutralization, she claimed, is really impossible, and thus her argument was that the language was becoming more rather than less masculinized. How widespread that view might be I do not know, but what struck me is Muchnik's experience of grammatical gender in modern Israeli Hebrew as deeply problematic for gender equity.

To what extent the kind of gender system in a language constrains or promotes gender equity is not clear. What is clear, however, is that the relation of sex to linguistic gender, whether 'grammatical' or 'notional', is a moving target: languages and those speaking them continue to change in ways that we still do not fully understand. Neither linguistic nor sociocultural gender is 'natural' if by that we mean impervious to change, isolated from human ideas and actions.

5 References

Adriaen, Monique and Ruth King. 1991. Job titles, ch. 5. In R. King, (ed.). 27–40.
Baron, Dennis. 1986. *Grammar and Gender*. New Haven: Yale University Press.
Baron, Naomi. 1971. A reanalysis of English grammatical gender. *Lingua* 27. 113–140.
Barrett, Rusty. 1997. The "homo-genius" speech community. In A. Livia & K. Hall (eds.), *Queerly Phrased: Language, Gender, and Sexuality*. 181–201. New York & Oxford: Oxford University Press.
Beardsley, Elizabeth Lane. 1973–74. Referential genderization. *Philosophical Forum* 5. 285–293.
Black, Maria and Rosalind Coward. 1981. Linguistic, social and sexual relations. *Screen Education* 39. 111–133.
Bloomfield, Leonard. 1933. *Language*. New York: Holt, Rinehart and Winston.
Boroditsky, Lera, Lauren A. Schmidt, and Webb Phillips. 2003. Sex, syntax and semantics. In Dedre Gentner & Susan Goldin-Meadow (eds.), *Language in Mind: Advances in the Study of Language and Cognition*, 61–80. Cambridge, MA: MIT. Press
Burr, Elisabeth. 2003. Gender and language politics in France. In Hellinger & Bussman, (eds.), vol. 3. 119–139.
Cameron, Deborah and Don Kulick. 2003. *Language and Sexuality*. Cambridge: Cambridge University Press.
Connors, Kathleen. 1971. Studies in feminine agentives in selected European languages. *Romance Philology* 24. 573–598.
Corbett, Greville. 1991. *Gender*. Cambridge: Cambridge University Press.
Curzan, Anne. 1999. Gender categories in early English grammars: Their message to the modern grammarian. In Barbara Unterbeck and Matti Rissanen, (eds.), *Gender in Grammar and Cognition*. The Hague: Mouton. 561–576.
Curzan, Anne. 2003. *Gender Shifts in the History of English*. Cambridge: Cambridge University Press.
Fausto-Sterling, Anne. 2000. *Sexing the Body: Gender Politics and the Construction of Sexuality*. New York: Basic Books.
Frank, Francine W. and Paula A. Treichler (eds.). 1989. *Language, Gender, and Professional Writing: Theoretical Approaches and Guidelines for Nonsexist usage*. New York: Modern Language Association.
Hall, Kira. 2003. 'Unnatural' gender in Hindi. In Hellinger & Bussmann (eds.), vol. 2, 133–166.
Hall, Kira and Veronica O'Donovan. 1996. Shifting gender positions among Hindi-speaking hijras. In Victoria L. Bergvall, Janet M. Bing, and Alice F. Freed (eds.), *Rethinking Language and Gender Research: Theory and Practice*. London and New York: Longman. 228–266.
Hellinger, Marlis and Hadumod Bussmann (eds.). 2003. *Gender across Languages*, Volumes 1–3. Amsterdam and Philadelphia: John Benjamins.
Khosroshahi, Fatemeh. 1989. Penguins don't care, but women do: a social identity analysis of a Whorfian problem. *Language in Society* 18. 505–525.

King, Ruth (ed.). 1991. *Talking Gender: A Guide to Nonsexist Communication*. Toronto: Copp Clark Pittman Ltd.

Livia, Anna. 2001. *Pronoun Envy: Literary Uses of Linguistic Gender*. New York and Oxford: Oxford University Press.

Livia, Anna and Kira Hall (eds.). 1997. *Queerly Phrased: Language, Gender, and Sexuality*. New York and Oxford: Oxford University Press.

Mathiot, Madeline (ed.). 1979. *Ethnolinguistics: Boas, Sapir and Whorf Revisited*. The Hague: Mouton.

Mathiot, Madeline, assisted by Marjorie Roberts. 1979. Sex roles as revealed through referential gender in American English. In M. Mathiot (ed.). 1–47.

Matossian, Lou Ann. 1997. *Burglars, Babysitters, and Persons: A Sociolinguistic Study of Generic Pronoun Usage in Philadelphia and Minneapolis*. Philadelphia: University of Pennsylvania PhD dissertation.

McConnell-Ginet, Sally. 2008. Words in the world: How and why meanings can matter. *Language* 84(3). 497–527.

McConnell-Ginet, Sally. [1979], 2011. Pronouns, prototypes, and persons. In S. McConnell-Ginet. chapter 9. 185–206.

McConnell-Ginet, Sally. [1988], 2011. Linguistics and gender. In S. McConnell-Ginet. chapter 2. 37–62.

McConnell-Ginet, Sally. 2011. *Gender, Sexuality, and Meaning: Linguistic Practice and Politics*. New York and Oxford: Oxford University Press.

McConnell-Ginet, Sally. 2012. Generic predicates and interest-relativity. *Canadian Journal of Linguistics* 57(2). 261–287.

Moore, Samuel. 1921. Grammatical and natural gender in Middle English. *Proceedings of the Modern Language Association* 36. 79–103.

Nevalainen, Terttu and Helena Raumolin-Brunberg. 1994. Its strength and the beauty of it: the standardization of the third person neuter possessive in Early Modern English. In Dieter Stein and Ingrid Tieken-Boon van Ostade (eds.), *Towards a Standard English, 1600–1800. Topics in English Linguistics* 12. Berlin: Mouton de Gruyter. 171–216.

Newman, Michael. 1997. *Epicene Pronouns: The Linguistics of a Prescriptive Problem*. Outstanding dissertations in linguistics series. New York: Garland Press.

Pastre, Genviève. 1997. Linguistic gender play among French gay men and lesbians. In A. Livia & K. Hall (eds.). 369–379.

Pollard, Carl and Ivan A. Sag. 1994. *Head-Driven Phrase Structure Grammar*. Chicago: University of Chicago Press and Stanford: CSLI Publications.

Rosch, Elinor. 1978. Principles of categorization. In Elinor Rosch and Barbara B. Lloyd (eds.), *Cognition and Categorization*. 27–48. Hillsdale, NJ: Erlbaum.

Rudes, Blair A. and Bernard Healy. 1979. Is she for real?: The concepts of femaleness and maleness in the gay world. In Madeline Mathiot (ed.). 49–61.

Treichler, Paula A. and Francine W. Frank. 1989. Guidelines for nonsexist usage. Part 2. In Frank and Treichler (eds.), 137–278.

Wagner, Suzanne. 2003. *Gender in English Pronouns: Myth and Reality*. Accessed at http://www.freidok.uni-freiburg.de/volltexte/1412/pdf/Diss_Freidok.pdf. 16 February 2011.

Michael Dunn
Gender determined dialect variation

1 Introduction

On the Telqep tundra of the Russian arctic in the early 20th century, a young man drives his reindeer sled towards a snow-covered *jaraŋə*, the traditional dome-shaped reindeer hide tent of the Chukchis. The elderly Chukchi herdsman whose home it is cries out *okkaj!* in surprise, and asks *meŋin pəkiryʔi?* 'Who has arrived?'. His wife comes out to look and echoes his question, *ii, meŋin pəkiccʔi?* 'Yes, who has arrived?'. The young man, seeing their confusion, shouts out *ətcajqaj, waj rayṭəɬʔeyəm!* 'Aunty, it's me, Rayṭəɬʔən'. They both call out to him in delight, *rayṭəɬʔeyət?!* 'It's you, Rayṭəɬʔən?!'. The aunt welcomes him, *qəcecqikwi! jaracyko! qəcajoccən!* 'Come inside, into the house, have tea!'; *ee*, agrees the uncle, *qərecqikwi, qəcajorkən!* This cozy scene of homecoming and tea-drinking is a pastiche of welcoming scenes from folktales, but illustrates some of the typical features of real Chukchi usage. There are small differences in the speech of men and women, such as how the uncle says *ee* for 'yes' while the aunt says *ii*. Mysteriously, many instances of *r* or consonant clusters with *-r-* in the uncle's speech correspond to the affricate *-c-* or *-cc-* in the aunt's speech. But the aunt's speech does include *-r-* too. Longer acquaintance with the old couple would convince you that these correspondences are completely regular: both of them say *jaraŋə* for 'house'; aunty never says **jacaŋə*. But whereas the old man says *mren* 'mosquito' the old woman would only ever say *mcen*.

In 1658 the author[1] of the *Histoire naturelle et morale des Iles Antilles* described a peculiar linguistic situation of the Garifuna people of the Caribbean islands. Men and women had, at least in part, different vocabularies, with the same object named in one way by men, and another by women so that "in much of their conversation, one could say that women speak a different language to men" (Rochefort 1658: 392; Section 3.9).

---

[1] The identity of this author is somewhat mysterious: the preface of the first edition of the book is signed LDP, presumed to be the initials of Philippe de Longvilliers de Poincy, the then Governor General of the French West Indies and by all accounts a very unlikely ethnographer. Later editions are signed C. Rochefort, probably for Charles de Rochefort, a Huguenot pastor travelling and writing in the West Indies at that time, but often confused with César de Rochefort, a prominent French lexicographer. The Dominican missionary and ethnographer/naturalist Jean Baptiste du Tertre further claimed that a considerable portion of the book is plagiarised from his own work.

Since at least the 17th century there have been sporadic reports in the ethnographic record of language communities where men and women speak significantly different forms of their language, so different, in fact, that it would be impossible to speak without signalling gender identity. While gender variation in language is common, perhaps ubiquitous, such obligatory, categorical dialect differences determined by gender are rarer, and tend to be poorly described. The complex correspondences between men's and women's Chukchi (above and Section 3.6) are described as a simple substitution by women of *c* for men's *r* and *č* (Skorik 1961: 33). Gender dialects are often poorly documented with respect to usage too. Many gender dialect systems occur in small, endangered languages, and the gender dialect systems themselves tend to drop out of use faster than the language itself does. This means that the rules for using gender dialects are often inferred from the recollections of elderly (e.g. Section 3.1, 3.4, 3.8) or extracted from older written sources (e.g. Sections 3.9, 3.12) rather than taken from direct observations.

The term 'dialect' is used in the variationalist tradition to refer to systematic linguistic variation statistically associated with a sociolinguistic parameter, and as such can be difficult to delimit (Labov 1972: 192). This paper approaches gender-determined language usage from the ethnographic extreme, examining a small set of instances of *categorical* gender dialects for which we have records. These gender dialects are easily recognized as being the same language: they are spoken by people who form a single speech community and their differences only affect parts of the language: grammar, phonology and perhaps lexicon. They differ from a frequentially characterised dialect in that they form complete linguistic systems whose use is determined by the gender affiliation of the speech participants (Section 2.1), and which is characterized by obligatory grammatical differences rather than statistical tendencies (Section 2.2; Sherzer 1987: 96). In languages which have such categorical gender dialects, to use language means to use language like a woman or to use language like a man. This means that each gender dialect must be learned separately (since presumably most individuals in a gender dialect language community will have at least passive command of the other gender dialect). This is interesting from an acquisitional perspective, because the mutual autonomy of gender dialects makes for a considerable cognitive load in acquisition and use. In turn, it is also indicative of the social/cultural importance of signalling gender through language.

In this paper I take a pragmatic, cross-cultural approach to the notion of gender. All known societies classify people at birth as "male" or "female" according to the anatomical distinctions indicating their potential reproductive role. But this is in practice a social classification, relating biological sex to a wider set of social practices, norms, and relations (Eckert and McConnell-Ginet

1992: 463, McConnell-Ginet *this volume*). The specifics of the social construction of gender vary from culture to culture, differing both in the manner of expression, and the magnitude of effect. But as a fundamental social category it is highly likely to have significant consequences for ways of being (e.g. acting, speaking) in any society.[2] They provide a significant example of language-culture interaction, and have an important role in the documentation of human cultural diversity.

Following from the strict categorical definition of gender dialect, I specifically exclude some phenomena called *gender dialect* or *genderlect* in the linguistic literature from this survey. For example, Yokoyama (1999: 402) uses the term "genderlect" to describe a gendered speech register in Russian which is a part of colloquial speech, and which comprises "merely 'typical', rather than absolute traits". Likewise Sen ([1928] 1979) describes "women's dialect in Bengali", but the description here shows a cluster of linguistic choices from within the range of variation of a single language, rather than a pair of related, but structurally different, systems. I will not consider gender-determined variation such as that in Yuchi, which shows morphological differences in possessive prefixes determined by speaker gender, but which only occur with certain kinship terms (Wagner 1934: 339–340). Forty years after Wagner's study, Ballard (1978: 107) could elicit few of these terms. An example is the pair of terms for 'my brother', *dzodane* in men's speech and *doda?one* in women's speech. Marking speaker gender in kinship terminology is not the same sort of social signal that it is in a gender dialect system. Kinship systems have an intrinsically egocentric orientation (e.g. Scheffler 1987: 217), and quite naturally form a dyad between ego and relative, where the sex of both participants in the relationship is relevant (see also the 'same sex sibling'/'different sex sibling' oppositions in many languages). The clearest examples of gender dialect have different phonological rules describable in historical linguistic terms as the product of different regular sound changes (e.g. Chukchi, Tangoan), or which have different morphological terms and grammatical categories (e.g Kũṛux, Yanyuwa).

Along with the recognition that gender is a culturally constructed category, whose relation to biological sex is not straightforward, there are some scholars

---

[2] The importance of biological sex in communication systems extends beyond humans too. For example, in many bird species the songs of males and females are distinct. Furthermore, it is not uncommon for birdsong to be transmitted through social learning, leading to vocal repertoires which are differentiated by geographical region – referred to as regional dialects. There is even an analogy to gender dialect amongst the birds: the slate-coloured boubou *Laniarius funebris* is highly unusual in that it combines these two characteristics: songs are learned through imitation of same-sex models, resulting in distinct male and female variants embedded within the geographical variation (Wickler and Lunau 1996).

arguing that genderlect is not a valid category (Glück 1979; Motschenbacher 2007, 2010). Since these authors appeal to evidence from the languages treated in this paper I will discuss the linguistic and ethnographic basis for their arguments (Section 3.6). It is notable that the societies I will discuss are largely non-western, non-technological and, in some cases, only attested historically. This is not by chance: it may be that the stable transmission of gender dialect distinction is only possible in languages which are used primarily as in-group codes, and not as languages of inter-cultural communication.

This paper will treat the range of attested categorical gender dialects from three interrelated perspectives. In Section 2.1 I will discuss the functional typology of gender dialects, addressing how gender dialects are actually used. In Section 2.2 I present a description of the typical structural characteristics of gender, and discuss whether any of these characteristics distinguish them from other kinds of dialects. Section 2.3 takes a diachronic perspective: where are the attested gender dialects and how have they come about? After the general characterization of gender dialects in Section 2, Section 3 is devoted to 14 case studies of languages with gender dialect distinctions.

2 Characteristics

2.1 Usage

Haas (1944: 147) provides a typology of gender dialect systems, whereby the speech-act participant's gender determines which gender dialect is used. She defines three types:
- Type I: Speaker-based systems
- Type II: Addressee-based systems
- Type III: Speaker-and-addressee-based systems

According to the Haas typology, systems based on gender of addressee are qualitatively different than speaker-based systems. Speaker-based systems comprise, in effect, two language communities cohabiting in space (with passive comprehension), while addressee-based systems constitute two systems coexisting in each speaker (and so are more akin to diglossia/bidialectalism). The Haas typology doesn't, however, seem to pick out the most common or important parameters from the distributional point of view, since almost all attested gender dialects belong to Type I. Type II systems intersect with notions of politeness and taboo: they are contextually sensitive social norms of speech and behaviour and may be difficult to fit in to the notion of "dialect" rather than "register". For this reason I treat Type I and Type III in this paper, although I do give a brief description of Island Carib, a Type II language, since this is by far the best known example of gender variation described as a gender dialect (Section 3.9).

In most language communities where gender dialects are used speakers are bidialectal, at least passively and maybe actively. There is a basic asymmetry here: in all the non-institutional language communities for which we have information, children learn to produce the women's dialect first, then male children have to learn to produce the men's dialect later. In most cases, boys' acquisition of the men's dialect accompanies social and ritual recognition of their entering the men's world. This probably contributes to the historical instability of gender dialects, as the interruption of traditional social practices may also interrupt men's dialect acquisition. A number of descriptions of gender dialects explicitly mention that in quoted speech the gender dialect of the person quoted may be used, even where this is otherwise not the gender dialect used by the speaker. In Chukchi at least this is not completely regular, and is presumably related to vividness of the direct speech. Irish Sign Language seems to offer an exception to this rule of bidialectalism, having developed from two different dialects spoken in gender segregated institutions. In post-institutional life the female speakers have adapted to the male speakers, and not vice versa (Section 3.1).

Japanese has strong social norms about gender-appropriate linguistic behaviour (Inoue 2011). Some form of gender distinct speech has existed in Japanese since at least as early as the Heian period (794–1185AD), although there is no strong evidence that the practice was followed outside of social elites over this entire period (Abe 1995: 654). It is however doubtful that Japanese gender dialect variation forms a categorical system, although amongst many features used differentially by male and female speakers, some scholars do identify some features which are present only in one of the gendered varieties. Examples of supposedly categorical phenomena in gender varieties of Japanese include distinctive sets of personal pronouns and the forms of sentence final particles. However, Abe (1995: 663) demonstrates that "[...] this categorization of sentence-final particles based on gender is nothing but a representation of longstanding stereotypes and fails to accurately represent the current usage by both women and men." The gender differences in Thai mentioned by Haas (1944: 147–148) may be similar.

2.2 Structural typology

Gender variation in language is often expressed phonetically. Biological differences between males and females in vocal tract length determine fundamental frequency: biological males have an average f_0 around 100–120hz, and biological females have an average f_0 around 200–220hz (Simpson 2009: 622). This is a statistical difference only, but is clearly used for social classification (Gelfer and Mikos 2005). Hillenbrand and Clark (2009) show that f_0 and formant frequencies are major determinants of speaker sex identification. Listeners would fairly reliably change their speaker sex identification from recordings when f_0 and formants were artificially manipulated. This effect was most reliable when both f_0 and formants were changed together, less so when just f_0 was changed, and weaker again when just the formants were changed. Interestingly, sex classification changes of manipulated recordings happened more often with recordings of isolated syllables than with entire sentences, demonstrating that there are other phonological factors contributing to sex identification beyond these two. Hillenbrand and Clark cite sources suggesting that women's speech is breathier, and (controversially) that women's speech has wider prosodic variation (2009: 1191). These features would seem to be under more conscious control, and I would expect them to be subject to considerable cross-cultural variation, and available for 'emicization' as overt socio-cultural gender markers.

While phonetic differences are outside the scope of this survey, many of the languages with gender dialects do have significant phonetic differences between men's and women's speech on top of phonological, morphological and lexical differences. Women's Chukchi has an affricate [ts] where men's Chukchi has (depending on the region) [s] or [tʃ]; Pirahã women's speech uses a smaller articulatory space than men's speech, with characteristic pharyngeal constriction and more retroflexed articulation (Everett 2004: 7).

In the *Journal of a second voyage for the discovery of a north-west passage from the Atlantic to the Pacific,* Parry (1824: 553) describes differences in the speech of Eskimo men and women,

> It is common for the Esquimaux to vary the pronunciation of their words at different times without altering the sense. The women, in particular, seem frequently to make such alterations as conduce to the softness of the words, as, for instance, by dropping the harsh final *k* which occurs so commonly, as *Inniloo* for *Innialook*; by changing it into a vowel, as *Ne-a-ko-a* for *Neakoke*, or by altering *Oo-ce-ga* into *Oo-inga-a* or *Oo-ee-ma*, and *Hee-u-teega* into *Hee-u-ting-a*.

This kind of non-systematic phonological difference in men's and women's varieties is attested widely. But categorical distinctions in men's and women's phonology are also attested. There are two different kinds of systematic phonological differences shown in the languages of this sample: Pirahã, Tangoan and (marginally) Gros Ventre show phonological collapses in the women's/common gender dialect, which male speakers have to 'undo' when they produce the adult male speech style. The phonological differences in Chukchi follow a different pattern: three ancestral phonemes of proto-Chukotian, *s, *r and *ð, are collapsed differentially into two in men's (*r, *ð > /r/) and women's (*s, *ð > /ts/) Chukchi. Unlike the Pirahã and Tangoan, neither Chukchi gender dialect can be structurally derived from the other.

Many gender dialect languages differ morphologically, either through having different morphological forms, as in Kokama-Kokamilla, Koasati and Awetí, or through expressing different morphological categories, as in Yanyuwa. Haas Type III systems, i.e. systems which are determined by gender of speaker and addressee together, are often expressed morphologically. Yanyuwa speakers have different morphological paradigms depending on the gender of both speaker and addressee; Kũṛux has an interaction of speaker gender, addressee, and grammatical subject (the latter applies in the third person, where speech act reference is neither speaker or addressee-oriented).

Some gender dialects possess lexical differences. These may be cryptic variants of the same word, where men's and women's forms of the lexeme are clearly related but have some distinctive mutation. For example, certain nouns in Awetí which are vowel initial in the women's dialect are pronounced with initial n- in the men's dialect. There are also cases where men's and women's lexemes have no obvious etymological relationship. This is also found sporadically in Awetí with the word for the parrot species *a. Amazonica*, which is *takänyt* in men's dialect and *takárï* in women's dialect. Often lexical differences in gender varieties resemble euphemism, avoidance language, or other forms of word substitution which are unlikely to be categorical (as found in Kalmyk, and yet other Awetí terms).

There are some cases where one gender dialect can be formally derived from the other – women's dialect can be derived from men's in the case of e.g. Pirahã (Section 3.11) and Tangoan (Section 3.5), and men's dialect can be derived from women's in the case of e.g. Yanyuwa (Section 3.4). But other gender dialect distinctions exist where neither men's nor women's systems are structurally derivable from the other, e.g. Irish Sign Language (Section 3.1), Chukchi (Section 3.6) and Kũṛux (Section 3.2).

2.3 Origins and distribution

In general, gender dialects are originally statistical phenomena of gender variation in language use which have at some historical point become categorical. Where the origins of gender dialects can be inferred, there seem to be three distinct evolutionary pathways:
- Dialect merger
- Internal change and conservatism
- Isolation and diversification

In some cases discussed below the historical source of the women's and men's dialect distinction is the merger of two different geographical dialects, or the fossilization of other types of language contact. Chukchi (Section 3.6), Island Carib (Section 3.9) and Kokama (Section 3.10) all provide examples of men's and women's dialects incorporating elements for different genealogical sources. In other cases, gender dialects have come about through long-term institutionalization of linguistic conservatism in the speech of one gender. The mapping of conservative or colloquial speech onto gender categories can go either way: men's dialect can be conservative and women's innovative (from the historical linguistic perspective), or vice versa. In Pirahã (Section 3.11) and Tangoan (Section 3.5) there is a learned phonemic distinction used by men, especially when speaking in an elevated register. Comparison with related languages shows that this phonemic distinction was present in the ancestral language, but subsequently lost in colloquial speech. In Yanyuwa (Section 3.4), women's language is more archaic, preserving morpho-syntactic categories which have been collapsed in the men's language. Irish Sign Language (Section 3.1) is the sole example I have of a gender dialect that evolved through neutral drift in isolation. While isolation and drift is probably the default mechanism for the diversification of geographically-based dialects, gender dialect could only develop this way in the kind of gender-segregated institutional context recorded for this language.

Gender dialect systems do not seem to be diachronically stable. If they were we might expect to see, for instance, entire linguistic subgroups with inherited gender dialect systems. Rather, the gender dialect systems we see seem to be sporadic. There are hints that high levels of gender variation in language may be an areal feature e.g. in Amazonia, and so the relatively frequent instances of gender dialect systems in the Americas may be significant (Map 1 on page 48; see also Kroskrity 1983: 88; Fleming 2012).

2.4 Language and other correlates of gender

Ochs (1988: 137–139) describes the effect of *gender* and social *rank* in Samoan society, showing that while gender has significant effects on language, these effects are outweighed by the effect of social rank. This demonstrates that while gender is always an important social category, it is not always the most important one. A similar phenomenon is found in ancient literary traditions. In Sanskrit (Indo-European, 1200–300 BCE) drama, only educated upper-class males speak Sanskrit, whereas women and lower-class males speak colloquial Prākrit (Hoch and Pandharipande 1978: 14–15). Likewise in Sumerian (language isolate, 2nd millenium BCE), men are portrayed as speaking high register Emeĝul and women are portrayed as speaking the colloquial Emesal variety (Whittaker 2002). It is probably no coincidence that the Sanskrit and Sumerian examples pertain to the written language, since literacy in ancient societies is a correlate of high social status, and so writing itself should be oriented towards a higher register.

The debate around the description of Koasati men's and women's speech by Haas (1944) illustrates the arbitrariness of 'gender' as the social category determining linguistic variation (Section 3.8; Kimball 1987; Saville-Troike 1988). The distinction between the two varieties of Koasati had all but disappeared at the time that these languages were being studied, and it seems impossible to decide conclusively whether gender or social status was at the root of the system. Luthin (1991; cited by Mithun 2001: 278) showed that the Yana gender dialect system described by Sapir (1929: 212) [as a Haas Type III system] was similarly a register marking formality.

Labov ([2001] 2010: 266) shows that for stable sociolinguistic variables, women show a lower rate of stigmatized variants and a higher rate of prestige variants than men. Evidence for this principle was drawn from a wide range of studies of common variables and a wide range of speech communities, rural and urban, western and non-western. The evidence from gender dialects contradicts this tendency however. In all the ethnographically attested cases of possible gender dialects with overtones of formality, it is the male (or male-to-male) variety which is the elevated one (cf. Koasati, and Yana, as well as Tangoan).

3 Case studies

Gender dialect is distributed sporadically around the world. I know of no gender dialects recorded in Africa, but the distribution in other parts of the world is so thin that there is no reason to think that this absence – even if true – is significant. The following case studies are ordered geographically, from west to east according to the Pacific-centred view of Map 1.

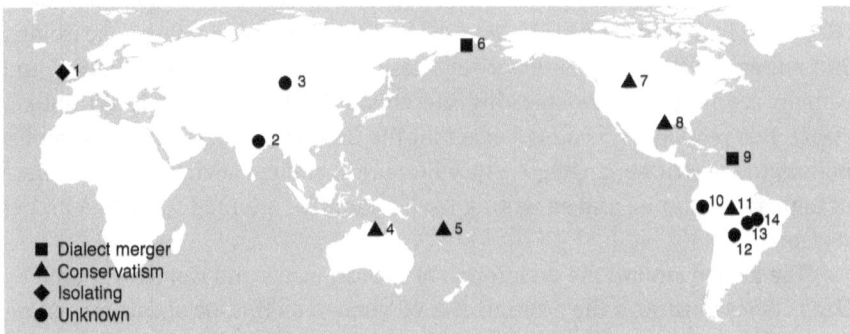

Map 1.: Distribution of attested gender dialects with evolutionary type where it can be inferred (from internal evidence or from comparison with related languages). Languages: 1. Irish Sign Language, 2. Kũṛux, 3. Kalmyk, 4. Yanyuwa, 5. Tangoan, 6. Chukchi, 7. Gros Ventre, 8. Koasati, 9. Island Carib, 10. Kokama, 11. Pirahã, 12. Chiquitano, 13. Awetí, 14. Karajá

3.1 Irish Sign Language

Irish Sign Language originated in a girls' school for the deaf founded in Dublin by a Dominican order of nuns in 1846. The nuns running the school were all hearing, adult learners of a sign language, trained at a school for the deaf run by the order in France. After the foundation of the girls' school, there was little or no further contact with sign languages from outside, so the language used at the school rapidly developed unique characteristics. A second link to this chain was added when a boys' school for the deaf was founded a decade later, in 1857. The language used at this school was based on a dictionary of signs produced by the nuns from the girls' school, but despite the physical proximity of the two schools there was very little interaction between them, and the language at the boys school likewise developed its own unique characteristics. From these divergent varieties a consensus variety was formed when these children grew up and began to socialize together. The consensus variety was based on the male dialect, but female speakers maintained female sign alternants for use as an in-group, women-only code. The linguistic differences that are documented are lexical: some meanings are indicated by entirely different signs, and some signs have different meanings in the two dialects (see LeMaster 1999: 69–70 for illustrations). In terms of usage, Irish Sign Language was a Haas Type III system: a woman talking to women would use the women's sign language; talking to men or a group containing men she would use the so-called 'men's language', the latter always being used by male speakers.

The two Irish Sign Language dialects were the sole medium of language socialization for many deaf Irish children for a century. In 1946 the girls' school abandoned sign language in favour of oralism, with the boys' school following suit in 1957 (although sign language continued to be used outside the classroom at the boys' school at least until 1987). LeMaster (1997, 1999) gives a description of the lexical characteristics of the Irish Sign Language gender dialects, based on dissertation research in 1990. At the time this research was carried out, the native speakers of Irish Sign Language were primarily women over 70 years and men over 55 years.

3.2 Kũṛux

Ekka (1972) describes a complex morphological interaction between speech act participants within the verbal paradigms in the Dravidian language Kũṛux. A sample is given in Table 1. This is a good example of a Haas Type III "speaker-addressee determined" gender dialect (Section 2.1). When this system is considered from the speaker's perspective, you can see that men and women have to make different morphological choices from each other. A male speaker must select different forms of the 2sg or 3sg.m agreement according to gender of the addressee (the 2sg form is coreferential with the addressee, but the 3sg.m form–presumably–is not). A female speaker uses distinct person-number agreement forms according to gender of addressee in all person-number combinations except for 1pl.in, and two of the 3rd person forms. Men's and women's forms only differ from each other when the addressee is a women; for a male addressee the agreement form is identical irrespective of the gender of the speaker.

It is unclear how this system developed. According to Ekka (1972: 31), there is no evidence of similar phenomena in any of the neighbouring Dravidian or Munda languages.

Table 1: Present tense of 'come' in Kũṛux, showing interaction of speaker and addressee gender with specification of gender, number and person of grammatical subject. MM = Man speaking to man, WM = Woman speaking to man, etc. (adapted from Ekka 1972: 26).

	MM, WM	MW	WW
1sg	barc-k-an		barc-ʔ-an
1pl.ex	barc-k-am		barc-ʔ-am
1pl.in		barc-k-at	
2sg	barc-k-ay	barc-k-i	barc-k-in
2pl		barc-k-ar	barc-k-ay
3sg.m	barc-Ø-a		barc-Ø-as
3sg.nm		barc-Ø-a(d)	
3pl		barc-Ø-ar	

3.3 Kalmyk

The Kalmyk (Mongolic) women's language is an example of an avoidance language (Aalto 1959: 3–4; Birtalan 2003: 227). The precise circumstances of its use are unclear, but it seems that is consciously and overtly derived from general Kalmyk. Many common terms are taboo, and replaced by near synonyms: for terms meaning 'girl, daughter' the word *nojɔxɔn* 'princess, lady' is used; *köwün* 'boy, son' is replaced by a word derived from the adjective *ajtɛ* meaning 'good, proper'. If no suitable or sufficiently unambiguous synonym is available, a word can be transformed phonologically, by replacing the initial consonant with /j/: *shaghä :: yaghä* 'ankle bone', *tend :: yend* 'there' and *shaar :: yaar* 'tea'. Certain words are referred to euphemistically or with cryptic paraphrases: *bū* "taxation" is called *ägaryɔdɔɢ* "the roisterer, rabble-rouser".

3.4 Yanyuwa

The Yanyuwa language (Pama-Nyungan) of northern Australia has a complex and well-described gender dialect distinction (Kirton 1988; Bradley 1988; Kirton and Charlie 1996). The main difference between the dialects is in syntactic categories and their morphological marking: The female dialect distinguishes two noun classes, 'male' and 'masculine', where the male dialect only has one.[3]

---

[3] See Mithun, *this volume,* for discussion of the culturally specific properties of gender as a grammatical category.

There is one exception in the male dialect, an archaic form suggesting to Kirton and Charlie (1996: 3) that the ancestor of the male dialect also distinguished two classes. Yanyuwa makes use of noun class prefixes, which differ according to case. In the female dialect "male" and "masculine" noun classes are indicated by different prefixes (see Table 2).

Table 2: Noun class prefixes in the female dialect of Yanyuwa

noun class	nominative	non-nominative
male	nya-	nyu-
masculine	ø	ji-

In the male dialect these correspond to a single noun class, marked by different prefixes in non-nominative cases and by zero in the nominative (see Table 3), like the women's masculine-class.

Table 3: Noun class prefixed in the male dialect of Yanyuwa

noun class	nominative	non-nominative
male/masculine	ø	ki-

The women's dialect also makes more distinctions in third-person pronouns than the men's dialect. These distinctions are highlighted in Table 4.

Table 4: Third-person pronouns in male and female Yanyuwa dialects

	women's dialect	men's dialect
he	yiwa	yiwa
she	anda	anda
it	alhi	anda

Bradley (1988: 127) gives a good example of how far-reaching the differences between the two dialects are, contrasting the women's dialect (1) with that of the men (2):

(1) Nja-ja   nya-wukuthu   nya-rduwarra   niya-wini
     this-M   M-short   M-initiated_man   his-name
     nya-Wungkurli   kiwa-wingka   wayka-liya   ji-wamarra-lu
     M-personal_name   he-go   down-wards   MSC-sea-ALL
     niwa-yirdi   na-ridiridi   ji-walya-wu
     he-bring   ARB-harpoon   MSC-dugong/turtle-DAT

(2) Jinangu   ø-wukuthu   ø-rduwarra   na-wini
     this   short   initiated man   his-name
     ø-Wungkurli   ka-wingka   wayka-liya   ki-wamarra-lu
     personal name   he-go   down-wards   MSC-sea-ALL
     na-yirdi   na-ridiridi   ki-walya-wu
     he-bring   ARB-harpoon   MSC-dugong/turtle-DAT

"The short initiated man whose name is Wungkurli went down to the sea, taking a harpoon with him for dugong or sea turtle"

The Yanyuwa language was no longer being transmitted at the time that the gender dialects were documented, so we only have speakers' reminiscences of how language acculturation happened rather than direct observations. But the situation seems to have been similar to that reported for Pirahã and Tangoan, where all children acquire the women's dialect first from their caretakers. In Yanyuwa society, boys underwent formal initiation at the age of ten, after which they were expected to speak men's dialect, and rebuked if they spoke the women's dialect by mistake. Older speakers could use the inappropriate gender dialect for various kinds of humorous or rhetorical effect.

3.5 Tangoan

Many of the languages of Santo and Malekula islands in Vanuatu have, or have had, distinctive apico-labial phonemes, a cross-linguistically rare type articulated with the tip of the tongue against the middle of the upper lip (described for the neighbouring language Araki in François 2002: 15). This areal feature is evidently unstable, as a number of the other languages of the region show apico-alveolar stops and nasals corresponding to proto-Oceanic bilabials, a change which can be explained by an intermediate apico-labial stage: $*p > *\underline{t} > t$ and $*m > *\underline{n} > n$ (Tryon 1976: 52). There is also evidence from the Tutuba language that the apico-labial consonants can revert back to bilabials, e.g. *p > *t̪ > p (Naito 2006: 224). This sound change would normally leave no trace, and was only detected because Naito (2006) was able to observe the phonological change in progress between generations.

The Tangoan language had a gender dialect distinction acquired by males during a protracted initiation period, during which boys lived in seclusion in all-male company (Baker 1928: 289–290). This distinction held only for phonological features: boys had to learn to produce apico-labials in the appropriate contexts, in effect undoing the historical collapse of the reflexes of e.g. *m and *m^w, as in Table 5.

Table 5: Phonological distinctions in Proto-Oceanic and Tangoan

	'eye'	'snake'
Proto-Oceanic	*mata	*m^w ata
Male Tangoan	t̪ata	mata
General Tangoan	mata	mata

To the phonologist, this is actually quite remarkable, since the irreversibility of phonological mergers is the basic diagnostic of directionality in phonological change. In the Tangoan case the knowledge of pre-merger phonological distinctions may have been supported by awareness of other languages in the vicinity in which the distinction is also preserved, as demonstrated in Table 6.

Table 6: Phonological correspondences in Proto-Oceanic and several Oceanic languages

		'eye'		'snake'
Proto-Oceanic	*m	*mata	*m^w	*m^w ata
Tolomako	n	nata-	m	mata
Araki	t̪	t̪ari-ku	m	mařa
Tangoa (male)	t̪	t̪ata-	m	mata
Tangoa (general)	m	mata-	m	mata
North Malo	m	mata	m	mata

William Camden described the male dialect as a prestige variety, used regularly for "oratory, serious discussion, traditional storytelling, etc., and with less consistency in ordinary speech." (1979: 113). He noted that women and children are not expected to use the phonological distinction, but implied that they occasionally did without sanction. Inconsistency in the use of the male dialect is attested in early sources. In his 19th century description of Tangoan, Joseph Annand (1891: 1–2) described the phonological characteristics of the apico-labials quite well, at least for the stop consonant. He went on to note, however, that [m] and [n] are often used interchangably, even by the same speaker. His examples – *lima/lina* 'hand', *mae/nae* 'come' and *magi/nagi* 'animal' – are all reflexes of *m, so provide the expected environment for the apico-labial nasals.

3.6 Chukchi

The Chukchi gender dialects (Dunn 2000) were introduced at the beginning of this chapter. They provide interesting evidence of pre-contact social dynamics. Chukchi is a Chukotko-Kamchatkan language, spoken in the tundras of the extreme north east of the Eurasian continent. Until the mid twentieth century most Chukchis lived as nomadic reindeer herders in family units of perhaps 20 people. On the northern coasts there was intermixture with sedentary Yupik Eskimo hunter-gatherers, the source of considerable Chukchi influence in the Siberian Yupik languages, and in the south a Chukchi expansion over recent centuries put pressure on culturally similar nomadic pasturalists speaking closely related Koryak languages. There are also contacts with other coastal and riverine groups speaking Chukotka-Kamchatkan languages: Kerek, Alutor, and further varieties of Koryak.

Male and female Chukchi are distinguished by differences in the phonological system. Two phonemes (men's /r/ and /s/, women's /r/ and /ts/) can be sorted in to three correspondence sets, as shown in Table 7.

Table 7: Male and female phonological correspondences in Chukchi

	Male Chukchi	Female Chukchi	Correspondence
mosquito	mren	mtsen	/r/ :: /ts/
polar fox	rekokalyən	tsekokalyən	/r/ :: /ts/
reindeer	qoraŋə	qoraŋə	/r/ :: /r/
s/he went home	raytayʔe	raytayʔe	/r/ :: /r/
trap	utkusʔən	utkutsʔən	/s/ :: /ts/
sister	sakəyet	tsakəyet	/s/ :: /ts/

Historical linguistic reconstruction of this family shows that the correspondences between male and female Chukchi phoneme variation are the product of regular sound change, albeit different sound changes in each dialect. In female Chukchi *r is realized as /r/, while *ð and *s are realized as /ts/. In male Chukchi the three-to-two phonological collapse has gone another way: *r and *ð are realized as /r/, while *s is realized as /s/. This means that there is a phonological contrast between male and female Chukchi in any word containing a reflex of *ð, as well as the phonetic contrast between the afficate /ts/ of the female dialect and the sibilant /s/ of the male.

Table 8: Sound changes in Chukchi and related languages

	Alutor	Palana Koryak	Female Chukchi	Male Chukchi	Chavchuv Koryak	Kerek
*t	t/tʃ	t/tʃ	t	t	t	t/tʃ
*ð	t/tʃ	t/tʃ	ts	r	j/tʃ	j
*r	r	r	r	r	j/tʃ	j
*s	s	ts	ts	s	tʃ	tʃ
*j	j	j	j	j	j/tʃ	ø/j

There is also a form class of adverbs and particles which is distinctive in having a final r ~ t alternation. This includes forms such as qənur/qənut, ewər/ewət, qənwer/qənwet, iyər/iyət, luur/luut, janor/janot and weler/welet. These are not diagnostic of male/female speech, but there are statistical preferences, with men using the -r final forms and women using the -t final forms, in each case by a ratio of about four to one. Historically, the final -r/-t in these forms is *ð, the proto-phoneme which is otherwise realized as /ts/ in female Chukchi. However, the word-final allophone of *ð is /t/ in Palana Koryak and Alutor, so the /t/ pronunciation is expected. What is surprising is that these forms are not recognized as categorically male or female dialect forms, despite being high enough frequency for the variants and the statistical associations with gender to be preserved. It seems that the salient feature of the gender dialects of Chukchi is the /r/ :: /ts/ contrast. The low-frequency /r/ :: /t/ contrast seems to be treated as a stylistic choice.

Using gender dialect correctly is part of being manly or womanly according to Chukchi construction of gender, but there is no taboo against using the other gender dialect in appropriate occasions. Chukchis freely quote speech in either gender dialect during vivid story-telling. In traditional society, and well into living memory, individual Chukchis sometimes change their gender affiliation as part of shamanic inspiration. The individual "doomed to being a shaman" adopts the distinctive characteristics of the other gender: clothing, work, social behaviour, and not least language (Bogoras 1901: 98–99).

Glück (1979) argues against the existence of gender dialects with some dubious data from Chukchi. He claims that Russian loanwords into Chukchi all enter in the form of the men's language, rather than the women's, on the basis that where these loanwords can contain *r* in Russian they always have *r* in Chukchi too (1979: 191). While it's true that loanwords from Russian never have the /r/ :: /ts/ correspondence, the most salient characteristic of the gender dialect distinction, Glück was unaware that Chukchi men's and women's languages also have a systematic /r/ :: /r/ correspondence. Naturally Russian loanwords with /r/ enter into the /r/ :: /r/ correspondence set, since the only words in the /r/ :: /ts/ correspondence set are words descending from proto-Chukotko-Kamchatkan /*ð/. Likewise, Motschenbacher's (2010: 45) observation that women and men can both use the other gender dialect in certain contexts (such as quotation) is true, but this is not a valid argument that a gender dialect distinction doesn't exist.

3.7 Gros Ventre

The description of men's and women's speech in Gros Ventre (Algonquian) provides an example of a marginal gender dialect from both phonological and functional perspectives (Flannery 1946; Taylor 1982). Phonologically, where women have *k* or *ky* men have *č* or (for elderly speakers who preserve the phoneme distinction) *ty*. The women's form is completely predictable from the men's, conditioned by the following vowel, as demonstrated in Table 9.

Table 9: Phonological correspondences in men's and women's speech in Gros Ventre

mens *č (ty)* corresponds to	women's *k* / __ e, i women's *ky* / __ a, æ, ʌ

This shift was perfectly reversable for most speakers during the 1960s to 1980s, since the phonological distinction between *č* and *ty* was only preserved by a few elderly men. While the *č* ~ *ty* distinction was preserved, this would seem to provide the same kind of acquisitional puzzle as in, e.g., Tangoan, where boys acculturated in the women's language would have to learn to reverse a phonological merger as they matured.

The contexts of use of the so-called "men's" and "women's" varieties of Gros Ventre are also not clear. While Flannery (1946: 133) describes them unproblematically as speaker-determined gender varieties, Taylor's (1982: 304) observations, in an admittedly highly endangered language situation, suggest that men might have used the so-called "women's" variety in certain sociolinguistic contexts too, including as "foreigner talk".

3.8 Koasati

Haas (1944) describes a morphological difference in the men's and women's speech of Koasati (Muskogean), comprising a set of correspondences between the respective forms for certain endings in the indicative and imperative. These rules produce pairs (women's form ~ men's form) like ka·hâl ~ ka·hás 'I am saying'. í·sk ~ í·sks 'you are saying', and ka· ~ ká·s 'he is saying'. Haas (1944: 145) gives internal comparative evidence from other verbal paradigms that the women's speech preserves more archaic features of the language than the men's. Haas notes that at the time of observation (up to 1939 according to Kimball 1987: 30) the women's system was only used by the middle-aged and elderly women.

This entire description was challenged by Kimball (1987). In fieldwork starting in 1977 Kimball found that the 'male' speech described by Haas was very nearly extinct, only used by people quoting the speech of deceased elders. He also concluded that rather than being a phonological transformation of certain positions in the verbal paradigm, the male speech forms were actually produced by a suffix serving as a phrase terminal marker. Two other phrase terminal markers – deletion or nasalization of the final verb – were in use at the time of Kimball's fieldwork, although neither was functionally connected to speaker gender. Kimball also established that this so-called 'male' marker was (i) not used by all men, (ii) also used by some women, and (iii) that usage was probably related to high social status.

Saville-Troike (1988: 242) contributed to this debate with observations from fieldwork in 1968–1969. At that time her consultants explicitly described the varieties as male and female terms, regretting:

> that Koasati boys were no longer learning to speak like males, and had not done so for about twenty years. He said that before then boys had learned the male forms when they accompanied their fathers and other men for hunting and daily activities. (The female forms were acquired first by both boys and girls in early childhood while with female caretakers in the home.)

Saville-Troike (1988: 242) suggests that Kimball's social status marking function might be a reanalysis of the markers by non-users as the markers themselves were dropping out of common speech.

3.9 Island Carib

Perhaps the most well-known example of a gender dialect is Island Carib. The documentation of the gender dialect difference comes entirely from the 17th century (Rochefort 1658; Breton [1667] 1877). The early sources related that the gender dialect was said to have come about as the result of Carib conquest of the Arawakan Iñeri speaking communities, with eradication of the male Arawaks and capture of the female. Later anthropological analysis has questioned this (Whitehead 2002).

Taylor (1954) and Hoff (1994) have reanalyzed the 17th century sources with a better understanding of comparative Carib and Arawakan linguistics, which gives us a reasonable picture of how the gender varieties were structured and used. They demonstrate that Island Carib is structurally an Arawakan language with a lexical stratum of Carib (where the etymologically Carib items correspond to the men's language, as would be expected). There are only a few morphological differences between men's and women's Island Carib in Breton's data (Taylor 1954: 29), and many of these may have been unwittingly recorded examples of code-switching to mainland Carib, rather than authentic men's style Island Carib (Hoff 1994: 163). There are only a few regularly incorporated Cariban morphological elements in Island Carib, and these are used in the same way as they are used in Carib pidgins, rather than as in Carib proper. Hoff concludes that Island Carib was a mixed language with gender determined diglossia that grew out of society wide bilingualism in Iñeri (Arawakan) and Pidgin Carib. Finally, Hoff (1994: 164) also interprets the sources to say that the gender variety choice is determined by addressee gender rather than speaker gender, making Island Carib a rare example of a Haas Type II language.

3.10 Kokama-Kokamilla

The Kokama-Kokamilla language is spoken in the Peruvian Amazon. It has been classified as a member of the Tupi-Guarani family (Campbell 1997: 200), although Cabral (1995: 2–3) has argued for a mixed origin, a conclusion only partially supported by Vallejos on the basis of a comprehensive description of the language carried out in a more vital language community (Vallejos 2010: 38). The men's and women's dialects of Kokama-Kokamilla differ in number particles, personal pronouns, demonstratives and connectors. Some of these forms seem to result from a semi-regular process where women's *y* corresponds to men's *r*, but other forms lack any obvious etymological connection, such as *penu ~ tana* '1 plural exclusive'.

Table 10: Particles used in the men's and women's dialects (Vallejos 2010: 42)

Gloss	F	M	Gloss	F	M
1sg.	ta	tsa, etse	distal dem.	yukun	yukan
1pl.excl.	penu	tana	indef. dem.	yama/yamua	rama/ramua
3sg. short form	ya [ja ~ za]	ra	'like this'	ajaya	ikiara
3sg. long form	ay	uri	'like that'	ya [ja]	ria
3sg. object	(=)ay	(=)ura	'also'	yay	riay
3pl.	inu	rana	'but'	iyan	urian
plural clitic	=kana	=nu	'there, then'	yaepe	raepe
proximal dem.	ajan	ikian	'after that'	yaepetsui	raepetsui

These grammatical function words are very common in speech, making for highly salient differences between men's and women's speech:

(3)   a. **uri**   tsenu   **ikian**   yawara=**kara**=uy   **tana**   ku=kuara
(male speaker)

b. **ay**   tsenu   **ajan**   yawara=**nu**=uy   **penu**   ku=kuara
(female speaker)

3SG.L hear   DEM   dogs=PL=PAS1   1PL   farm=INE
'She heard the dogs on our farm.' (Vallejos 2010: 41–42)

There are also minor phonological differences. In the Kokamilla dialect, women have a tendency to produce the phoneme /r/ as a lateral rather than as a tap. Vallejos speculates that this might be a residue of an earlier difference between the Kokamilla dialect and the Kokama dialect (2010: 102), which if true would add support for the hypothetical role of dialect mixing in the origins of the Kokama-Kokamilla gender dialects.

3.11 Pirahã

The Pirahã language has gender differences on phonetic and phonological levels (Everett 1979, 1986, 2004). On the phonetic level, Everett (2004: 7) reports that women use more retroflexed points of articulation in comparison to men, and they have a characteristic 'guttural' articulation caused by pharyngeal constriction. Phonologically, where men have two phonemes /s/ and /h/ women have a single phoneme /h/.

In a personal communication (22 April 2011), Everett filled in some more of the background to this. He confirms that early in language acquisition, Pirahã boys speak using the women's variety. Their later shift to the men's variety seems to be motivated by the desire to affiliate more with adult men's society; there are no formal social structures reinforcing this, however, but Everett gives anecdotal evidence of an individual male who, along with other unconventional (for Pirahã) social preferences, uses the women's dialect.

The simplest historical scenario to produce /h, s/ :: /h/ correspondence between male and female dialects of Pirahã is a simple phonological collapse, which is consciously resisted and reversed by adult men. The source of the phonological collapse is likely to be language-internal change, rather than contact with another language or dialect, since the pharyngeal constriction characteristic of womanly speech would act to reduce the distinctiveness of s and h in female pronounciation, from which the full collapse of /s/ and /h/ phonemes would be a small step.

3.12 Bésɨro (Chiquitano)

Bésɨro is an endangered language isolate spoken in south-eastern Bolivia (Adelaar and Muysken 2004: 477; Sans 2009). Nineteenth century forms of the language are documented as having morphologically and lexically distinguished gender variants (Adam and Henry 1880). It is not however clear that the system ever included obligatory variation rather than a just register choice, and the examples by Adam and Henry (1880: 67) show variation between the notional men's and women's varieties even in a single utterance.

Adelaar and Muysken interpret this as a men's variety and a general variety, rather than a women's variety (Adelaar and Muysken 2004: 479). The men's variety had morphological class and number markers which were used only in elevated speech, when talking of men or of divine entities. The general dialect is used by men in other contexts, as well as by women in all contexts. The gender varieties also had other differences. These include: nouns never used by men; pronouns and adverbs only used by men; nouns that women use inflected and men uninflected, and vice versa (Adelaar and Muysken 2004: 478–479, excerpted from Adam and Henry 1880: 67–68). New data is coming available on the Bésɨro gender dialects which casts doubt upon the earlier sources. While gender varieties are not treated in a sociolinguistic survey of the contemporary language by Sans (2009), a complete description of the gender dialects will be presented in a grammatical description currently under preparation by the same author. Rose (submitted) contains a summary of this updated account which shows that Bésɨro does in fact have a categorical gender dialect distinction.

3.13 Awetí

Drude (2002) describes another Amazonian gender dialect in the Awetí language. This dialect difference, determined by speaker gender, manifests itself both morphologically, with differences in the pronoun, verbal prefix and, deictic paradigms, and lexically. The differences in the personal pronouns are illustrated in Table 11.

Table 11: Personal pronoun differences by gender in Awetí

	M	F
1sg	atit	ito
2sg	en	
3sg	nã	i
1pl.ex		kajã
1pl.in		ozoza
2pl		e'ipe
3pl	tsã	ta'i

Unlike the morphological distinctions between men's and women's Awetí, the lexical distinctions are variational tendencies rather than categorical differences. There are two types of lexical alternatives. The first type comprises pairs consisting of entirely different words in the male and female dialects. In some cases, the alternatives have transparent morphological structure. The men's dialect tends to form these morphologically complex, metaphorical terms by reference to function, whereas the women's dialect refers to source material/species, as exemplified in Table 12.

Table 12: Lexical differences by gender in Awetí

Gloss	Male dialect form	Female dialect form
drinking gourd	y'a'jýt = 'little round thing for water'	mopo'j ýt = 'small gourd'
thatch	tawypepo'apy (< tawypé, 'roof, large mat')	tapaj'jypo'apy (< tapaj'jyp, plant species used for thatching)
curica (parrot species)	takänyt	takárï

The second type of lexical difference relates to form class: vowel-initial words in the women's dialect correspond to n- initial words in the men's dialect. The words entering this class are mostly species' names and tools, three examples of which can be found in Table 13.

Table 13: Phonological differences in lexical items by gender in Awetí

Gloss	Male dialect form	Female dialect form
duck	nypék	ypék
parrot	napúryt	apúryt
bow	nyzapát	yzapát

Drude (2002: 189) suggests that the vowel-initial forms are ancestral, and that the n- initial forms are innovated by analogy to the third person singular inalienable noun prefix.

3.14 Karajá

The Karajá language of central Brazil has a well documented gender dialect system in a highly gender-segregated society (Fortune and Fortune 1975; Fortune 1998; Ribeiro 2012). The differences are highly salient, with the gender dialect differences showing up in every second or third word of running speech (Fortune and Fortune 1975: 112). The most frequently occurring difference is a simple correspondence between *k* in the women's dialect and *ø* in the men's dialect. There is one exception to this, a small set of interjections and grammatical words where the men's form has the same *k* as the women's form. There is also an irregular correspondence between women's *č* and men's *ø, č* or *j*; a conditioned rule for dropping *n* in the men's dialect; and a few words which are etymologically unrelated in the two dialects (Table 14).

These phonological correspondences (at least those involving dropping women's *k* in the men's dialect) are the product of synchronically active phonological rules (Ribeiro 2012: 130–139), and act equally on Portuguese loanwords, e.g. women's *kararu* :: men's *araru* (< *cabalo* 'horse'); women's *nobiku* :: men's *nobiu* (< *domingo* 'Sunday').

Ribeiro (2012: 149) describes how speakers may use gender-incongruent dialect forms, for example, when quoting speech by a member of the opposite sex. Interestingly, this also seems to be used as part of gender dialect socialization: men may use women's speech when baby-talking to baby girls and women may use men's speech when baby-talking to baby boys (Ribeiro 2012:149).

Table 14: Phonological and lexical comparison of men's and women's Karajá (Fortune and Fortune 1975: 116–118)

correspondence	women's Karajá	men's Karajá	gloss
k :: ø	kǝtora	ǝtora	'fish'
k :: k	kohe	kohe	'yes'
	kai	kai	'you'
č :: ø	ričɔre	riɔre	'child'
č :: č	ričoko	ričoko	'doll'
č :: ǰ	ičorɔθa	iǰorɔθa	'dog'
n :: ø / a__o	anobo	aobo	'what'
lexical	-bu-	-hi-	'cry'
	-sira-	-bu-	'to be angry'
	bebe!	mi!	surprise
	wu	ku	calling form

4 Conclusion

Women's and men's dialects are a poorly documented phenomenon in language, which, while rare, is nevertheless important to an understanding of the range of possible culture and language interactions in a broad ethnographic perspective. In many of the cases described above, language dialect distinction is clearly a reflex of wider social gender segregation. Physical separation of the genders, e.g. with the "men's houses", found in traditional Tangoan society as well as in Karajá, contribute to mutual reinforcement of gendered practices in culture and language. The Irish Sign Language situation was different: the gender varieties developed under isolation from each other, so didn't have the distance-creating function present in their origins. I know of no other languages like this, but they might be expected to show up in places with e.g. gender-segregated monastic traditions, Cossack-style military societies, etc.

Gender dialects are only attested in relatively small communities. Most likely gender dialects are only stable in small scale societies, what Trudgill refers to as "societies of intimates" (2011: 185). Maintaining a gender dialect distinction in a language is evidently costly: a community must preserve society-wide bidialectalism, and growing children must relearn basic linguistic principles of their native language. As a result of this gender dialect systems are diachronically unstable, and rarely survive major social upheavals within a speech community. Nevertheless, it is clear that gender dialect is a possible outcome of gendered sociolinguistic variation, which demonstrates the relative importance of the social signaling function of language compared to acquisitional ease and communicative efficiency.

5 Acknowledgements

Thanks to Agata Blichewicz and Kate Bellamy-Dworak for assistance in assembling materials, and to Kate Bellamy-Dworak and the participants in the 'Expression of Gender' workshop (4 March 2011) at the Max Planck Institute for Psycholinguistics, Nijmegen for their questions and comments.

6 References

Aalto, Pentti. 1959. Über Die Kalmückische Frauensprache. *Studia Mongolica* 1(3). 1–8.
Abe, Hideko Nornes. 1995. From Stereotype to Context: The Study of Japanese Women's Speech. *Feminist Studies* 21(3). 647–671.
Adam, Lucien and Victor Henry. 1880. Arte y vocabulario de la lengua Chiquita, con algunos textos traducidos y explicados compuestos sobre manuscritos inéditos del XVIIIo Siglo. *Bibliothèque Linguistique Américaine VI*. Paris: Maisonneuve.
Adelaar, Willem and Pieter Muysken. 2004. *The Languages of the Andes*. Cambridge: Cambridge University Press.
Annand, J. 1891. A Grammar of the Tangoan-Santo Language. In Donald MacDonald (ed.), *South Sea Languages: A Series Of Studies On The Languages Of The New Hebrides And Other South Sea Islands*. 1–14.
Baker, John R. 1928. Depopulation in Espiritu Santo, New Hebrides. *The Journal of the Royal Anthropological Institute of Great Britain and Ireland* 58. 279–303.
Ballard, William L. 1978. More on Yuchi Pronouns. *International Journal of American Linguistics* 44(2). 103–112.
Birtalan, Ágnes. 2003. Oirat. In Juha Janhunen (ed.) *The Mongolic Languages*. 210–228. London: Routledge.
Bogoras, Waldemar. 1901. The Chukchi of Northeastern Asia. *American Anthropologist* 3(1). 80–108.
Bradley, John. 1988. Yanyuwa: 'Men Speak One Way, Women Speak Another. *Aboriginal Linguistics* 1. 126–134.
Breton, Raymond. [1667]1877. Grammaire Caraibe. In Charles Leclerc and Lucien Adam (eds.), *Grammaire Caraibe*. Paris: Maisonneuve et Cle.
Cabral, Ana Suelly. 1995. *Contact-induced Language Change in the Western Amazon. The Non-genetic Origin of the Kokama Language*. PhD dissertation, University of Pittsburgh.
Camden, W. G. 1979. Parallels in Structure of Lexicon and Syntax Between New Hebrides Bislama and the South Santo Language as Spoken at Tangoa. In Peter Mühlhäusler (ed.), *Papers in Pidgin and Creole Linguistics*, 2. 51–117. Pacific Linguistics Series A. Occasional Papers 57.

Campbell, Lyle. 1997. *American Indian Languages: The Historical Linguistics of Native America.* Oxford: Oxford University Press.
Drude, Sebastian. 2002. Fala Masculina e Feminina Em Awetí [Male and female speech in Awetí]. In Aryon Dall'Igna Rodrigues and Ana Suelly Arruda Camara Cabral (eds.), *Línguas Indígenas Brasileiras: Fonologia, Gramática e História,* 177–190. Belém: EDUFPA.
Dunn, Michael. 2000. Chukchi Women's Language: A Historical-Comparative Perspective. *Anthropological Linguistics* 42(3). 305–328.
Eckert, P. and S. McConnell-Ginet. 1992. Think practically and look locally: Language and gender as community-based practice. *Annual Review of Anthropology* 21. 461–490.
Ekka, Francis. 1972. Men's and Women's Speech in Kũṛuk. *Linguistics* 81. 25–31.
Everett, Daniel L. 1979. *Aspectos Da Fonologia Do Piranhã* [Aspects of Piranhã phonology]. PhD dissertation, Universidade Estadual de Campinas. Instituto de Estudos da Linguagem.
Everett, Daniel L. 1986. Pirahã. In Desmond Derbyshire (ed.), *Handbook of Amazonian Languages* 1. 200–325.
Everett, Daniel L. 2004. Coherent Fieldwork. In Piet van Sterkenberg (ed.) *Linguistics Today – Facing a Greater Challenge.* 141–162. Amsterdam: John Benjamins.
Flannery, Regina. 1946. Men's and Women's Speech in Gros Ventre. *International Journal of American Linguistics* 12(3). 133–135.
Fleming, Luke. 2012. Gender indexicality in the Native Americas: Contributions to the typology of social indexicality. *Language in Society* 41. 295–320.
Fortune, David L. and Gretchen Fortune. 1975. Karajá Men's-Women's Speech Differences with Social Correlates. *Arquivos De Anatomia e Antropologia* 1. 111–124.
Fortune, Gretchen. 1998. *Sex-exclusive differentiation in the Karaja language of Bananal island, Central Brazil.* PhD dissertation. Lancaster University.
François, Alexandre. 2002. *Araki: A Disappearing Language of Vanuatu.* Pacific Linguistics, Research School of Pacific and Asian Studies, Australian National University.
Gelfer, Marylou Pausewang and Victoria A. Mikos. 2005. The Relative Contributions of Speaking Fundamental Frequency and Formant Frequencies to Gender Identification Based on Isolated Vowels. *Journal of Voice* 19(4). 544–554.
Glück, Helmut. 1979. Der Mythos von den Frauensprachen. *Osnabrücker Beitrage Zur Sprachtheorie* 9. 60–95.
Haas, Mary R. 1944. Men's and Women's Speech in Koasati. *Language* 20(3). 142–149.
Hillenbrand, James M., and Michael J. Clark. 2009. The Role of F0 and Formant Frequencies in Distinguishing the Voices of Men and Women. *Attention, Perception, and Psychophysics* 71(5). 1150–1166.
Hock, Hans Henrich and Rajeshwari Pandharipande. 1978. Sanskrit in the Pre-Islamic Sociolinguistic Context of South Asia. *International Journal of the Sociology of Language* 16. 11–26
Hoff, Berend J. 1994. Island Carib, an Arawakan language which incorporated a lexical register of Cariban origin, used to address men. In Peter Bakker and Maarten Mous (eds.), *Mixed Languages: 15 Studies in language intertwining.* 161–168. Amsterdam: IFOTT.
Inoue, Miyako. 2011. What does language remember? Indexical inversion and the naturalized history of Japanese women. In Bambi B. Schieffelin and Paul B. Garrett (eds.), *Anthropological Linguistics: Critical concepts in language studies.* Volume III. Talking about language. 212–235 London, New York: Routledge.
Kimball, Geoffrey. 1987. Men's and Women's Speech in Koasati: A Reappraisal. *International Journal of American Linguistics* 53(1). 30–38.
Kirton, Jean F. 1988. Men's and Women's Dialects. *Aboriginal Linguistics* 1. 111–112.

Kirton, Jean F. and Bella Charlie. 1996. *Further Aspects of the Grammar of Yanyuwa, Northern Australia*. Dept. of Linguistics, Research School of Pacific Studies, Australian National University.

Kroskrity, Paul V. 1983. On Male and Female Speech in the Pueblo Southwest. *International Journal of American Linguistics* 49(1). 88–91.

Labov, William. 1972. *Sociolinguistic Patterns*. Philadelphia: University of Pennsylvania Press.

Labov, William. [2001]2010. *Principles of Linguistic Change, Volume II, Social Factors*. Wiley-Blackwell.

LeMaster, Barbara. 1999. Reappropriation of Gendered Irish Sign Language in One Family. *Visual Anthropology Review* 15(2). 69–83.

LeMaster, Barbara. 1997 Sex Difference in Irish Sign Language. In Jane H. Hill, P. J. Mistry and Lyle Campbell (eds.), *The Life of Language: Papers in Linguistics in Honor of William Bright*. (Trends in Linguistics 108), 67–86. Berlin Mouton de Gruyter.

Luthin, Herbert. 1991. *Restoring the Voice of Yanan Traditional Narrative: Prosody, Performance, and Presentational Form*. PhD dissertation, University of California, Berkeley.

Mithun, Marianne. 2001. *The Languages of Native North America*. (Cambridge Language Surveys). Cambridge: Cambridge University Press.

Motschenbacher, Heiko. 2007. Can the Term 'Genderlect' be Saved? A Postmodernist Re-definition. *Gender and Language* 1(2).

Motschenbacher, Heiko. 2010. *Language, Gender and Sexual Identity: Poststructuralist Perspectives*. Amsterdam: John Benjamins.

Naito, Maho. 2006. Tutuba Apicolabials: Factors Influencing the Phonetic Transition from Apicolabials to Labials. *Oceanic Linguistics* 45(1) (June 1). 217–228.

Ochs, Elinor. 1988. *Culture and Language Development: Language Acquisition and Language Socialization in a Samoan Village*. (Studies in the Social and Cultural Foundations of Language 6). Cambridge: Cambridge University Press.

Parry, Sir William Edward. 1824. *Journal of a Second Voyage for the Discovery of a North-west Passage from the Atlantic to the Pacific*. John Murray, publisher to the Admiralty, and Board of Longitude.

Ribeiro, Eduardo. 2012. *A Grammar of Karajá*, PhD dissertation, Chicago University.

Rochefort, Charles de. 1658. *Histoire naturelle et morale des îles Antilles de l'Amerique. Enrichie de plusieurs belle figures des raretez les plus considérebles qui sont d'écrites. Avec un vocabulaire Caraïbe*. Rotterdam: Arnout Leers.

Rose, Françoise. submitted. On male and female speech and more. A typology of categorical gender indexicality in indigenous South American languages.

Sans, Pierric. 2009. *Éléments de sociolinguistique du bésɨro (chiquitano). Approche bibliographique et approche de terrain d'une langue en danger de Bolivie*. MA thesis. Lyon: Université Lumière Lyon II.

Sapir, Edward. 1929. Male and Female Forms of Speech in Yana. In Josef Schrijnen and St. W. J. Teeuwen, *Donum Natalicium Schrijnen*. 79–85. N. V. Dekker and van de Vegt.

Saville-Troike, Muriel. 1988. A Note on Men's and Women's Speech in Koasati. *International Journal of American Linguistics* 54(2). 241–242.

Scheffler, Harold W. 1987. Markedness in Systems of Kin Classification. *Journal of Anthropological Research* 43(3). 203–221.

Sen, Sukamara. [1928]1979. *Women's Dialect in Bengali*. Calcutta: Jijnasa.

Sherzer, Joel. 1987. A Diversity of Voices: Men's and Women's Speech in Ethnographic Perspective. *Language, Gender, and Sex in Comparative Perspective*. 95–120.

Simpson, Adrian P. 2009. Phonetic Differences Between Male and Female Speech. *Language and Linguistics Compass* 3(2). 621–640.

Skorik, Pjotr Ja. 1961. *Grammatika čukotskogo jazyka. Tom 1, Fonologija i morphologija* [Grammar of the Chukchi language. Volume 1. Phonology and Morphology]. Leningrad: Nauka.

Taylor, D. 1954. Diachronic Note on the Carib Contribution to Island Carib. *International Journal of American Linguistics* 20(1). 28–33.

Taylor, Allan R. 1982. 'Male' and 'Female' Speech in Gros Ventre. *Anthropological Linguistics* 24(3). 301–307.

Trudgill, Peter. 2011. *Sociolinguistic Typology: Social Determinants of Linguistic Complexity*. Oxford, New York: Oxford University Press.

Tryon, Darrell T. 1976. *New Hebrides Languages: An Internal Classification*. Australian National University, Department of Linguistics Research School of Pacific Studies.

Vallejos Yopán, Rosa. 2010. *A Grammar of Kokama*. PhD dissertation, University of Oregon.

Wagner, Günter. 1934. Yuchi. In Franz Boas (ed.), *Handbook of American Indian Languages*. Part 3. 293–384. Columbia University Press.

Whitehead, Neil L. 2002. Arawak Linguistic and Cultural Identity Through Time: Contact, Colonialism, and Creolization. In F. Santos-Granero and J. Hill (eds.), *Comparative Arawakan Histories: Rethinking Language Family and Culture Area in Amazonia*. 51–73. University of Illinois Press.

Whittaker, G. 2002. Linguistic Anthropology and the Study of Emesal as (a) Women's Language. In Simo Parpola and R. M. Whiting (eds.), *Sex and Gender in the Ancient Near East*. 633–634. Helsinki: Neo-Assyrian Text Corpus Project.

Wickler, W. and K. Lunau. 1996. How do East African Bush Shrikes Laniarius funebris recognize Male and Female Tutors during Gender Dialect Development? *Naturwissenschaften* 83, 12(12). 579–580.

Yokoyama, Olga. 1999. Russian Genderlects and Referential Expressions. *Language in Society* 28(3). 401–429.

Peter Hegarty
Ladies and gentlemen: Word order and gender in English

1 Introduction

Why do speakers of English like their homes to be spic and span rather than span and spic? Drink gin and tonic in the pub rather than tonic and gin? Stagger home from that same pub in a zig-zig rather than zag-zig fashion? Or stop for fish and chips rather than chips and fish on the way home? Linguists have long been fascinated by preferences to order words in binomial phrases; "sequence[s] of two words pertaining to the same form-class, placed on an identical level of syntactic hierarchy, and ordinarily connected by some kind of lexical link" (Malkiel, 1959: 113). Speakers reference couples – such as Jack and Jill, Romeo and Juliet, and The Queen and Prince Philip – and gender categories – such as ladies and gentlemen, men and women, and boys and girls, in binomial phrases. In his classic paper on binomials Malkiel (1959: 145) described the preference to name men before women in Indo-European and Semitic languages as paradigmatic of the way that pairs of words get ordered "with a hierarchy of values inherent in the structure of a given society." In a recent study, Mollin (in press) found that *men and women* was the most common binomial including the conjunction *and* in modern written English. Making sense of order preferences in binomials requires an analysis of gender. In this chapter, I review past studies and present some new evidence that semantics determines the order in which women and men are referenced in binomials.

2 Order Preferences in Binomials Referring to Gender Categories

Is the preference for *men and women* over *women and men* a "natural" feature of the English language, or something conventional that is subject to historical and situational change? Very different answers to this question are suggested by two essays, both published in 1975; Cooper and Ross' (1975) chapter on preferences for order in "frozen" binomials in English, and Bodine's (1975) article on the history of gendered conventions in English. Cooper and Ross' (1975) chapter has been, by far, the more influential of these two texts and I review it first. These authors proposed hypotheses about both semantic and phonological constraints that would tend to fix or "freeze" order in a particular direction. They considered semantic constraints to be primary and phonological ones to be secondary. Among the twenty-six semantic constraints that Cooper and Ross (1975: 67) hypothesized, several could be glossed by a parsimonious "me first" principle in which "first conjuncts refer to those factors which describe the prototypical speaker." This principle is evidenced by preferences to first name things that are closer in space (*here and there*), closer in time (*now and then*), or more friendly to the self (*pro and con*). The authors also listed seven phonological features – listed in order of presumed strength – that would be likely to distinguish first placed from second placed elements in frozen binomials. Compared to first named terms, second named terms were predicted to have (1) more syllables, (2) more resonant nuclei, (3) more initial consonants, (4) more obstruent initial segments (if both words start with the same consonant), (5) a vowel containing lower second formant frequency, (6) fewer final consonants and (7) a less obstruent final segment.

Gender was not a particular focus of Cooper and Ross' (1975) analysis, but their assumptions about gender are theoretically interesting. Like Malkiel (1959), these authors described the hypothesis that semantically male things would be named before semantically female ones. On the way to deriving the "me first" principle, Cooper and Ross (1975: 4–5) explicitly reject the possibility of a more general rule to position prototypical unmarked terms first, partially on the grounds of the male first preference. By so doing, they seemingly overlooked how a male-first hypothesis fits with the me-first principle for men better than for women. In other words, Cooper and Ross' (1975) analysis is characterized by androcentrism, "that is, males and male experience are treated as a neutral standard or norm for the culture of the species as a whole, and females and female experience are treated as a sex-specific deviation from that allegedly universal standard" (Bem, 1993: 41).

In addition, Cooper and Ross (1975) described the male-first preference as both general and natural. In the context of explaining deviations from this preference, they note that the preference for *mother and son* over *son and mother*, runs counter to "the general law of males first" (p. 94, my emphasis). (Elsewhere the authors explain preference to position mothers first by noting that "We believe that mothers are special" p. 105.) In a footnote on another exception, *ladies and gentlemen*, they hypothesize that the phrase is likely a result of a politeness convention, and that such conventions are "in general contrary to natural tendencies" (p. 105, my emphasis). In other words, they described idiomatic language that positions women first as conventional and idiomatic language that positions men first as natural.

Were Cooper and Ross (1975) aware of this androcentrism? In their concluding paragraph, they note:

> Finally ... we attempt to relate our findings to a general framework of man's view of himself in the world. The principle of Me First, which appears to account for a fairly wide range of freezing constraints, coupled with the assumption that place 1 conjuncts reflect the traits of the prototypical speaker, might give some indication about how we view this speaker. Although we have up until now been tacit on this matter, we hereby forsake the guise of linguistics proper and admit to being card-carrying Whorfers (p. 103).

Here, at last, Cooper and Ross distinguish the "me first" and "prototypical first" rules, and note that both rules are required. This conclusion could be read as recognizing earlier androcentric assumptions about the extent to which 'me' is a male person. But regardless of the authors' intentions, their analysis was tacit about the possibilities of future analysis beyond "linguistics proper."

The second essay from 1975 was more concerned with hierarchical gender relations in those societies where English is spoken. Bodine (1975) argued against the view that the use of generics such as *he* and *man* to refer to all were neutral or "traditional" uses of English (see also McConnell-Ginet, this volume). In so doing, she traced the prehistory of the prescription to use *he* as a generic in the 1850 Act of the British Parliament, which contracted binomial phrases such as *he and she*, on the grounds that the male term covered all legal persons. Bodine (1975) described grammarians' arguments for the correctness, naturalness, and propriety to name male entities before female ones in English in the 16th and 17th centuries. Wilson (1553, cited in Bodine, 1975) is typical of the earlier grammarians she cites. Like Cooper and Ross some four centuries later, Wilson (1553, cited in Bodine, 1975) proscribed that "in speaking at the leaste, let us kepe a natural order, and set the man before the woman for manners sake." Thus Bodine's (1975) suggests that the use of English is historical, and that gendered preference for referring to men first in binomials might be dictated by conventions, just as much as the polite phrase *ladies and gentlemen*. The difference is not that one is natural and the other conventional, but that preferences for male-first binomials have, from 1553–1975 been ontologized as natural and general, whilst female-first binomials have been ontologized as conventional and exceptional, most often by authors who, unlike Malkiel (1959), recognized that gender is a hierarchical social relationship in many English-speaking societies.

3 Empirical Studies of Binomial Order Preferences

Since 1975, several useful empirical studies have added to our knowledge of why English language speakers order terms in binomials the way that they do. Within this literature, Bodine's (1975) historical research is rarely mentioned, whilst Cooper and Ross' (1975) work is routinely positioned as foundational. Both psychologists and linguists have pursued the goal of teasing apart which conventions truly account for order preferences. As a consequence of this strategy, scholars in both disciplines have said comparatively less about situational and historical change in such preferences.

Three sets of psychology experiments are particularly worthy of attention within this literature. First, Pinker and Birdsong (1979) explored the strength of Cooper and Ross' (1975) hypotheses about phonology by asking speakers of English and speakers of French to indicate their preferences for sentences containing nonsense syllables within French and English sentences. Participants consistently preferred sentences with binomial phrases in which the word with fewer syllables was positioned first in each language. Cooper and Ross' (1975) hypotheses about phrases with particular vowel sounds or consonant sounds in the first and second term received far more qualified support or no support at all. These results constitute confirming evidence for the hypothesis that word length is primary over other phonological determinants of order preferences.

A second set of experiments provided support for the semantic rule to position prototypical things first and atypical things second in binomial phrases. Kelly, Bock and Keil (1986) argued for a model of lexical access in which more prototypical category members are more accessible than atypical ones because they are more easily called to mind (Rosch and Mervis, 1975). They presented participants with sentences including binomial phrases in which either a prototypical or an atypical item was named first (e.g., *apples and lemons* or *lemons and apples*). Participants systematically mis-remembered these sentences to position more prototypical things first. In a second study, participants reported a preference for sentences that positioned prototypical things first.

Finally, McDonald, Bock, and Kelly (1993) examined both semantic and phonological features concurrently in their experiments. These authors examined preferences by testing speakers' memory for binomial phrases and noting when order was spontaneously reversed in memory. They found that participants were particularly likely to reverse word order to place animate people and animals before inanimate things, consistent with Cooper and Ross' (1975) "animate first" rule. However, there was no preference to put shorter words before longer ones. In toto, this body of evidence confirms Cooper and Ross' (1975) hypothesis that phonological features can affect preferences for order

(Pinker and Birdsong, 1979), but are outweighed when semantic factors are relevant (McDonald et al., 1993).

Linguists have also examined order preferences by studying the frequency of their occurrence within corpora. Fenk-Oczlon (1989) introduced the new hypothesis that more frequently used words in the language are positioned first in binomial phrases, a preference that explained 84% of the cases in her corpus, more than any other single rule could explain. Benor and Levy (2006) examined a large number of semantic, metrical and phonological features that might constrain word order. Their findings confirmed Cooper and Ross' broad generalization in that semantic features appeared to be the primary determinants of order preferences. Similar conclusions were drawn from a recent study of the British National Corpus, where again "[s]emantic features tend to trump metrical ones" and "[t]he phonological principles, on the other hand, clearly operate on a subordinate level and only have influence on binomial order in the absence of the other, more important factors" (Mollin, 2012, p. 94). Among the semantic factors, Mollin noted particularly strong tendencies to position less marked, more powerful, and more iconic entities first. Her definition of markedness distinguished perceptual markedness, such as the "me first" principle, from formal markedness, in the sense of the term with the more specific rather than the more general meaning. Her findings regarding both markedness and power are consistent with the psychological studies mentioned above (Kelly et al., 1986, McDonald et al., 1993).

Recent studies of corpora have also oriented attention toward the question of how flexible or 'frozen' order preferences can be. Some binomials – such as *spic and span* – appear to be relatively fixed in a particular order, whilst others – such as *Bill and Mary* – do not. Benor and Levy (2006) posited that order preferences might be more frozen when Cooper and Ross' (1975) rules align, and less frozen when those rules are misaligned. Mollin (2012) found that only 18% of the binomial pairs in her corpus were truly irreversible in the sense of appearing in the same order 100% of the time. The other 82% were "distributed on a cline of reversibility." Most recently, Mollin (in press) used the Google Books n-gram to examine the reversibility of binomials in written modern English between 1800 and 2000. She examined each decade for the frequency of occurrence of each order of the most commonly-occurring binomials within the 1800–2000 period. Of the 206 common binomials for which trends could be analyzed, 101 showed trends towards freezing order preferences, 52 toward unfreezing, 10 showed nonlinear trends and 43 showed no trend at all. Thus, historical change toward both freezing and unfreezing are ordinary in English. In sum, the literature on binomials in English increasingly converges on the view that order preferences are primarily a result of semantic features, particularly beliefs about agency, animacy, power, prototypicality, and closeness to the self.

Unsurprisingly, such preferences can and do change over historical time. The preference for *ladies and gentlemen* is a case in point. Mollin notes that there is a strong preference for *ladies and gentlemen* over *gentlemen and ladies* in 1800–2000, but also that Potter (1972, cited in Mollin, in press) had earlier observed a preference for *gentil men* before *ladies* in Chaucer's texts. My suspicion that this binomial may have reversed in the late 1800s was sparked by the on-line OED's quotation from 1808, in the entry on *gentlemen*, to the effect that "All public addresses to a mixed assembly of both sexes, till sixty years ago, commenced Gentlemen and Ladies: at present it is Ladies and Gentlemen." A combined searches of the following British Library databases: 17th–18th Century Burney Collection Newspapers, The Times Digital Archive, and the Times Literary Supplement Digital Archive for articles using the phrases *ladies and gentlemen* and *gentlemen and ladies* over the period 1700–1900 confirmed that the OED informant was a reliable informant as to patterns of late 18th century English. Figure 1 shows a clear change of what Mollin (in press) has called 'freezing with changing preference.' Within this period, *ladies and gentlemen* becomes preferred. The number of newspaper articles including the phrase *gentlemen and ladies* and *ladies and gentlemen* are both strongly correlated with chronological year over the period 1705–1800, Pearson's r (51) = – .79, +.78 respectively, both p <.001. Correlation statistics of this magnitude are only observed in the absence of genuine correlation in less than 1 in a 1000 cases.

4 Explaining Order for Names in Binomials, I: Phonological and Frequency

> Thus, assuming there exist, in real life or in fiction, two playmates, Ván'a, and Mít'a the reasons for any mention of them, in conversation, report, oral story, or fine literature as R[ussian] Ván'a i Mít'a rather than Mít'a i Ván'a may be effectively explored in sociological, psychological or esthetic terms (margin of age, order of appearance, closeness to narrator, importance of rôle, etc.) If there emerges a schema of definite preference, linguistic conditions are likely to have acted, as best, as a lubricant (Malkiel, 1959: 119).

Given that preferences for binomial phrases that name categories can change over time, it would be remarkable if preferences to name individual men before women – such as *Bill and Mary* – were not yet more situation-specific. After all, Bill and Mary could be anybody. Malkiel (1959) suggested that psychological factors such as roles and closeness to the speaker might be more determinative of order preferences than any 'lubricating' effects of the linguistics of names. Similarly, Allan (1987: 52) suggested that proximity might be the primary determinant of order in binomials and that pairs of people are named with the closer partner first. And yet, the most sustained linguistic investigation of the preference to name men before women in English de-emphasized semantic constraints. Wright et al. (2005) noted how Cooper and Ross' phonological hypotheses overlapped with statistical differences between women's and men's names in English. In English, men's names have fewer syllables, and are more likely to begin and end with consonants. These statistical differences may reflect different historical roots (Hough, 2000), but whatever their source, the differences are sufficiently robust that connectionist models, and children and adults who speak English can all consistently predict the gender of real names and nonsense names (Cassidy, Kelly and Sharoni, 1999; Lieberson and Mikelson, 1995; Whissell, 2001). Fenk-Oczlon's (1989) hypothesis about word frequency may also explain a preference to name men first. In English, the most popular names for boys are given to more children than are the most popular names for girls (Lieberson and Bell, 1992). Wright et al. (2005) described how these differences between the phonology of conventional women's and men's names lead to a "conspiracy" to prefer to name pairs of people with the man's name first.

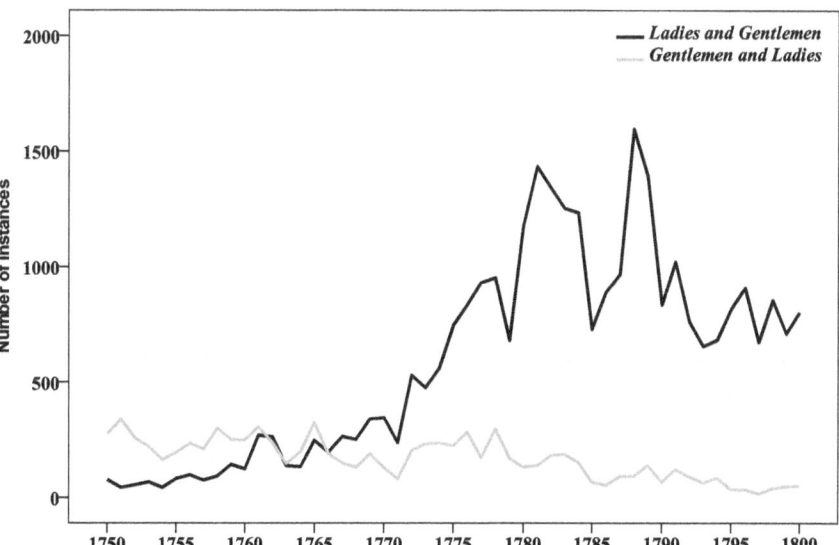

Figure 1: Number of Articles Mentioning *Ladies and Gentlemen* and *Gentlemen and Ladies* in 18th Century English Newspapers.

This hypothesis has received some support in empirical studies. Wright and Hay (2002) used internet searches to document a preference to name opposite-sex pairs with men's names first (e.g., *Bill and Mary*) rather than women's names first (e.g., *Mary and Bill*). Wright et al. (2005) reported two experiments that tested their hypotheses that phonological features and name popularity explain why people prefer binomial phrases in which men's names precede women's names. In the first, forty-six students ordered two names (e.g, *Tammy and Freddy*) in a binomial phrase to complete a sentence (e.g., _____ and _____ went to the yogurt factory). Participants, particularly men, demonstrated a preference to position men's names first when a man's and a woman's name were presented. When the names were of the same gender, participants, particularly women, showed a preference to position the shorter name first. Post hoc analysis also suggested a preference to position the name with longer vowel sounds second. In a second experiment with twenty-eight student participants, the obstruency of consonants was varied across the names used as stimuli. This experiment replicated the preference to name men first. When the names were of the same gender, participants preferred to position the name with a final obstruent consonant sound first. Post hoc analysis of both experiments showed a preference to position more common names first.

5 Explaining Order for Names in Binomials, II: Semantics

Wright et al.'s (2005) phonological features could not completely account for the strength of the preference to name men before women, nor for the particular strength of this preference among men. Yet they concluded that "a number of phonological constraints condition the optimal ordering of binomial pairs" and that "male names tend to be characterized by first position phonology, whilst female names tend to be characterized by second position phonology" (Wright et al., 2005: 558). However, the conclusion that features of names rather than semantic beliefs about the people being named affect order preferences seems unlikely for several reasons. First, it is inconsistent with the primacy of semantics in the literature (Benor and Levy, 2006; Cooper and Ross, 1975; McDonald et al., 1993; Mollin, 2012). Second, Wright et al.'s (2005) experiments may have included "demand characteristics" (Orne, 1962) to focus on features of the names to a greater extent than is typical in everyday use of English. As Hilton (1995) notes, Gricean pragmatics shape the communication between experimenters and researchers. Wright et al.'s (1995) demand that participants express a preference for one of two sentences that vary only in the order of names implicitly communicates that the experimenter is interested in order preferences, directing attention toward features of the names. This demand may not be relevant to situations in which people discuss trips to yogurt factories and their attention is focused on the actors named in the account, rather than the names of those actors per se.

Cooper and Ross' (1975) work also predicts why men might be named before women for semantic reasons. Several of their rules are relevant to the common stereotype that men are more agentic kinds of people than are women (Diekman and Eagly, 2000; Eagly, 1987; Hoffman and Hurst, 1990), including their "agentic first rule" and "power source first" rule. Subsequent research has confirmed these hypotheses about preferences to put animate things first (McDonald et al., 1993) and powerful things first (Mollin, 2012). Can gender stereotypes explain how the social gender hierarchy is translated into binomial order preferences? Such a hypothesis would suggest that preferences for name order will be relatively unfrozen, because people are not always viewed through the lens of gender stereotypes. Rather, such stereotypes colour judgment about strangers about whom we know little individuating information and not very much about people that we know well (Fiske and Neuberg, 1990; Deaux and Major, 1987). Two empirical studies demonstrated how the constraints on name order preferences vary in predictable ways depending on whether speaker are addressing strangers in public or referring to people that they know well (Hegarty, Watson, Fletcher, and McQueen, 2011, Studies 1 & 2).

The first study was a replication of Wright and Hay's (2002) internet search using 200 popular name pairs (Hegarty et al., 2011, Study 1). Approximately three times as many hits were retrieved for men-first name combinations (e.g., *John and Mary*) than for equivalent women-first combinations (e.g,. *Mary and John*). On the internet, there is a clear preference to name men before women. However, preferences for order look different when we address the people we know and love the most, as theories of gender stereotyping would predict. In a second study, seventeen informants who inhabited opposite-sex couples shared the greeting cards received over one Christmas period, and told us whether each card was sent by someone closer to them, to their partner, or equally close to both (Hegarty et al., 2011, Study 5). Among the 492 cards that were sent by someone closer to one of the partners, 433 cards, or 88% of the total, addressed the closer partner first. These findings are harder to square with a phonological theory of name order based on statistical difference between women's and men's names. However, they accord perfectly with gender stereotyping theory; people stereotype men as agentic people and position their names first in relatively anonymous communication only (Deaux and Major, 1987; Fiske and Neuberg, 1990). Other semantic rules, such as the "me first" rule affect private communication with people we know well as individuals and are unlikley to stereotype.

Earlier, I noted that Cooper and Ross' (1975) theory had failed to fully explore the consequences of the fact that the "me first" rule and the "prototypical first" rule were mismatched for women and matched for men speakers. Another study examined consequences of the 'me first' rule for ordering names of couples of varying levels of familiarity (Hegarty et al., 2011, Study 6). Thirty nine women and thirty-eight men each listed the names of five couples in their families, five couples among their friends, and the names of five imaginary couples. Men positioned men's names first when naming family and friend couples in 62% and 73% of cases respectively. However, women positioned women's names first in these two contexts, 66%, 68% respectively. Typically, people have more close friendships with members of the same gender (Caldwell and Peplau, 1982). A me first preference might lead to a male-first preference for most men and a female-first preference for most women when naming well-known people.

In this same study, men more often positioned men's names first when naming imaginary couples than women did (74%, 55% respectively). This gender difference is consistent with Wright et al.'s (2005) finding. Possibly, people call imaginary couples to mind in ways that are influenced both by their habits of naming friends and family, and by their gender stereotypes. Both factors lead men to name men first, but the two factors have opposing effects on the order preferences of women. In support of this interpretation, I present three more experiments that evidence a direct influence of gender stereotypes on the order in which members of imaginary couples are named.

6 Direct Evidence of the Effects of Stereotyping on Order in Binomials

If gender stereotypes affect order preferences in binomials, then men should be positioned first in those binomials when the couple being described is believed to conform to gender stereotypes, but not when the couple are perceived to live in a way that disconfirms those same stereotypes. In the first experiment to test this hypothesis, eighty-six women and thirty-five men British students were randomly assigned to read instructions to think about a couple who either 'are quite traditional, and who conform strictly to gender scripts about how the two genders should behave' or who 'are quite non-traditional and who deviate radically from gender scripts about how the two genders should behave' (Hegarty et al., 2011, Study 2). In both conditions, participants answered a series of questions about the division of labour and personal interests of the imagined couple that confirmed that they had called to mind a relatively traditional or non-traditional heterosexual couple. Next, participants listed five name combinations for the imaginary couple. Confirming predictions, combinations of names for traditional couples included a disproportionate number of male first combinations whilst those for non-traditional couples did not (69%, 49% respectively). As in the study described above, men positioned men's names first more often than women did (73%, 53% respectively), independent of the stereotyping manipulation, $F < 1$ (see Table 1).

The second study used historical time as a proxy for gender stereotypicality, and drew on the finding that students typically consider gender norms to be eroding over historical time (Diekman and Eagly, 2000). Consequently, we predicted that students would be more likely to list men's names first when considering couples who lived in earlier periods of time. Eighty women and eighty men listed the names of ten couples living in either the 1920s, 1950s, 1980s or the 21st century (Hegarty et al., 2011, Study 3). Again we calculated the percentage of combinations that positioned the man's name first. As in the first study, men produced more male-first name combinations than women did. Moreover, the historical time manipulation affected the way women, but not men ordered names for these couples (see Table 1).

The third study addressed a more subtle prediction from gender stereotyping theory. Gender stereotypes are not simply implicit beliefs about the attributes of women and men, or 'conceptual baggage' associated with those terms (McConnell-Ginet, this volume). Rather, gender stereotypes are 'notional gender systems' that are not directly tied to the physical attributes that conventionally define sex (see also McConnell-Ginet, this volume). Gender stereotypes are networks of association that lead people to believe that a wide range of features; physical attributes, interests, occupational choices, and sexual orientations will all co-vary as if they made up a single dimension of masculinity-femininity (Deaux and Lewis, 1984). Gender categories (e.g., women, men) are not the most persistently active nodes in gender stereotypes. When placed under cognitive load, semantic associations between other elements of gender stereotypes remain active even after associations between such traits and gender categories have become inactive (Pratto and Bargh, 1991). Consequently, gender stereotyping research predicts that people will tend to name the more masculine partner in a romantic couple first, even when naming partners in a same-sex couple.

Table 1: Proportion of Couples Named with Male Name First by Participant Gender and Imagined Decade (Historical Study).

Decade	1920s	1950s	1980s	21st Century
Participant Gender				
Female	.69*	.68*	.39	.42
Male	.63	.70**	.76***	.84***

* $p<.05$, **$p<.01$, ***$p<.001$. Significance tests are two-tailed t-tests testing deviation from a theoretical mean of .50 within each cell of the experiment's design.

To test this hypothesis, forty-seven women and thirty-nine men were randomly assigned to conditions in which they called to mind either an imaginary lesbian couple or an imaginary gay couple (Hegarty et al., 2011, Study 4). In all cases, partners were given names using the following prompt: 'My imaginary couple are called ____ and ____.' Next, six items required participants to describe differences between the partners that were relevant to gender stereotypes by writing the partner's names into six comparative statements, endowing each attribute to one partner more than to the other. For example, the final two items pertaining to physical attributes were presented as follows:

      ____ is physically smaller than ____
      ____ is physically stronger than ____

Listing a partner's name first in the first item suggests that the partner was considered stereotypically feminine. Listing a partner's name first in the second item suggests that this partner was considered stereotypically masculine. Notice that these items were carefully written so that a participant who positioned one partner's name first in responding to all items would endow that partner with an equal number of stereotypically feminine and stereotypically masculine attributes.

Consistent with predictions, first named partners were endowed with attributes that were more likely to be masculine than feminine (68% vs. 32%), irrespective of whether participants were women and men, or were asked to imagine a lesbian or a gay couple. Some participants were recruited on one British campus and others participated in a psychology of gender class at a second British campus. Recruitment method did not affect this pattern or results. This experiment provides strong evidence of an association between notional gender and the order of names in binomials. Thus, even when same-sex couples are named, the partner deemed to be masculine is named first.

7 The Phonological Conspiracy Re-Examined

Jointly, these three studies provide compelling evidence of an influence of gender stereotypes on the ways that we name couples that we do not know well. Next, I report a new analysis of these data that tests elements of Wright et al.'s (2005) theory. First, recall that in English, men's names typically have fewer syllables than women's names (Cutler et al., 1990), and that Wright et al. (2005) found a preference for sentences in which shorter names appeared first. In the three studies described above, the names that were generated for men partners consistently had fewer syllables than the names produced for women partners (see Table 2). There were weak trends to position shorter women's names first in all three studies, but to put shorter men's names first in only one of three studies. Overall, these data do not support the preference to position shorter words first in binomials.

Wright et al. also found preferences to position names with longer vowels in the second name and final obstruent consonants in the first name. Table 3 shows how more of the men's names than women's names began and ended with obstruent consonants, whilst more of the women's names began and ended with vowels. Some supporting evidence for the phonological conspiracy emerged only in the historical study. Chi-square tests confirmed that among the women's names in this study, a significantly greater number of those positioned first ended in obstruent consonants and a significantly greater number of those positioned second ended in vowels, χ^2 (1, 1600) = 4.59, 6.45 respectively, both $p<.05$. Among male names, a significantly greater number of those positioned first ended in obstruent consonants and a significantly greater number of those positioned second ended in sonorant consonants, χ^2 (1, 1600) = 6.33, 7.57 respectively $p<.05$, $p<.01$ respectively. These findings are consistent with Wright et al.'s (2005) predictions. However, it is notable that they emerge only in this study in which participants were briefed that the study concerned knowledge about naming traditions. A demand to focus on features of names may have been evident in this study as in Wright et al. (2005), but not in the other experiments.

Finally, I tested Fenk-Oczlon's (1989) hypothesis about word popularity. The UK census office recorded the one hundred most popular names given to girls and to boys in England and Wales across the 20th century, every ten years, in years ending with the number 4. As study participants were largely born between 1984 and 1994, I used both the 1984 and 1994 data as proxy measures of name popularity. Table 3 shows both the proportion of names mentioned by participants among the top one hundred names, and the mean rank of those names according to both the 1984 and 1994 lists. As participants in Study 2 were briefed that the study tapped knowledge of naming trends, only data from the 21st century condition of that study were analyzed here. Table 2 shows that men's names produced in the studies were more popular than women's names produced in the studies. There are considerable differences in trends across studies, and across the year used to operationalize the popularity measure. This analysis lends little support to the idea that men's names are positioned first because they are more popular than women's.

Table 2: Phonological Characteristics and Popularity of First and Second Named Female and Male Names (Studies 4–6).

Study	Study 4				Study 5				Study 6			
Gender of Names	Female		Male		Female		Male		Female		Male	
Position	1	2	1	2	1	2	1	2	1	2	1	2
Count of Names	230	353	353	230	575	1025	1025	575	42	42	44	44
Syllables	1.99	2.20	1.51	1.50	2.18	2.22	1.65	1.63	1.79	1.93	1.38	1.45
Name Beginning												
PVowel	.157	.136	.105	.087	.151	.179	.126	.134	.149	.190	.159	.091
PSonorant	.242	.252	.181	.213	.252	.247	.232	.236	.238	.333	.182	.159
PObstruent	.622	.615	.714	.700	.597	.574	.642	.630	.619	.476	.659	.750
Name Ending												
PVowel	.609	.632	.091	.078	.508	.573	.127	.125	.619	.595	.114	.114
PSonorant	.270	.240	.456	.496	.252	.233	.350	.417	.262	.262	.455	.386
PObstruent	.110	.127	.453	.426	.240	.193	.523	.457	.119	.143	.432	.500
Name Popularity (1984)												
PMention	.477	.491	.537	.543	.810	.638	.433	.622	.452	.428	.409	.636
Rank	41.7	40.2	31.5	29.5	31.7	33.4	38.0	32.0	43.2	53.0	34.1	34.2
Name Popularity (1994)												
PMention	.365	.337	.567	.568	.608	.575	.488	.500	.286	.333	.409	.568
Rank	36.0	32.0	38.7	37.8	30.7	30.7	40.0	41.5	32.3	46.7	46.6	31.0

Note: PVowel = Proportion of names beginning or ending in a vowel, PSonorant = Proportion of names beginning or ending in sonorant consonants (i.e., /l/, /m/, /n/, /ŋ/, /ɹ/, /w/, /j/), PObstruent = Proportion of names beginning of ending in obstruent consonants (i.e., all other consonants). PMention = Proportion of names mentioned among 100 most popular baby names for girls and boys in 1984 or 1994, Rank = Mean rank of mentioned names among lists of most popular baby names.

8 Conclusions

I have argued that people order names and category terms that reference gendered people in situation specific ways that are influenced by historical and situation-specific beliefs about groups and individuals. Whilst the literature on binomials has repeatedly commented on the reasons why it is idiomatic to name men before women in many contexts, that literature has tended to emphasize features of the words (including names), rather than speaker's beliefs about the people whom they reference. In particular, studies with nonsense terms (e.g., Pinker and Birdsong, 1979) and studies using names without any semantic content (e.g., Wright et al., 2005) can yield results which isolate phonological features affecting order preferences. However, the consensus emerging from analyses of corpora (Benor and Levy, 2006; Mollin, 2012), and from experiments (Hegarty et al., 2011; McDonald et al., 1993) is that semantic beliefs about the people and things that we talk about affects the order in which we talk about them. I want to conclude by positioning these findings in three broad contexts.

First, rules for naming people in binomials in English are variable and subject to psychological and sociological explanation as Malkiel (1959) predicted. Speakers of English are guided by their beliefs about whom they are closest to and by gender stereotypes when they chose one of two orders to use when talking about a romantic couple. These rules may not be conscious choices by English speakers, just as speakers of Mohawk often fail to notice that they have two different ways of referring to women, or that they use these two systems in different social contexts depending on familiarity, politeness, status and other factors (see Mithun this volume). English speakers who may choose to address their Christmas cards to *Mary and Bill* or to *Bill and Mary* are similar to speakers of Mohawk in this regard.

Second the influence of semantics on word order in binomials that reference gender is consistent with a growing body of psychological evidence about the ways that semantic beliefs influence the way that information is ordered in both linguistic and pictorial representations. People who read languages written left-to-right or right-to-left learn spatial schemas that associate action with the direction of their written language, and agency with the starting position in their language (Chatterjee, Southwood, and Basilico, 1999; Maass and Russo, 2003). When couples are imagined to inhabit gender stereotypes they are not only named with men first, but depicted as such (Maass, Suitner, Favaretto, and Cignacchi, 2009). Even when graphing gender differences, stereotypes about power lead men to be graphed first and women second (Hegarty, Lemieux, and McQueen, 2010). Consistent with the stereotyping approach adopted here, conventions for representing women and men in portraits can change with time and vary with gender. For example, in recent centuries European women artists have increasingly broken with the convention to represent men facing to the right and women facing to the left (Suitner and Maass, 2007). Within the context of this body of evidence, the effects of gender stereotypes on a form of linguistic order that is also affected by semantic beliefs about agency are less surprising.

Finally, the gender stereotyping orientation presented here suggests the merit of McConnell-Ginet's (this volume) argument to de-couple assumptions about "sex" and "gender" in linguistics. It is important to recognize that the sexist proscriptions for male-first binomials described by Bodine (1975) continue to resonate in English, because male-first binomial terms are often taken to be a non-sexist alternative to masculine generics. Malkiel (1959, p. 144) noted that such expansions from *man power* to *man and woman power* in his own time were rare. However, the increased attention to masculine generics as sexist language in the late 20th century has not always been coupled with a recognition of the sexist conventions that congeal in the male-first binomials that masculine generics truncated.

Finally, I wish to return to Cooper and Ross' vague conclusion about the status of normative women and men speakers of English in their analysis. Prescriptive gender stereotypes exclude or marginalize some people systematically; gay men, lesbians, transgender people, and hjiras, for example. By analyzing the language use of all groups on an equal footing, then the notional gender system that is meted out in noun and pronoun use comes into view (McConnell-Ginet, this volume). Similarly, asking people to name partners of imaginary same-sex couples helped to decouple the effects of the semantics, phonology, and popularity that are confounded with conventionally gendered names in English. As such, I hope that this work spurs the impulse within English language scholarship to queer the disciplines by taking the experiences of lesbian, gay and queer subcultures as reference points in their own right rather than assuming them to be deviations or particulars that cannot serve as paradigms or general frameworks (Butler, 1990; De Lauretis, 1991). I wish to end this chapter being explicit on this point, much as Cooper and Ross (1975) were implicit in the end.

9 References

Allan, Keith. 1987. Hierarchies and the choice of left conjucts (with particular attention to English). *Journal of Linguistics* 23. 51–77.
Bem, Sandra L. 1993. *The lenses of gender: Transforming the debate on sexual inequality*, New Haven, CT: Yale University Press.
Benor, Sarah B. and Roger Levy. 2006. The chicken or the egg? A probabilistic analysis of English binomials. *Language* 82. 233–278.

Bodine, Anne. 1975. Androcentrism in prescriptive grammar. *Language in Society* 4. 129–146.
Butler, Judith. 1990. *Gender trouble*. New York: Routledge.
Caldwell, Mayta A. and Letitia Anne Peplau. 1982. Sex differences in same-sex friendship. *Sex Roles* 8. 721–732.
Cassidy, Kimberley W., Michael H. Kelly, and Lee'at J. Sharoni. 1999. Inferring gender from name phonology. *Journal of Experimental Psychology: General* 128. 362–381.
Chatterjee, Anjan, M. Helen Southwood, and David Basilico. 1999. Verbs, events, and spatial representations. *Neuropsychologia* 37. 395–402.
Cooper, William E. and John Robert Ross. 1975. World order. In: Robin E. Grossman, L. James San and Timothy J. Vance (Editors). *Chicago Linguistic Society: Papers from the Parasession on Functionalism*. 63–111. Chicago, IL: Chicago Linguistic Society.
Cutler, Anne, James McQueen, and Ken Robinson. 1990. Elizabeth and John: Sound Patterns of men's and women's names. *Journal of Linguistics* 26. 471–482.
de Lauretis, Teresa. 1991. Queer theory: Lesbian and gay sexualities. *differences: A Journal of Feminist Cultural Studies* 3. iii–xviii.
Deaux, Kay and Laurie L. Lewis. 1984. Structure of gender stereotypes: Interrelationships among components and gender label. *Journal of Personality and Social Psychology* 46. 991–1000.
Deaux, Kay and Brenda Major. 1987. Putting gender into context: An interactive model of gender-related behaviour. *Psychological Review* 94. 369–389.
Diekman, Amanda B. and Alice H. Eagly. 2000. Stereotypes as dynamic constructs: Women and men of the past, present, and future. *Personality and Social Psychology Bulletin* 26. 1171–1188.
Eagly, Alice H. 1987. *Sex differences in social behavior: A social-role interpretation*. Hillsdale, NJ: Erlbaum.
Fenk-Oczlon, Gertraud. 1989. Word frequency and word order in freezes. *Linguistics* 27. 517–556.
Fiske, Susan T. and Steven L. Neuberg. 1990. A continuum of impression formation from category-based to individuating processes: Influences of information and motivation on attention and interpretation. In: Mark P. Zanna (ed.), *Advances in Experimental Social Psychology* 1–74. San Diego, CA: Academic Press.
Hegarty, Peter, Anthony F. Lemieux, and Grant McQueen. 2010. Graphing the order of the sexes: Constructing, recalling, interpreting, and putting the self in gender difference graphs. *Journal of Personality and Social Psychology* 98. 375–391.
Hegarty, Peter, Nila Watson, Katie Fletcher, and Grant McQueen. 2011. When gentlemen are first and ladies are last. Effects of gender stereotypes on the order of romantic partners' names. *British Journal of Social Psychology* 50. 21–35.
Hilton, Denis J. 1995. The social context of reasoning; Conversational inference and rational judgment. *Psychological Bulletin* 118. 248–271.
Hoffman, Curt and Nancy Hurst. 1990. Gender stereotypes: Perception or rationalization? *Journal of Personality and Social Psychology* 58. 197–208.
Hough, Carole. 2000. Towards an explanation of phonetic differentiation in masculine and feminine personal names. *Journal of Linguistics* 36. 1–11.
Kelly, Michael H., J. Kathryn Bock, and Frank C. Keil. 1986. Prototypicality in a linguistic context: Effects on sentence structure. *Journal of Memory and Language* 25. 59–74.
Lieberson, Stanley and Eleanor O. Bell. 1992. Children's first names: An empirical study of social taste. *American Journal of Sociology* 98. 511–554.

Lieberson, Stanley and Mikelson, Kelly S. 1995. Distinctive African-American names: An experimental, historical, and linguistic analysis of innovation. *American Sociological Review* 60. 928–946.

Maass, Anne and Aurore Russo. 2003. Directional bias in the mental representation of spatial events: Nature or culture? *Psychological Science* 14. 296–301.

Maass, Anne, Catarina Suitner, Xenia Favaretto, and Marina Cignacchi. 2009. Groups in space: Stereotypes and the spatial agency bias. *Journal of Experimental Social Psychology* 45. 496–504.

Malkiel, Yakov. 1959. Studies in irreversible binomials. *Lingua* 8. 113–160.

McDonald, Janet L., Kathryn Bock, and Michael H. Kelly. 1993. Word and world order: Semantic, phonological, and metrical determinants of serial position. *Cognitive Psychology* 25. 188–230.

Mollin, Sandra. 2012. Revisiting binomial order in English: Ordering constraints and reversibility. *English Language and Linguistics* 16. 81–103.

Mollin, Sandra in press. Pathways of change in the diachronic development of binomial reversibility in late modern American English. *Journal of English Linguisitics*.

Orne, Martin. 1962. On the social psychology of the psychological experiment; With particular reference to demand characteristics and their implications *American Psychologist* 17. 776–783.

Pinker, Steven and David Birdsong. 1979. Speakers' sensitivity to rules of frozen word order. *Journal of Verbal Learning and Verbal Behavior* 18. 497–508.

Potter, Simeon. 1972. Chaucer's untransposable binomials. *Neuphilogoische Mitteilungen* 73. 309–314.

Pratto, Felicia and John A. Bargh. 1991. Stereotyping based on apparently individuating information: Trait and global components of sex stereotypes under attention overload. *Journal of Experimental Social Psychology* 27. 26–74.

Rosch, Eleanor and Carolyn B. Mervis. 1975. Family resemblances: Studies in the internal structure of categories. *Cognitive Psychology* 7. 573–605.

Suitner, Catarina and Anne Maass. 2007. Positioning bias in portraits and self-portraits: Do female artists make different choices? *Empirical Studies of the Arts* 25. 71–95.

Whissell, Cynthia. 2001. Cues to referent gender in randomly constructed names. *Perceptual and Motor Skills* 93. 856–858.

Wright, S. and Hay, J. 2002. Fred and Wilma: A phonological conspiracy. In: Sarah Benor, Mary Rose, Devyani Sharma, Julie Sweetland, and Quing Zhang (eds.), Gender and Linguistic Practice. 175–191. Stanford, CA: CSLI Publications.

Wright, Saundra K., Jennifer Hay, and Tessa Bent. 2005. Ladies first? Phonology, frequency, and the naming conspiracy. *Linguistics*, 43. 531–535.

Greville G. Corbett
Gender typology

1 Introduction: Is gender special?[1]

If we compare gender with the other morphosyntactic features, it seems evident that gender stands out. As Ranko Matasović puts it: '... gender is perhaps the only grammatical category that ever evoked passion – and not only among linguists.' (2004: 13). Non-linguists as well as linguists argue about what is "right" or appropriate in the use of gender, whether they are concerned with the appropriate recognition of the status of women, or with the agreement found with recent loanwords. In the same source, however, besides suggesting that gender is 'unlike all other grammatical categories of nouns', Matasović (2004: 18) also writes: '... there is a sense in which gender is just one grammatical category among others.' This is clearly right too, as I shall show. I shall take a canonical approach (Corbett 2011), examining what the canonical morphosyntactic feature would look like, and the possible deviations from this canonical ideal. From this typological perspective, we can contrast gender with the other morphosyntactic features. Current terminology would suggest that the different types of deviation give grounds to separate off gender as different from other morphosyntactic features. However, at this level of abstraction, we see that the variations in gender systems are in fact interestingly similar to those of other features. Gender is indeed special, but it is not as different as is sometimes believed.[2]

I first outline the main ideas of Canonical Typology (§2); then look at the two main issues in the typological analysis of gender systems. The first of these is the analysis problem, which is concerned with whether a particular language has a gender feature, and if so, how many values it has; we tackle this in §3. As will already

---

[1] The support of the European Research Council (grant ERC-2008-AdG-230268 *MORPHOLOGY*) and of the AHRC (grant: From competing theories to fieldwork: the challenge of an extreme agreement system, and grant: Combining Gender and Classifiers in Natural Language) is gratefully acknowledged. I thank Marina Chumakina for help with Russian and Archi, Anna Thornton for suggestions for improving a draft, and Sebastian Fedden for advice on Mian, for helpful comments on a draft and especially for discussion of recategorization. Versions were read at the Workshop "The Expression of Gender", Max Planck Institute for Psycholinguistics, Nijmegen, 4 March 2011, the Workshop "Exploring Grammatical Gender" within the 15th International Morphology Meeting, Vienna, 9–12 February 2012, and the Third Summer School of the Marie Curie Initial Training Network "Language, Gender and Cognition", Potsdam, 14 June 2012. I am grateful to all three audiences for their comments.
[2] For a detailed recent bibliography on gender see Audring (2011).

be clear, I use 'feature' for constructs like gender, number, case and person (some, like Matasović above, use the term '(grammatical) category'). Within each feature there is a set of 'values': masculine, feminine, neuter and so on for gender, singular, plural, dual, paucal and so on for number, and similarly for other features. Then to the second main problem, the assignment problem, which covers the general system according to which gender values are assigned to nouns, and the particular rules for each value in a given language (§4). There is a brief conclusion (§5).

2 Canonical Typology

Let us think of a hypothetical language where every single verb, adjective and adposition showed clear agreement in gender. We would propose a morphosyntactic feature gender, with certainty. If we did not, it would be hard to give a convincing account of the syntax. On the other hand, if our hypothetical language showed evidence of gender only in the personal pronoun, we would think harder about proposing a gender feature. There are many real languages which fall between these two extremes. With these we may be too ready to treat them as though they were instances of the first type. The morphosyntactic features, including gender, often have a 'penumbra' where the evidence is not straightforward, and needs careful analysis.

Typologists are naturally attracted to clusterings of properties. Certainly where there is a problem with a particular feature it is often problematic in more than one way. We want to establish whether these are significant clusterings of properties or are no more than coincidences. One way in which we can address this issue is to extend the theoretical space: then the clusters can be pulled apart. In order to anchor this space, we start from the type of instance we mentioned earlier – the clearest instance of a feature. We use it to set up the properties of a canonical feature and its values; we then have a point from which we can measure the real examples we find. Naturally, the closer our real example is to being canonical, the easier it is to argue for the use of a morphosyntactic feature.

As has been hinted at, to adopt a canonical approach is to take definitions to their logical end point, which is the way we can build theoretical spaces of possibilities. Only then do we investigate how this space is populated with real instances. Canonical instances are those that match the canon: they are the best, clearest, the indisputable ones. Given that they have to match up to a logically determined standard, they are unlikely to be frequent. They are more likely to be rare, and may even be non-existent. This is not a difficulty. The convergence of criteria fixes a canonical point from which the phenomena actually found can be calibrated. This approach has been worked out particularly for inflectional morphology, as well as for syntax. Inflectional morphology has been treated by Baerman, Brown and Corbett (2005: 27–35), Spencer (2005), Stump (2005, 2006), Corbett (2007a), Nikolaeva and Spencer (2008), Stump and Finkel (2008) and Thornton (2011). In syntax, agreement has occupied centre stage, for instance in Corbett (2003, 2006), Comrie (2003), Evans (2003), Polinsky (2003), Seifart (2005: 156–74) and Suthar (2006: 170–198). There has been interesting work in other areas of linguistics too, from phonology (Hyman 2009, 2011) to formal semantics (Fortin 2011) and computational modeling (Sagot and Walther 2011). A working bibliography of this growing body of research can be found at http://www.surrey.ac.uk/LIS/SMG/CanonicalTypology/index.htm, and a volume of relevant work has appeared (Brown, Chumakina and Corbett 2013). Particularly relevant to the current issue is the discussion of morphosyntactic features in Corbett (2011).

I should stress that canonical is not identical to prototypical (as the term is normally used) since we have no requirement to produce a canonical exemplar; rather we need to be able to define and so identify the canonical point. We should also not confuse canonicity with being easy to find: the example which is frequently cited may not be a fully canonical instance of a phenomenon.

3 The analysis problem

We need to be able to determine first, whether a particular language has a given feature, and of course our main focus will be on gender, and second, how many values that feature has. 'Gender' derives from Latin 'genus' via Old French 'gendre', and it originally meant 'sort' or 'kind'. Nouns come in many different kinds: those with initial stress, those ending in a consonant, those with an irregular plural, those denoting instruments, and so on. These are not gender values. 'Gender' is normally used for kinds of noun which are 'reflected in the behavior of associated words' (Hockett 1958: 231). This point is important, accepted by many, and often forgotten. In order to compare across languages in a sensible way, we need this means of classification which is motived from outside the noun itself. What then does Hockett's definition mean? The relevant 'reflection' in the associated words is agreement (which for some linguists includes antecedent-anaphor relations). That is, we divide the inventory of nouns into different kinds according to the different agreements they control. This demonstrates the existence of a gender system, and we can then ask about which gender values it contains. If we apply this type of analysis, we find that some familiar languages, the different gender values have a semantic core based on sex (thus Russian nouns divide into three kinds, and nouns denoting males, though not only these, group together, and those denoting females also group in another gender value). In other languages the structures may be very similar but the semantic core is based not on sex, but for instance on human versus non-human or animate versus inanimate. Thus a language has a gender system only if noun phrases headed by nouns of different types control different agreements. No amount of marking on a noun can prove that the language has a gender system; the evidence that nouns have gender values in a given language lies in the agreement targets which show gender.

3.1 A clear instance of evidence for a gender system

Let us take first a clear example from Russian:

Russian

(1) Žurnal by-l zdes'.
    magazine be-PST[M] here.
    'The magazine was here.' (And now it's gone.)

(2) Kniga by-l-a zdes'.
    book be-PST-F here.
    'The book was here.'

(3) Pis'mo by-l-o zdes'.
    letter be-PST-N here.
    'The letter was here.'

In these three examples we see different forms of the verb: the bare stem in (1) and different inflections in (2) and (3). The number of the head nouns has been kept constant, as have all other potentially interfering factors. It follows that the language has a gender system, and the three nouns have different gender values.

The approach to gender which I have outlined rests on the notion of 'agreement class' (Zaliznjak 1964). For nouns to be in the same agreement class they must take the same agreements under all conditions, that is, if we hold constant the values of other features such as case and number. If two nouns differ in their agreements, when all other relevant factors are held constant, they belong to two different agreement classes. Normally this will mean that they have different gender values. In our Russian examples, it is clear that *žurnal* 'magazine', *kniga* 'book' and *pis'mo* 'letter' have different gender values. Each of these nouns represents several thousand more. In (1) we could replace the noun with *otec* 'father' and many other nouns denoting males; this gender value is conventionally called 'masculine', even though most nouns it includes, like *žurnal* 'magazine', do not denote males. Similarly in (2), in place of *kniga* 'book' we could have a noun like *mat'* 'mother', and these nouns are members of the feminine gender. Again, the majority of the nouns involved do not denote females. Finally the nouns like *pis'mo* 'letter' comprise the neuter gender value.

There are languages where we can see quite easily that they have a gender system, and the number of gender values is evident. However, for some languages the number of gender values has given rise to debate, even the passionate debate of which Matasović speaks. A good example is Romanian, about which there has been a long and sometimes quite heated discussion. The analytical problem posed by Romanian is genuinely interesting, as we shall see shortly. It matters that we are consistent in our analyses, since otherwise when we move to typology we are not comparing like with like. For instance, it is regularly stated that the Nakh language Batsbi (also known as Tsova Tush) has eight gender values. In a way it does. However, if we were to analyse French in the same way, we would say that French has three gender values. Alternatively, if we were to analyse Batsbi as French is normally analysed we would find that Batsbi has five gender values.

Thus the analytical decisions are not always straightforward. We think of features and values as being clean and neat. However they can have a less clear area, a penumbra around the clear core. To investigate this tricky area it proves helpful to start from the clearest examples, the canonical ones.

3.2 Principles for canonical features and their values

It will be helpful to have a yardstick against which to measure the examples we find. We therefore consider the ideal morphosyntactic feature and how it would behave. I suggest three overarching principles (Corbett 2011: 450, 458):

I: Canonical features and their values are clearly distinguished by formal means.

II: The use of canonical morphosyntactic features and their values is determined by simple syntactic rules.

III: Canonical morphosyntactic features and their values are expressed by canonical inflectional morphology.

Non-canonical instances may deviate in terms of the feature as a whole (thus gender may be non-canonical in particular respects in a given language) and particular values may also be non-canonical (neuter might be non-canonical in a way that did not affect other gender values). We shall not consider all the possibilities, but rather home in on some which are particularly interesting for gender, in comparison with the other morphosyntactic features. We shall concentrate on Principle I and on some of the more specific criteria which it covers.

According to Principle I, canonical features and their values are clearly distinguished by formal means; given the general philosophy of the approach, it follows that if we compare the formal means by which a feature or value is distinguished, then the clearer they are the more canonical that feature or value. But what does 'clear' mean here? It means that there is a straightforward and regular mapping from form to function. As a result, in the canonical situation there is clear evidence for a given feature, gender for instance, and its values. We shall consider four of the criteria which make this general principle more specific.

Criterion 1
Canonical features and their values have a dedicated form

We might very reasonably assume that in order to postulate a feature, and its values, we should be able in each instance to point to an inflected form as justification; ideally, it should be possible to explain this form only in terms of the particular feature and value. Values that can be justified in this way may be termed 'autonomous' (Zaliznjak 1973: 69–74; Mel'čuk 1986: 66–70). Naturally we can look for non-canonical situations where there is no unique form to make the value autonomous. Consider this situation, first at the abstract level, applicable to any morphosyntactic feature:

a	d
a	e
b	e

Figure 1: A non-autonomous case value

In Figure 1, 'a', 'b' and so on represent fully inflected forms. The paradigm represents two orthogonal features. For the feature represented by the rows, the issue is whether there are three values or only two. Looking just at the left column, we see there two values, and similarly in the right column. And yet, many linguists would accept three values, based on the combinations a-d, a-e, and b-e; of these, the combination a-e has no autonomous form. Let us check first with regard to case values: Zaliznjak (1973: 69–74) discusses several instances. Here we will look at Classical Armenian:

SINGULAR	PLURAL	
am	amkʻ	NOMINATIVE
am	ams	ACCUSATIVE
ami	ams	LOCATIVE
ami	amacʻ	DATIVE

Figure 2: Classical Armenian *am* 'year' (partial paradigm)

In this example (from Klein 2007: 1053, see also Baerman, Brown and Corbett (2005: 42–44) and references there) there is no unique form for the accusative; its forms are always syncretic, with the nominative or with the locative, depending on number. Yet we accept an accusative case value. The alternative, to avoid all this, would be to say that transitive verbs take a nominative object in the singular and a locative object in the plural, but that would not allow simple rules of syntax (Principle II). In terms of canonicity, we can say that the accusative is a less canonical case value than the nominative or dative in this system.[3]

How does this relate to gender? A very clear comparable instance is the gender system of Romanian. Key examples follow:

Romanian (Adina Dragomirescu and Alexandru Nicolae, personal communication)

(4)   bărbat   bun
      man(M)[SG]   good[M.SG]
      'a good man'

(5)   film   bun
      film(N)[SG]   good[M.SG]
      'a good film'

(6)   femei-e   bun-ă
      woman(F)-SG   good-F.SG
      'a good woman'

---

[3] For nouns of this type the locative similarly does not have a unique form; however, elsewhere in the system, there are nouns which do have a distinct locative. Daniel Kölligan points out (personal communication) that Classical Armenian has a preposition *z-*, used to distinguish objects which are specific (for examples, see Jensen 1959: 146–150). This is an instance of differential object marking but it does not make the accusative autonomous: it does not have a unique inflectional form. For pronouns the preposition is obligatory.

(7) bărbaț-i   bun-i
     man(M)-PL   good-M.PL
     'good men'

(8) film-e   bun-e
     film(N)-PL   good-F.PL
     'good films'

(9) femei   bun-e
     good woman(F)[PL]   good-F.PL
     'good women'

If we had only the evidence from singular noun phrases we would conclude that Romanian had two gender values. Similarly, if we had only plural noun phrases we would propose two gender values. When we put the two together, we see the need for three gender values, even though the third gender value has no unique form to justify it. This third gender value is non-autonomous, just like the accusative of Classical Armenian. This can be seen in Figure 3:

SINGULAR	PLURAL	
bun	bun-i	MASCULINE
bun	bun-e	NEUTER (AMBIGENERIC)
bun-ă	bun-e	FEMININE

Figure 3: A non-autonomous gender value: Romanian *bun* 'good'

Further discussion and sources can be found in (Corbett 1991: 150–154).[4] This type of gender value, what we are calling here a non-autonomous gender value, is also known as *genus alternans* (as in Igartua 2006); once we recognize that gender is not different in having such values, but is just like case (and as we shall see shortly, like person too), we may prefer the term 'non-autonomous', since it is common to the different morphosyntactic features. Given the nature of this third gender value in Romanian, some prefer the term 'ambigeneric' to neuter.

It is important that from the point of view of the noun inventory Romanian clearly has three gender values. There are substantial numbers of nouns in each

---

[4] And more recently see Maiden (2011: endnote 36, pp. 701–702), and Nedelcu (2013) on Romanian, and Loporcaro and Paciaroni (2011), for discussion of the development of such instances elsewhere in Indo-European.

of the three genders, and the neuter gender is gaining new members through borrowings into the language. What is noteworthy about the Romanian gender system is the means of agreement for one gender value: the distribution across the lexicon is straightforward. Compare this with French, which arguably also has nouns which are masculine in the singular and feminine in the plural: these are: *délice* 'delight', *orgue* 'organ' and less clearly *amour* 'love'. There is some question about whether we are dealing with different lexical items, since they are not straightforward singular-plural pairs and there is some variability. It seems clear that these nouns should be treated as lexical exceptions and that the traditional account which has two gender values for French is correct. But now consider the Nakh language Batsbi, mentioned earlier. In various sources it is said that Batsbi has eight genders. This can be found, for example, in the grammar by Dešeriev (1953: 138–145), but the view goes back to the nineteenth century. Batsbi has just four gender-number markers, and yet these occur in remarkable combinations (Corbett 1991: 171). These combinations give eight agreement classes, all but one of which are non-autonomous. The tradition has been to treat each of these agreement classes as a gender value.

This traditional analysis may be represented as in Figure 4 (note that this cannot be presented as in Figure 3, because of the 'crossed' relations between some forms):

SINGULAR   PLURAL

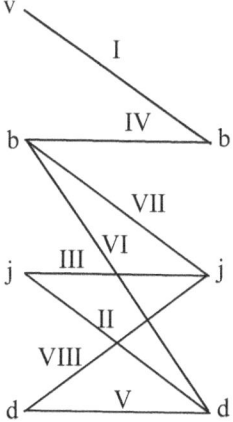

Figure 4: Agreement classes in Batsbi

However, the vast majority of nouns are found in just five gender values. The remaining three agreement classes (all of which are non-autonomous) account for around twenty nouns between them. None of these three classes should be recognized as a gender value, since they have insufficient members: they are "inquorate". Each of the twenty or so nouns can be labeled as a lexical exception; this is the analysis in Holisky and Gagua (1994: 162–163) and in Corbett (1991: 170–172). This analysis can be represented as in Figure 5:

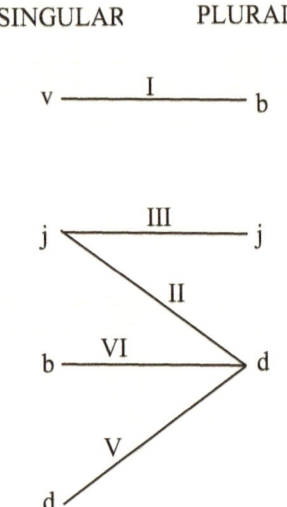

Figure 5: Gender in Batsbi (excluding inquorate genders)

Recall the earlier point about Batsbi and French. It is reasonable to say that Batsbi has eight gender values (including the inquorate ones) provided we say also that French has three gender values (also to include the inquorate gender for the very few nouns which are masculine in the singular and feminine in the plural, noted earlier). I believe it is preferable to treat French as having two gender values, in which case Batsbi has five.

Having considered inquorate gender values, let us return to the main point, that of non-autonomous values; we have seen a non-autonomous case value in Classical Armenian and a non-autonomous gender value in Romanian. To demonstrate the similarity across the features here let us look briefly at a non-autonomous person value, as found in Old Nubian (Figure 6); the source is Browne (2002: 50), as cited in Baerman, Brown and Corbett (2005: 75):

SINGULAR	PLURAL	
dollire	dolliro	1
dollina	dolliro	2
dollina	dollirana	3

Figure 6: A non-autonomous person value: Old Nubian present indicative (*doll-* 'wish')

Old Nubian was a Nilo-Saharan language, with texts dating from the eighth to the fifteenth centuries AD (according to Browne 2002: 1). The picture seen in Figure 6 is fully comparable to that seen in Classical Armenian and in Romanian; just the features have changed. Given only the singular, we would say that Old Nubian makes a two-way distinction of morphosyntactic person, and similarly in the plural. When we put the two together we recognize three person values, the second person being non-autonomous. Thus non-autonomous gender values are certainly interesting, but they are not unique to gender.

Criterion 2
Canonical features and their values are uniquely distinguished across other logically compatible features and their values.

This criterion makes intuitive sense. We know that in some instances, demonstrating the existence of a particular feature or values means looking at a limited set of environments, determined by combinations of other features and values. In other languages, a particular feature and its values is evident almost wherever one looks. The latter is the more canonical situation, since it is then easy to argue that the particular feature and its values are required. This will be clear from these Italian examples:

Italian (Marco Bertinetto, personal communication)

(10) il   terren-o   bass-o
      DEF.M.SG   ground(M)-SG   low-M.SG
      'the low ground'

(11) i   terren-i   bass-i
      DEF.M.PL   ground(M)-PL   low-M.PL
      'the low grounds'

(12) la   port-a   bass-a
      DEF.F.SG   door(F)-SG   low-F.SG
      'the low door'

(13) le   port-e   bass-e
      DEF.F.PL   door(F)-PL   low-F.PL
      'the low doors'

Let us ask whether we need a number feature. Just comparing (10) and (11) suggests that we do, and that we need the values singular and plural. Equally, if we compare (12) and (13) we reach the same result. Now consider gender. A comparison of (10) and (12) suggests that we need gender, and further work would confirm masculine and feminine as appropriate values. Equally, comparing (11) and (13) would give the same result. In other words, we find evidence for number across the different gender values, and we find gender across the different number values. We do not have to look, say, within the singular to find evidence for gender. The situation is as in (14):

(14) Gender and number in Italian adjectival forms (both uniquely distinguished)

GENDER	NUMBER	
	SINGULAR	PLURAL
MASCULINE	basso	bassi
FEMININE	bassa	basse

Note that not all Italian adjectives are like *basso* 'low'. *Basso* 'low' is canonical in respect of Criterion 2. We return to other non-canonical Italian adjectives in our discussion of Criterion 4 below.

Continuing with Criterion 2, according to which features and values are uniquely distinguished across other logically compatible features and their values, we now look for contrast as a clearly non-canonical instance. (15) shows selected forms of the Archi verb *aχas* 'lie down' (data from Chumakina, Brown, Quilliam and Corbett 2007: ix-xi and Marina Chumakina, p.c., following Kibrik (1998: 457–458)):

(15)　　　Gender marking in Archi (*aχas* 'lie down')

NUMBER	GENDER	IMPERFECTIVE	PERFECTIVE
SG	I	w-a‹r›χa-r	a‹w›χu⁸
	II	d-a‹r›χa-r	a‹r›χu
	III	b-a‹r›χa-r	a‹b›χu
	IV	a‹r›χa-r	aχu
PL	I	b-a‹r›χa-r	a‹b›χu
	II		
	III	a‹r›χa-r	aχu
	IV		

We can extract the verbal gender/number markers, which may be prefixal (indicated X-) or infixal (<X>), as in Figure 7:

GENDER (and assignment)	NUMBER	
	SINGULAR	PLURAL
I (male human)	w-/‹w›	b-/‹b›
II (female human)	d-/‹r›	
III (some animates, all insects, some inanimates)	b-/‹b›	Ø-/‹Ø›
IV (some animates, some inanimates, abstracts)	Ø-/‹Ø›	

Figure 7: Gender and number in Archi (evidence from verbs)

We should still recognize four gender values in Archi; however, it is clear that the way in which they are realized in the morphology is less canonical than in Italian. To see the four-way distinction, we must look at the singular, and even here some markers are syncretic with other gender/number markers. Another example is Lavukaleve (discussed in more detail in §4.2.2 below), which distinguishes three gender values in the singular and dual but not in the plural (Terrill 2003: 142).

Again we find comparable non-canonical behaviour with other morphosyntactic features: that is, instances where their values are distinguished fully only in an environment defined by other morphosyntactic feature values. Examples

---

5 Realized as /uwχu /.

for number (from Biak, based on van den Heuvel 2006: 66), from person (from Belhare, following Bickel and Nichols 2005: 51) and for case (from Russian) are given in Corbett (2011: 462–464).

Criterion 3
Canonical features and their values are distinguished consistently across relevant parts of speech (word classes).

In the canonical situation we find the same distinctions whichever part of speech we look at. For instance, Russian nouns, adjectives, verbs and pronouns all show two number values, singular and plural. From the perspective of systems like the Russian number system, it may seem hard to imagine an alternative. And yet there are various systems, gender systems and other morphosyntactic systems, where different parts of speech behave differently.

Let us start with a problem which is relatively well known, concerning case. In Guugu Yimidhirr (a language of North Queensland described in Haviland 1979), we find pronouns which, as part of a larger case system, distinguish subjects and objects according to a nominative-accusative system. The forms are given in (16):

(16)   Guugu Yimidhirr pronouns (partial: Haviland 1979: 66–67)

	NOMINATIVE	ACCUSATIVE
1 SINGULAR	ngayu	nganhi
2 SINGULAR	nyundu	nhina(an(in))
3 SINGULAR	nyulu	nhinhaan(in)

The nouns, however, are different, distinguishing ergative and absolutive:

(17)   Guugu Yimidhirr nouns (partial: Haviland 1979: 47–51)

	ERGATIVE	ABSOLUTIVE
'girl'	gabirr-inh	gabiirr
'head'	ngaabay-il	ngaabaay

Given just the pronoun, we would imagine that Guugu Yimidhirr had a NOMINATIVE-ACCUSATIVE system. With just the evidence of nouns we would say that it was ERGATIVE-ABSOLUTIVE. And indeed, such systems are sometimes treated as 'split ergative'. This makes sense if we are discussing the lexicon; it is true that the lexicon is split between items with different morphological patternings of case. However, if we are concerned with syntax (especially the simple syntax of our Principle II), it is unlikely that we would allow different case values for different controlees: we do not expect verbs to 'peek' at the type of a noun phrase in order to establish which case they govern. Rather, we can consider pronouns and nouns together: the data above give evidence for three distinct case values (Guugu Yimidhirr has several additional simpler case values). This makes good sense, and might be called a 'combined case system'.

	NOM		ACC
PRONOUN 1SG	ngayu		nganhi
	ERG	ABS	
NOUN 'girl'	gabirr-inh	gabiirr	
combined case values	ERG	NOM-ABS	ACC

Figure 8: Guugu Yimidhirr (as a combined case system): set-theoretical analysis

As we see in Figure 8, Guugu Yimidhiir has case values distinguishing the following:
1. the subject of a transitive verb stands in the ERGATIVE
2. the object of a transitive verb stands in the ACCUSATIVE
3. the single argument of an intransitive verb stands in the NOMINATIVE-ABSOLUTIVE; this name is only a helpful mnemonic: it is a single case value, which we could have labeled simply ABSOLUTIVE.

This type of analysis is argued for in Goddard (1982). It is established by combining the evidence gained from pronouns with that gained from nouns.

Can we find similar situations with the other morphosyntactic features? Few examples have been identified to date. For number there is Mele-Fila (data from Ross Clark) see Corbett (2011: 467) and for person consider the Maybrat data (from Dol 2007: 65) presented in Corbett (2011: 468). Of course, we are most interested in instances of combined gender systems. One that has been discussed in some detail is Mba (see Corbett 2011: 465–466 for sources and analysis), and a second is Michif (Bakker 1997: 106–107 discussed in Corbett 2006: 269–270). Here we examine an equally interesting example, which has been less discussed, namely Burmeso, a language of the Mamberamo River area of Western New Guinea. The material on Burmeso is entirely from Donohue (2001). Consider first these instances of verb agreement (according to an ergative system):

Gender marking on verbs in Burmeso (Donohue 2001: 99–101):

(18) da nawak g-ihi-maru
 1SG woman.SG II.SG-see-TODAY'S.PAST
 'I saw a woman.'

(19) da mibo j-ihi-maru
 1SG banana.SG V.SG-see-TODAY'S.PAST
 'I saw a banana.'

(20) jamo nawak n-akwa-ru
 dog.SG woman.SG II.SG-bite-TODAY'S.PAST
 'The dog bit a woman.'

In these few examples (see Donohue 2001 for the full set) there is evidence that Burmeso has a gender system, and also that gender agreement is marked differently according to verb class. There are two inflection classes, as shown in Figure 9:

	assignment	inflection class 1		inflection class 2	
		e.g. -ihi- 'see'		e.g. -akwa- 'bite'	
		SG	PL	SG	PL
I	male	j-	s-	b-	t-
II	female animate	g-	s-	n-	t-
III	miscellaneous	g-	j-	n-	b-
IV	mass nouns	j-	j-	b-	b-
V	banana, sago tree	j-	g-	b-	n-
VI	arrows, coconuts	g-	g-	n-	n-

Figure 9: Full set of gender markers on Burmeso verbs (Donohue 2001: 100, 102)

These inflection classes are of great typological interest (see Corbett 2009), but they are not our main concern here. The point which matters for us is that the agreements of each inflection class show that there are six agreement classes of nouns, labeled I-VI in (Figure 9). One of these, agreement class V can be considered inquorate, since it contains only two nouns, and the agreements are simply an irregular combination: IV in the SINGULAR and VI in the PLURAL. This system of gender agreement, is rather different from that shown on adjectives: (Donohue 2001: 105):

(21) Da   de   koya   bek-abo
      1SG   1SG.POSS   grandfather.SG good-M.SG
      'My grandfather is well.'

(22) Da   d-asia   bek-an.
      1SG   1SG.POSS-grandmother.SG   good-F.SG
      'My grandmother is well.'

(23) Da   de   koysorad   bek-odo
      1SG   1SG.POSS   grandson.PL   good-ANIM.PL
      'My grandsons are well.'

Again, I will not repeat all the examples to show the full system; the possible suffixes are as follows:

(24)   Gender agreement suffixes on adjectives (Donohue 2001: 106)

GENDER	SINGULAR	PLURAL
MASCULINE	-ab	-od(o)
FEMININE	-an	-od(o)
NEUTER	-ora	-or(o)
MASCULINE INANIMATE	-ab	-or
FEMININE INANIMATE	-an	-or
NEUTER ANIMATE	-ora	-od

It is evident that the distinctions made by Burmeso adjectives do not match those of the nouns.[6] However, they are not fully orthogonal either, as we see if we plot the two against each other (Figure 10). I give the distinctions made on the basis of verbs as I-VI on the left, and the adjectivally-induced distinctions along the top:

In each cell I give the number of nouns found in Donohue's representative word-list. This means that the figures are indicative, but not more.[7] From

---

[6] The adjective 'white' marks both gender systems.
[7] For instance, the number of nouns in GENDER VI is actually higher; all terms for arrows belong in GENDER VI (Donohue 2001: 102) but only the generic term *kasarar* appears in the representative word list.

Figure 10 we see clearly that it is not a matter of two systems combining freely. Of the 36 possibilities, instances have been found of only 16. (It is possible, of course, that with a larger noun inventory a few more cells might be filled, but the distribution within Figure 10 shows considerable skewing.) Thus Burmeso shows a combined gender system, comparable to the combined case system of Guugu Yimidhirr; to see the full system we have to look at the differing evidence of verbs and adjectives. Both systems are far from canonical: in a canonical system, the evidence gained from each controllee or target would be the same.

	M	F	N	M INAN	F INAN	N ANIM
I	44 plus all male kin terms	5 (4 birds)		1 ('neck')		2 ('sea', 'wound')
II		7 plus all female kin terms	4		1 ('small goanna')	2 ('sago rinser (lower)', 'string. shapes')
III	3		28, mainly inanimate	10, inanimate	1 ('goanna')	
IV	9, inanimate					
V				2 ('banana', 'sago tree')		
VI			1 ('arrow')	1 ('coconut')		

Figure 10: The combined gender system of Burmeso

It is not just larger systems that can be non-canonical in this way. Consider the apparently simpler system of Dutch. Different targets distinguish different numbers of gender values, as shown in Figure 11.

Dutch is non-canonical in that the targets are sensitive to different numbers of gender values; the system appears relatively straightforward in that the smaller system of two values is nested within the larger. There are additional very interesting complications, however, in that several different combinations of gender agreements are possible, for which see Audring (2009). See also De Vos and De Vogelaar (2011) on the special interest of Dutch, and Schiller (this volume) for some unexpected psycholinguistic results from its gender system.

agreement target (type)	attributive			relative pronoun	personal pronoun
agreement target (category)	indefinite article	definite article	adjective	relative pronoun	personal pronoun
example forms	een	de [c] het [n]	mooi-e [c] mooi [n]	die [c] dat [n]	hij [m] zij [f] het [n]
number of gender values	0	2	2	2	3

Figure 11: Gender values of different agreement targets in Dutch (Audring 2009: 52)

Since we are discussing situations where different targets behave differently, we should pause briefly to consider classifiers. In the clearest instances classifiers are rather different from gender systems, since they are free forms; see Dixon (1982: 212–218) and Corbett (1991: 136–137) for ways of distinguishing gender from classifiers. And the best known classifier systems and gender systems are found in languages of different types (isolating and fusional respectively), which was taken to suggest rather different functions. Since those accounts the typology has become much more interesting. Classifiers are of various types, and interesting examples have been found of each. For comparison with gender, the most relevant are noun classifiers (or generics). There have been two particularly significant steps forward. First, more and more instances have been found of languages with both gender and classifiers. These include Tariana (North Arawakan; Brazil; Aikhenvald 1994, 2000), which has a gender system and three sub-types of classifier, Retuarã (Tucanoan; Columbia; Strom 1992: 10–11, 34–36, 45–47), Tidore (West Papuan; Halmahera, Indonesia; van Staden 2000: 77–81) and Mian (Trans New Guinea; Papua New Guinea, Fedden 2011: 185–201). Ngan'gityemerri (Daly; northern Australia) shows the development from generic classifiers into genders (Reid 1997).[8] Such a development points to the second step forward, namely that systems have been found which fall between the earlier ideas of gender and classifier. A good example is Miraña (North West Amazon), as analysed by Seifart (2005). Consider these examples:

---

[8] See Sansò (2009) for discussion of an embryonic classifier construction in Ancient Greek, whose development was cut short.

Miraña (Seifart 2005: 78–79)

(25) í-ːbaj úβi-ːbaj
 PRX-SCM_CONT basket-SCM_CONT
 'this one (container), a basket'

(26) úβi-ːbaj oːkɛ ɯ áhkɯ-ːbaj
 basket-SCM_CONT 1SG.ACC 2SG.SUB give-SCM_CONT
 'the basket that you gave to me'

(27) kátúɨːβɛ-ːbaj úβi-ːbaj
 fall-SCM_CONT basket-SCM_CONT
 'The basket fell down.'

Note: CONT: container, PRX: proximal demonstrative, SCM: specific class marker;

Miraña has 66 specific class markers, mainly concerned with shape, which makes one think of a classifier system; in addition, it has six general markers, based on animacy, natural gender and number (Seifart 2005: 77); in terms of assignment, then, this part of the system is like a gender system. Examples (25)-(27) are particularly interesting in terms of the targets involved: the markers are found on a range of targets: on demonstrative pronouns (25), on the predicate of a relative clause (26) and that of a main clause (27). (They also occur on the controller noun, as all three examples show.) Their occurrence on different controllers makes the system like a gender system. As Seifart (2005) shows, the canonical approach is particularly fruitful here, since it allows to separate out the different parts of the system, as more or less like a canonical gender system, rather than trying to determine the typology of this complex system as a whole.

The final criterion we consider concerns lexemes. When we say that a language has a gender system, we should consider what this means for individual lexemes. In a canonical system, the following holds:

Criterion 4
Canonical features and their values are distinguished consistently across lexemes within relevant parts of speech.

In the canonical system, then, if a particular part of speech – say the verb – marks gender, then every verb does, and it can mark all the values. This implies two ways to be non-canonical, in terms of (a) the feature or (b) a value of a feature. We discuss each in turn.

In Archi, almost every part of speech can agree in gender. I will illustrate some of the less familiar targets:

Archi: agreeing adverb: Kibrik (1977: 186); Chumakina and Corbett (2008: 187) where original *bala* is amended to *balah*

(28) o‹b›qˤa-tːu-b   balah   **ditːa‹b›u**
     ‹III.SG›leave.PFV-ATR-III.SG trouble(III)[SG.ABS] **soon‹III.SG›**

     b-erχin
     III.SG-forget.IPFV
     'Past trouble gets forgotten quickly.'

Archi: agreeing postposition (Kibrik, Kodzasov, Olovjannikova and. Samedov 1977: 227)

(29) to-w-mi-s   sin-t'u   ɬːʷak-du-t
     that.one-I.SG-OBL.SG-DAT know-NEG   near-ATR-IV.SG

     duχriqˤa-k   **e‹b›q'en**
     village(IV).SG.INTER-LAT **‹III.SG›up.to**

     b-i-tːu-b   deq'ˤ
     III.SG-be.PRS-ATR-III.SG road(III)[SG.ABS]
     'He does not know the way to the next village.' (how far it is)

Archi: agreeing emphatic particle (Kibrik 1977: 326)

(30) arša   horoːk=**ej‹b›u**   iškul
     Archi.IN   long.ago=**EMPH.PTCL‹III.SG›** school(III)[SG.ABS]

     dabɬu
     OPEN.PFV
     'A school was opened in Archi already long ago.'

Even the personal pronoun, in some of its forms, agrees with absolutive argument:

Archi: agreeing pronoun (Chumakina and Corbett 2008: 188)

(31) **d-ez**   un   malgan
     II.SG-1SG.DAT 2SG.ABS   be.dear
     'You (female) are dear to me.' (uttered by a male)

Thus all these parts of speech, together with verbs (the agreement forms for which we saw earlier in (15)) and adjectives (too familiar cross-linguistically to deserve illustration) can in principle agree in gender. However, that is true at the level of the part of speech. Individual lexemes may or may not agree; this appears to be partly predictable, and partly lexically specified. Figures for the parts of speech which are easier to count are given in Table 1; I omit the pronouns, because it is not evident how to count the fact that some cells in the paradigm agree while most do not.[9] The data are derived from the Archi dictionary (Chumakina, Brown, Quilliam and Corbett 2007), reported in Chumakina and Corbett (2008: 188):

Table 1: Non-canonical at the feature level: agreement targets in Archi

	total	agreeing	% agreeing
adjectives	446	313	70.2
verbs	1248	399	32.0
adverbs	397	28	7.1
enclitic particles	4	1	(25.0)

Thus while these different parts of speech can agree in Archi, the system is less canonical in respect of lexemes: many do not show gender (or number) agreement. Earlier we noted the highly canonical behavior (in several respects) of Italian adjectives. However, they too are less canonical when we look at the level of lexemes. There is the type we saw in (10)-(13), which is canonical in respect of Criterion 2. That is the main pattern, but there are others too, which give a picture like Macedonian for Criterion 4. Thornton, Iacobini and Burani (1997: 74) give the following statistics for a total of 1129 adjectives:

Table 2: Types of Italian adjectives (Thornton, Iacobini and Burani 1997: 74)

Four distinct forms, *basso/ bassa/ bassi/ basse* 'low' as in (10)–(13)	65.3%
Two forms, singular versus plural: *verde/verdi* 'green'	31.7%
One form, invariable: *blu* 'blue'	1.9%
Others	1.1%

---

[9] In addition, there are 34 postpositions, of which one, namely *eq'en* 'up to', which shows infixal agreement (as in (29)). However, its part of speech status is not fully clear, and so I have not included postpositions in the table.

We see that many Italian adjectives do not agree in gender (while agreeing in number in most instances), which shows again that items which are fully canonical in one respect can be non-canonical in respect of others.

Let us turn to the other type of non-canonical behaviour, that which concerns values. Consider these Latin adjectives:

(32) Latin adjectives of inflection class 3 (NOMINATIVE SINGULAR forms)

MASCULINE	FEMININE	NEUTER	gloss
acer	acris	acre	sharp
facilis	facilis	facile	easy
vigil	vigil	vigil	alert

Latin has three gender values, as shown by many adjectives (though not in all of the case values). Other adjectives, those traditionally grouped in the third inflection class because of similarities elsewhere in the paradigm, show various possibilities. *Acer* 'sharp', and others like it distinguish three gender values; adjectives like *facilis* 'easy', on the other hand, show no distinction between MASCULINE and FEMININE. *Vigil* 'alert' and similar adjectives show no evidence of gender agreement in the NOMINATIVE SINGULAR (though certain other forms distinguish NEUTER from the other gender values). Thus we have some adjectives which are non-canonical in that they do agree in gender, but do not differentiate all the available gender values.

Let us sum up the types of non-canonicity we have surveyed. Figure 12 includes for completeness other instances which were not illustrated above, since we concentrate on gender. For full data see Corbett (2011).

	Criterion 1: autonomous	Criterion 2: distinguished across features/ values	Criterion 3: distinguished consistently across PoS	Criterion 4: distinguished consistently across lexemes
NUMBER		Biak	Mele Fila	Bezhta
GENDER	Romanian	Archi	Burmeso	Archi
PERSON	Old Nubian	Belhare	Maybrat	English
CASE	Classical Armenian	Russian	Guugu Yimidhirr	Russian

Figure 12: Non-canonical feature values and the four criteria

The picture in Figure 12 shows that typologists have identified an interesting set of phenomena. In terms of gender, we see that there are various ways in which we may say that a language has a gender system, but where accuracy requires us to specify this further. At another level of abstraction, gender shows the same characteristics as the other morphosyntactic features. Each of them can have a 'penumbra' of unclear behaviour around the more canonical core.

4 The assignment problem

For any feature, we have to give the rules for the use of each of its values, the assignment system. This is particularly interesting for gender, because typically values are assigned to nouns as a lexical matter. Thornton (2009: 14–15) points out that assignment, particularly gender assignment, can be thought of in two ways: nouns are assigned to gender values, conceptualizing gender as containers; or gender values are assigned to nouns, where a feature value is part of the specification needed for the noun to function properly in syntax. Both views are important: the first deals with cognitive classification, the second is more to do with the function of the feature in the grammar. It is the second perspective which concerns us here: given a noun, which gender value can be assigned to it.

When we analyse assignment systems of languages from different families we find that genders always have a semantic core. This may involve biological sex, or animacy, with other features also having a role (see McConnell-Ginet, this volume, for discussion of the sociocultural aspect of this relation). In some languages genders are assigned to nouns solely on the basis of semantics, but in others this semantic information is supplemented by formal information, and this may be phonological or morphological. Given this typology, we can see that gender is distributed in interesting ways across the world's languages.

4.1 Semantic assignment systems

Consider these examples from the Daghestanian language Bagwalal (from Kibrik 2001: 64–66):

(33) w-eš:a-w   waša
      M.SG-plump-M.SG   boy
      'a plump boy'

(34) j-eš:a-j   jaš
      F.SG-plump-F.SG girl
      'a plump girl'

(35) b-eš:a-b   ʕama
      N.SG-plump-N.SG donkey
      'a plump donkey'

Evidence from the attributive modifier gives us three agreement classes, each of which should be recognized as a gender. If we look at the verb, we find evidence for the same three classes. Bagwalal is a particularly clear instance of a consistent type of assignment system; the examples given are representative of the whole system. Nouns denoting male humans (and only those) are masculine, those denoting female humans are feminine. All remaining nouns are neuter. Thus *waša* 'boy' is masculine, *jaš* 'girl' is feminine, and *ʕama* 'donkey' is neuter (its sex is not relevant because it is not human). The meaning is sufficient, and no information about the form of a noun is needed to determine its gender. This is what we term a 'semantic assignment system'.

Bagwalal has a strict semantic system, since no other information is needed, and such systems are found in various parts of the world. Kala Lagaw Ya, spoken on the Western Torres Straits Islands, has a two-gender system, also with strict semantic assignment: nouns denoting males (and the moon) are masculine and all others belong in the feminine gender (Bani 1987). In Diyari, a language of South Australia, we find the converse: there is a gender for nouns with female referents (such as women, girls, doe kangaroos), and the other is for all remaining nouns (Austin 1981). Strict semantic systems are particularly prevalent in the Dravidian family, where there are three-gender systems (as in Kannada and Tamil) and two-gender systems (as in Parji). The semantic distinction at the heart of the assignment system of the languages discussed so far is biological sex (applying just to humans or to animals too), and this is true both for strict semantic systems and for those where other factors also have a role. Sex is the majority choice – three quarters are of this type.[10] There is another possibility, namely human vs non-human or animate vs non-animate. These systems are found in the Niger Congo and Algonquian families, but also in Khoisan and Austro-Asiatic, for instance.

---

10 There is variation as to what counts as being sex-differentiable: in Russian sex-differentiability operates where it matters (as with humans, domesticated animals and those where there is a striking difference), but shark is feminine and dolphin is masculine. In Tidore (Papuan, north Moluccas), on the other hand, anything non-human is grammatically neuter.

Besides these strictly semantic systems, we find others that we call 'predominantly semantic' assignment systems. These are again clearly based on semantics, but the rules are more complex and typically do not cover the full noun inventory so successfully. A complex and interesting system is that of Bininj Gun-wok (previously Mayali), a non-Pama-Nyungan language of northern Australia as described in detail by Evans, Brown and Corbett (2002).[11] To give a less well known example, we turn to Mian. Mian is a member of the Ok family (part of Trans-New-Guinea), spoken in Sandaun Province Papua New Guinea. Fedden (2011) describes the eastern dialect, which has around 1400 speakers. Fedden (2011: 169–184) presents evidence for four genders:

(36)   The four gender values of Mian (Fedden 2011: 170)

GENDER	example	gloss
MASCULINE	naka	'man'
FEMININE	unáng	'woman'
NEUTER 1	imen	'taro'
NEUTER 2	am	'house'

When we examine the assignments for the first two genders, the picture is straightforward, as we see in Figure 13:

	criteria		GENDER
animate	human	biological sex	MASCULINE e.g. *naka* 'man'
	animal (sex obvious or relevant)		FEMININE e.g. *unáng* 'woman'
	animal (sex not obvious or irrelevant)	conventionalized gender	MASCULINE e.g. *tolim* 'eagle'
			FEMININE e.g. *koból* 'cassowary'

Figure 13: The masculine and feminine genders in Mian (Fedden 2011: 172)

---

11 Bininj Gun-wok also shows a complex interaction of assignment to gender and to morphological class: it has four genders and five morphological classes for nouns. This has been successfully implemented; for details of a formal model of this system see Evans, Brown and Corbett (2002). Modelling has tended to be concentrated on synchronic assignment systems. However, there is also interesting work on modeling the development of assignment systems over time, as in Polinsky and van Everbroeck (2003).

These follow biological sex in the main. Compare this with the remaining two genders, which Fedden calls Neuter 1 and Neuter 2, as presented in Figure 14:

	criteria	GENDER
inanimate	count nouns (e.g. *mén* 'string bag', *imen* 'taro')	NEUTER 1
	liquids, body fluids/wastes, substances (e.g. *aai* 'water'; *ilem* 'blood', *as* 'wood')	
	places (e.g. *am* 'house', *mon* 'old garden', *dafáb* 'summit')	NEUTER 2
	masses (e.g. *afobèing* 'goods, property', *monî* 'money')	
	body decoration (e.g. *eit* 'decoration', *baasi* 'pig's tusk')	
	weather phenomena (e.g. *sók* 'rain', *ayung* 'mist')	
	illnesses (e.g. *kweim* 'fever')	
	intangibles/abstracts (e.g. *āns* 'song'; *kukub* 'way, custom')	
	verbal nouns (e.g. *fumin* 'activity of cooking'	
	some tools and weapons (e.g. *káawa* 'steel axe', *mōk* 'stone adze', *skemdâng* 'knife')	

Figure 14: The Neuter 1 and Neuter 2 genders in Mian (Fedden 2011: 172)

Compared with the first two genders, the two neuter genders are harder: count nouns tend to be in the first neuter gender, and there are other semantic indicators, but this is all less clear than in Bagwalal. Such systems are termed 'predominantly semantic assignment systems'. While this is fine as a characterization of the system as a whole, Mian suggests that the assignment to different gender values can be rather different within the same system. Indeed, the type of split we find in Mian is similar to that found in several languages of Daghestan.

A famous example of this type was Dyirbal, with four genders apparently requiring complex semantic assignment rules. This system has been reanalyzed by Plaster and Polinsky (2010) and we return to it shortly (in §4.2.1).

4.2 Formal assignment systems

In many languages, the semantic rules assign the appropriate gender value to many nouns but they also simply fail to apply for others. In Russian, and for many other Indo-European languages, there are semantic assignment rules for sex-differentiables (those where sex is salient or of importance to humans);

these are that nouns denoting males are masculine and those denoting female are feminine. But these rules have nothing to say about the majority of the noun inventory. In languages like Bagwalal, the nouns not assigned a gender value by the semantic rules (the 'remainder' or 'semantic residue'), all belong to a single gender value. However, in languages like Russian they are found in more than one gender, even in all the genders (as is the case in Russian). Here we find additional rules for assigning gender values to nouns, but according to their form. Languages may use semantic assignment rules, or semantic *and* formal rules, but not just formal assignment rules. In no language are genders assigned to nouns by purely formal rules. An example would be a language in which there were two agreement classes, and the nouns in the first all ended in a consonant cluster, and those in the second did not, and there was no semantic regularity for the distribution of nouns. I claim that this hypothetical type does not exist. Formal assignment rules, which always operate alongside semantic assignment rules, may appeal to two types of information: phonological and morphological.

4.2.1 Phonological

The clearest example of assignment depending on phonological information yet found is provided by Qafar (Afar), an East Cushitic language spoken in northeastern Ethiopia and in Djibouti (data from Parker and Hayward 1985). I repeat the evidence briefly here, since it is such a dramatic example, and then move on to a more recently published analysis of a comparable system.

Qafar has semantic assignment rules which are unsurprising: for sex-differentiable nouns, those denoting males are masculine and those denoting females are feminine. We are interested in the nouns which these rules do not cover, the semantic residue. These nouns are covered by phonological assignment rules: nouns whose citation form ends in an accented vowel, like *catò* 'help', are feminine; all others are masculine. Thus *gilàl* 'winter' does not end in a vowel and so is masculine, as is *tàmu* 'taste', which ends in a vowel, but an unaccented one. These rules, semantic and phonological, operate with few exceptions. The interaction in Qafar is particularly significant. Nouns denoting males and females typically fit with the phonological assignment rules too: *bàqla* 'husband' would be masculine by either set of rules and *barrà* 'woman, wife' would be assigned feminine gender by either. We might wonder whether we could do without semantic assignment rules for Qafar, though typologically that would mean Qafar was quite different from the languages we have discussed so far. However, there are key examples where the two types of rule are in conflict. First consider *abbà* 'father': the semantic assignment rules would predict masculine; given that it ends in an accented vowel, the phonological rules would predict feminine. It is masculine. Similarly, *gabbixeèra* 'slender-waisted female', where the semantic prediction is feminine, and the phonological predicition is masculine (the accent is non-final), is feminine. When the semantic and phonological rules are in conflict, which is relatively rare in Qafar, it is the semantic rules which take precedence. This is the normal situation in gender assignment systems.

There are many more examples of phonological assignment, including for instance Gujarati (Modi 2003), though few if any as clear as those of Qafar. At the other extreme we find French, often claimed to have no system to its gender assignment. Yet French has a phonological assignment system. For example, of 938 nouns ending in /ɛ̃/, 99% are masculine, like *le pain* [pɛ̃] 'the bread' (for details see Tucker, Lambert and Rigault 1977 and Hardison 1992).

As a less familiar example of a phonological assignment system, let us return to Dyirbal (from Queensland, Australia). This is a famous gender system, first analysed by Dixon in his grammar of the language (1972: 44–47, 60–62, 306–312), and taken up by many writers since. There are four genders, with these basic rules of semantic assignment:

(37)   Basic rules of semantic assignment in Dyirbal (from Dixon 1972: 306–312)

gender I:	male humans, non-human animates
gender II:	female humans, water, fire, fighting
gender III:	non-flesh food
gender IV:	residue

While these rules cover a good proportion of the nouns, many would be incorrectly assigned. In addition, Dixon proposes principles of association. For example, in mythology, the moon is the husband of the sun. The sun is in gender II because of the association with fire and light. Why then would the hairy mary grub be in gender II? According to this account, because the grub has a sting which, it is said, feels like sunburn, so by association with the sun it is in gender II (Dixon 1972: 310). The general idea was treated at length by Lakoff (1987), as an instance of radial categories.

This famous analysis has been questioned on the basis of how the language could be acquired. Plaster and Polinsky (2010) suggest that the age at which children acquire gender is too early for them to have access to radial categories. By looking more closely at the purely linguistic data, and taking account of the now established typology of gender assignment, they propose an account using just semantic and formal rules of assignment. Their assignment rules are as in Figure 15.

Semantic assignment	
1.	nouns denoting males → gender I
2.	females, fresh water, fire, stinging → gender II
3.	edible → gender III
4.	remaining inanimates → gender IV
Formal assignment (remaining animates)	
1.	nouns in *bi-*, *gugu-*, *ma-*, *yi-*, *-gan* → gender II
2.	remainder → gender I

Figure 15: Gender assignment in Dyirbal (Plaster and Polinsky 2010: 135)

Plaster and Polinsky's analysis accounts for 573 of the 597 documented nouns. It does so without any need for radial categories, by appealing to semantic and formal assignment rules. It is motivated in diachronic terms, since it suggests that the system arose as a result of the collapsing of a classifier system. And it has typological plausibility, since Dyirbal now fits into a well-attested type, requiring just semantic and formal assignment rules, such as we see in many gender systems; the elaborate radial categories are no longer required.[12]

4.2.2 Morphological

The morphological assignment system which has received the most attention is probably that of Russian. Again, since it is such a fine example of its type, I repeat the evidence briefly, and then go on to more recently discovered examples of this general type. In Russian, as in many other Indo-European languages, for sex-differentiable nouns, those denoting males are masculine and those denoting females are feminine. But unlike the situation in languages like Bagwalal, the nouns not covered by these rules – the semantic residue – are not simply assigned to the neuter gender. Rather in Russian the residue is shared between the three genders, with the neuter gender not even receiving the majority. This is represented in Figure 16:

---

[12] For an account of the gender system of the Daghestanian language Tsez, which also uses a combination of semantic and formal factors, see Plaster, Polinsky and Harizanov (in press).

MASCULINE	FEMININE	NEUTER
Sex differentiables denoting males PLUS part of the semantic residue	Sex differentiables denoting females PLUS part of the semantic residue	Part of the semantic residue

Figure 16: Gender assignment in Russian

It seems unlikely that we are failing to spot additional semantic criteria; in the past I have cited various 'triplets' of nouns with similar semantics but belonging to different genders (for instance in Corbett 2007b). Here are some further examples, to demonstrate that they are indeed numerous (Table 3):

Table 3: Russian nouns belonging to the semantic residue

MASCULINE	FEMININE	NEUTER
xor 'chorus'	pesnja 'song';	solo 'solo'
klarnet 'clarinet'	skripka 'violin'	fortep'jano 'piano'
kostjum 'suit'	jupka 'skirt'	plat'e 'dress'
nomer 'hotel room'	gostinica 'hotel'	foje 'foyer'
braslet 'bracelet'	cepočka 'chain'	kol'co 'ring'
jačmen' 'barley'	rož' 'rye'	pšeno 'millet'
sir 'cheese'	smetana 'sour cream'	maslo 'butter'
žurnal 'magazine'	gazeta 'newspaper'	pis'mo 'letter'
lokot' 'elbow'	kost' 'bone'	koleno 'knee'

If instead we consider the inflectional morphology of these nouns it becomes possible to find the assignment rules. Russian has four main inflection classes of noun, each with thousands of members. The singular forms are given in Table 4 (the nouns given for illustration were included in the triplets in table 3 above):

Table 4: Inflection classes in Russian

	I	II	III	IV
NOMINATIVE	žurnal	gazeta	kost'	pis'mo
ACCUSATIVE	žurnal	gazetu	kost'	pis'mo
GENITIVE	žurnala	gazety	kosti	pis'ma
DATIVE	žurnalu	gazete	kosti	pis'mu
INSTRUMENTAL	žurnalom	gazetoj	kost'ju	pis'mom
LOCATIVE	žurnale	gazete	kosti	pis'me
gloss	'magazine'	'newspaper'	'bone'	'letter'

It is important to stress that gender is not the same as inflection class. Gender is accessible to the syntax (for agreement), while inflection class is purely morphological. The two sometimes get confused in accounts of Indo-European languages where there are relatively few inflection classes; in languages like Kuot, discussed below, the larger number of inflection classes contrasts more strongly with the number of genders and there is less likelihood of confused analyses.

It is evident that the speaker must know the inflectional behaviour of a noun (its inflection class), and given that information, the assignment rules are straightforward. Gender can be assigned on the basic of inflection class, but not vice versa. Nouns in inflection class I are masculine, those in classes II and III are feminine, and those in IV are neuter. Since *otec* 'father' is in class I, while *sestra* 'sister' is in class II, and *mat'* 'mother' is in class III, we can see that many sex-differentiable nouns would be assigned their gender value correctly by the morphological assignment rules. And so, as we did with Qafar, we should ask whether we could do without the semantic assignment rules. This would not work because of nouns like *deduška* 'grandfather'; this noun denotes a male but is in class II, whose nouns are typically feminine; it is masculine. Nouns like this show, once again, that we do not find languages where formal assignment rules are sufficient. Further rules are required in Russian for indeclinable nouns (like *taksi* 'taxi', which is indeclinable and neuter); for fuller details see Corbett (1991: 34–43). The outline of gender assignment in Russian is given in Figure 17.[13]

When the system of inflection classes is not reliably available, as is the case with heritage speakers of Russian, the effect on the assignment system is dramatic, as Polinsky (2008) demonstrates convincingly.[14] More generally, the way in which semantic assignment rules take precedence is helpfully clarified in Thornton (2009); see also Enger (2009).

---

[13] The interesting question of how children acquire conflicting assignment rules is addressed in an experimental study (Rodina 2007). Rodina investigated 25 Russian children 2;6–4;0, and included Russian nouns like *papa* 'daddy' where semantic and formal assignment rules conflict. She suggests that children first apply the formal rule, and gradually add the semantic rule. Thus, according to this view, the semantic core to the gender system, which the typological evidence shows is always key to assignment, is not acquired first. For recent work on the acquisition of the Bantu language Sesotho, again showing the vital role of phonology, see Demuth and Wechsler (2012).

[14] And for a recent careful study of the decline of gender in Cappadocian Greek see Karatsareas (2009).

Semantic assignment (as before)
1. sex differentiable nouns denoting males → M
2. sex-differentiable nouns denoting females → F

Formal (morphological) assignment
1. nouns of inflection class I → M
2. nouns of inflection classes II & III → F
3. remainder → N

Figure 17: Gender assignment in Russian

So much is well established. Later work has helped to confirm and clarify this position.[15] Take, for instance, Lindström (2002: 147–164, 176–194) on Kuot, a language isolate of New Ireland. In some respects Kuot is even more convincing than Russian as an instance of morphological assignment, since it has few gender values and more inflection classes. Not surprisingly, however, the system is less well studied than that of Russian, and there are more uncertain instances.

Kuot has two gender values. Semantic assignment is as expected: sex differentiables (humans and major animals) are assigned gender according to sex. Of the semantic residue, a substantial number of nouns have their gender assigned according to morphological class. Lindström gives useful statistics, based on a list of 869 nouns. The inflection classes rest on number formation: nouns have singular and plural, and then there is a dual, used mainly for animates, which is for most nouns formed from the plural. Lindström gives eleven inflection classes, determined by the final syllable of the singular, and its relation to the plural form. For instance, nouns in the "ma-declension" form the plural using the normal plural marker -*p*, dropping the -*ma*, for instance:

(38) Examples of the *ma* declension in Kuot (Lindström 2002: 153)

SINGULAR	PLURAL	gloss
ima	ip	subclan; river
laukima	laukip	tooth
pipiduluma	pipidulup	bird (species)
adaima	adaip	dance mask

---

[15] Morphological assignment systems are found widely in Indo-European. In Arabic too, gender is assignable in the main according to morphology (Cowell 1964, 372–375); we now look at less familiar data.

Lindström lists 142 nouns in this inflection class; they are all masculine except *bunima* 'last born' which is covered by the semantic assignment rules (it takes its gender according to the sex of the referent), and *arəma* '(species of) pandanus fruit', which is exceptionally feminine (plus eight for which the gender value is not known). Statistics on the relations between inflection class and gender are given in Table 5:

Table 5: Inflection class and gender in Kuot (Lindström 2002: 149)

	F	M	F/M	?	Total
plain	237	172	39	28	476
ma	1	132	1	8	142
na	3	29	2	2	36
bun	17	0	0	0	17
bu	8	1	2	0	11
uom	8	0	0	0	8
bam	21	0	0	3	24
nəm	35	0	0	4	39
nim	12	0	0	2	14
n	40	25	10	6	81
m	16	2	2	1	21
Total	398	361	56	54	869

In Table 5, 'F/M' indicates that either gender value is possible, or that Lindström has conflicting information, while '?' indicates that the gender value is not known.

If we look first at the lower part of the Table 5, all but the 'plain' row, the picture is fairly clear. The inflection class of a noun gives a strong prediction as to its gender. The predictions are stronger than might first appear, because the nouns covered by the semantic assignment rules have not been excluded: several apparent exceptions to the morphological assignment rules are covered by the semantic rules. The picture is more straightforward than that seen in Russian because we have many inflection classes predicting just two gender values: there is no question of the prediction being in the other direction.

On the other hand, the picture is less clear in another respect, as we see when we consider the 'plain' inflection class. There are nouns which do not end in any of the sequences listed for the ten other classes in the table; in the main, these form the plural according to regular rules: the ending is -(i)p, with labialization assimilation of /i/ to /u/ under certain conditions. It is in this plain class that there is the least predictability of gender value. Lindström (2002: 183–190) considers various possible semantic groupings here, some of which are weakly predictive. For instance, most nouns denoting liquids are feminine, as are most abstract nouns, including nominalizations.

To sum up, Kuot is a clear instance of a morphological assignment system. In one respect it is more straightforward than Russian, in that the predictions go from eleven inflection classes to two gender values; in another respect it is less clear, since one substantial inflection class does not lead to a clear prediction of gender value.

Another significant and interesting assignment system is found in Lavukaleve, a Papuan language of the Central Solomons language described by Terrill (2003: 131–147). Lavukaleve has three gender values, with roughly equal numbers of nouns in each. There are semantic assignment rules for each gender, not only based on sex, but also, for instance, all mammals and turtles are masculine, while abstracts are neuter. However, apart from the main rules based on sex, semantic principles are more 'weak tendencies' (2003: 137). 'Formal assignment principles are more regular and transparent than semantic assignment principles.' (2003: 137). These formal principles are mainly phonological, but also appeal to derivational morphology. For comparison see also Terrill (2002) on gender systems in Papuan languages of this area more generally.[16]

It is worth spending a moment on the assignment of gender to loanwords. The simplest hypothesis is that they would be treated exactly as other nouns. Often this is the case, and such instances confirm the validity of the assignment rules. However, there can be respects in which loanwords are different from native words, and here there are interesting issues. For careful discussion see Thornton (2009), analyzing Italian data and Stolz (2009) working on Maltese. For the ways in which gender assignment can change, a recent reference is Visser (2011), who describes changes in West Frisian;[17] changes over a long time stretch are documented for the Iroquoian family by Mithun (this volume).

4.2.3 Recategorization

We noted that assignment is something which partly sets gender apart. At least in the more familiar languages, nouns have a single gender value; similarly personal pronouns have a single person value. On the other hand, nouns have access to all (or many of) the case and number values. However, there are also instances

---

[16] In addition to studies of gender systems in broad outline, others concentrate on the detail of gender use: see for instance Stein (forthcoming) and references there for gender and its significance in Biblical Hebrew texts.
[17] See also Rovai (2012) for Latin.

of less rigid assignment or – to think of it in the context of other features – recategorization. While in canonical gender systems, each noun is allotted to a single gender value, there are some very interesting systems, often described only quite recently, where there is more going on. Once again, there are intriguing parallels with other morphosyntactic features. Let us begin with number. There are familiar examples like *two coffees please* where *coffees* has a unit reading and is said to show recategorization. This is easier to see with the plural, as here. But the effect is more subtle. The non-count noun *coffee* is recategorized as a count noun, which means that instead of lying below the threshold of number differentiability, and so having only one number value, it is 'moved up' as it were to have a full set of number values (singular and plural for English). Thus the recategorization is to being a count noun, so that alongside the obvious plural there is also a unit reading for the singular, as in *a coffee please*.

The most obvious analogy for gender systems is the threshold of sex-differentiability. Languages may allow items below the threshold to be reclassified as being above it, and thus to have additional gender possibilities. We are used to animals and even inanimate objects being personified in stories, and then referred to with *he* and *she*. However, languages differ dramatically in how ready they are to allow such recategorizations, and there are interesting gradations. If we consider first the limits, we have languages like English where such recategorization is easily accepted: if the rhyme in which the dish ran away with the spoon were extended into their later lives, we can imagine one being referred to with *he* and the other with *she*. At the other end of the scale, Comrie (2005) reports on the Daghestanian language Tsez; in a story in which a rooster has an affair with a frog, no recategorization is possible. Given the following gender system: male humans – gender I, female humans – gender II, nouns denoting animals – gender III, but nouns denoting inanimates distributed over three genders, namely II, III and IV. Within this system, the rooster and the frog are both treated as gender III, as in normal situations, throughout the story. Compare this with Bininj Gun-wok (Mayali), a language of the Gunwinyguan family of northern Australia, where *alwanjdjuk* 'emu' is feminine, irrespective of sex. However, in exceptional circumstances, as in an account of what happens when emus divorce, and the wife emu marries another male emu, the use of the masculine is possible (Evans, Brown and Corbett 2002: 130–131). Finally, in certain Southern Bole-Tangale languages (part of West Chadic, spoken in northeastern Nigeria), with two-gender systems, Leger (1998) reports that personification is possible, but only for a small list of animals. Thus in Kupto (Kutto), animals are usually of feminine gender, but when personified 'a few selected animals' are treated as masculine: these are *túlúm* 'hyena', *yèd'dè* 'dog', *kúngú* 'leopard' and *gàandùk* 'mouse', but not *mbòlè* 'dove', *yóŋné* 'elephant or *kúglú* 'tortoise', which remain feminine, even if they are personified. In the related Kushi, *də̀ɓɓò* 'hyena', *jàŋàní* 'leopard' and *ʔàkùmóm* 'hedgehog' can change their gender to masculine, but not *jûr* 'squirrel' or *jèy* 'porcupine', which must retain their feminine gender. Other nouns may be taken into the sphere of the sex-differentiables; for instance, in Mian: 'Cross-classification for inanimates extends to body parts, which are generally (but not obligatorily) assigned to a gender reflecting the sex of their owner ...' (Fedden 2011: 177).

It is not only sex-differentiability which can be the basis for recategorization. Savosavo, which is the easternmost Papuan language, and is spoken in the Solomon islands, has two genders, masculine and feminine. Nouns denoting inanimates are by default masculine. However, recategorization is possible, according to a diminutive/affective classification. Nouns which are normally masculine (since inanimate) are occasionally made feminine; this may function to indicate that the referent is small compared with normal expectation or that it is in some way special (Wegener 2008: 65–67). The less that gender agreement is fully determined by unique gender values, the greater its role in constructing meaning. Other languages where this can happen include Lavukaleve (Terrill 2003: 140–141), and Walman (Brown and Dryer 2008a: 530; 2008b), where recategorization according to a diminutive/affective classification is widespread, and for which there is a set of diminutive gender agreement forms. Other interesting examples include Mawng (a member of the Iwaidjan family, spoken to the east of Darwin, Singer 2010) and Yawuru (a member of the Nyulnyulan family, non-Pama-Nyungan, of the west Kimberley region of Australia, Hosokawa 1996).

What then of the other morphosyntactic features? Recategorization in person is found in certain types of address; for instance, addressees "should" be treated as second person, but they can be recategorized as having other options, as in the doctor's *How are we today?* And full noun phrases, which "should" be third person, may be recategorized as having a person choice, as in Spanish. This was pointed out, for instance, by Harmer and Norton (1957: 270). These examples were found recently on the web (I am grateful to Enrique Palancar for the examples and analysis):

(39) Los   hombre-s   no   pode-mos   hac-er
      DEF.M.PL   man(M)-PL   NEG   can.PRES.IND-1PL   do-INF

      dos   cosa-s   a   la   vez
      two   thing(F)-PL   at   DEF.F.SG   time(F)
      'We men cannot do two things at the same time.'

(40) La-s mujer-es so-is muy rar-a-s
    DEF.F-PL woman[F]-PL be.PRES.IND-2PL very weird-F-PL
    'You women are very weird.'

These examples nicely show plural noun phrases recategorized as first person (39) and as second person (40).

We do not often think of recategorization for case, but the phenomena of Differential Object Marking and Differential Subject Marking show the availability of choices in case marking, driven by semantic and information structure factors, in place of uniquely determined syntactic government. Thus recategorization may be found in gender systems as well as in number systems, and it has analogues in person and case too.

4.2.4 Distribution of gender systems

Given this typology of gender systems, we can now ask how they are distributed over the world's languages. There is relevant information in the World Atlas of Language Structures (WALS), which contains 142 world maps, produced by 40 authors. In a sample of 256 languages (Corbett 2005), somewhat over half (144) have no gender system. Certain parts of the world are rather arid in terms of gender: the areas where Sino-Tibetan and Austronesian languages are spoken have few gender systems. Yet even here, some are found. Schapper (2010) documents the appearance of gender in several Austronesian languages, from contact with Papuan languages in her view. To have a gender system requires two genders at least, and two-gender systems are common, with 50 examples in this sample. Three genders is around half as common (26 examples) and four genders, about half as common again (12). Larger systems, with five or more genders, represent a substantial minority (24 languages in the sample). Fula (a Niger-Congo language) has around twenty genders, depending on the dialect.

If we ask about the semantic core of the gender system, we find that the majority have an assignment system based on sex (84),[18] but 28 languages in the sample, notably in the Niger-Congo and Algonquian families, have systems based on animacy. And as for the type of assignment system, taking strictly semantic and predominantly semantic assignment systems together, we find these in just under half the languages (53), while a slight majority (59) have semantic and formal assignment. The distribution of the systems across the world leads me to suggest that

---

[18] It is noteworthy that sex as a constant property of referents is central in many gender systems; in contrast, it is rare for the sex of the interlocutors to have a key role (see Dunn this volume).

new systems are always semantically based; they may persist over considerable periods, as in Dravidian languages, or evolve into semantic and formal systems. Older semantic and formal systems may in turn become primarily semantic (as is happening in various Germanic languages), but this is a later stage. To date there is no evidence for original systems having partially formal assignment.

5 Conclusion

The typology of gender reveals considerable diversity. And data from languages which, until recently, were less well studied, reveal that gender is even more varied and interesting than was earlier believed. On the other hand, the typology has been somewhat simplified since we have reduced the types of semantic relations permitted. Gender is indeed remarkable, but to appreciate this we need to see it in the context of the other morphosyntactic features; the deviations we find, as measured against the canonical construct, are challenging and interesting. In many ways, however, they are comparable to non-canonical behaviour we can find with other morphosyntactic features. To make further progress we need to maintain both perspectives: gender being unlike other features, and gender being one morphosyntactic feature among a small number of comparable features.

6 References

A **working bibliography** on canonical typology can be found at:
    http://www.surrey.ac.uk/LIS/SMG/canonical_bibliography.htm.
Aikhenvald, Alexandra Y. 1994. Classifiers in Tariana. *Anthropological Linguistics* 36. 407–465.
Aikhenvald, Alexandra Y. 2000. *Classifiers: A Typology of Noun Classification Devices*. Oxford: Oxford University Press.
Audring, Jenny. 2009. *Reinventing pronoun gender*. PhD thesis, Vrije Universiteit, Amsterdam. Utrecht: LOT.
Audring Jenny. 2011. Gender. In *Oxford Bibliographies Online: Linguistics*,
    http://www.oxfordbibliographiesonline.com/view/document/obo-9780199772810/obo-9780199772810-0066.xml (accessed 4-Jan-2012).
Austin, Peter. 1981. *A Grammar of Diyari, South Australia*. Cambridge: Cambridge University Press.
Baerman, Matthew, Dunstan Brown, and Greville G. Corbett. 2005. *The Syntax-Morphology Interface: A study of syncretism*. Cambridge: Cambridge University Press.
Bakker, Peter. 1997. *A Language of Our Own: The Genesis of Michif, the Mixed Cree-French Language of the Canadian Métis*. Oxford: Oxford University Press.
Bani, Ephraim. 1987. Garka a ipika: masculine and feminine grammatical gender in Kala Lagaw Ya. *Australian Journal of Linguistics* 7. 189–201.

Bickel, Balthasar and Johanna Nichols. 2005. Inclusive-exclusive as person vs. number categories worldwide. In Elena Filimonova (ed.) *Clusivity: Typology and Case Studies of the Inclusive–Exclusive Distinction* (Typological Studies in Language 63), 49–72. Amsterdam: John Benjamins.

Brown, Dunstan, Marina Chumakina and Greville G. Corbett (eds.) 2013. *Canonical Morphology and Syntax*. Oxford: Oxford University Press.

Brown, Lea and Matthew S. Dryer. 2008a. The verbs for 'and' in Walman, a Torricelli language of Papua New Guinea. *Language* 84. 528–565.

Brown, Lea and Matthew S. Dryer. 2008b. *Diminutive as an inflectional category in Walman*. Ms. University at Buffalo. Available at: linguistics.buffalo.edu/people/faculty/dryer/dryer/BrownDryerWalmanDimin.pdf. [Accessed 19.1.2009.]

Browne, Gerald M. 2002. *Old Nubian Grammar* (Languages of the World/Materials 330). Munich: Lincom Europa.

Chumakina, Marina, Dunstan Brown, Harley Quilliam and Greville G. Corbett. 2007. *Slovar' arčinskogo jazyka (arčinsko-anglo-russkij)* [A dictionary of Archi: Achi-Russian-English]. Makhachkala: Delovoj Mir. [Available as a WWW version on the SMG website].

Chumakina, Marina and Greville G. Corbett. 2008. Archi: the challenge of an extreme agreement system. In A. V. Arxipov, L. M. Zaxarov, A. A. Kibrik, A. E. Kibrik, I. M. Kobozeva, O. F. Krivnova, E. A. Ljutikova and O. V. Fëdorova (eds.) *Fonetika i nefonetika: K 70-letiju Sandro V. Kodzasova*. 184–194. Moscow: Jazyki slavjanskix kul'tur.

Comrie, Bernard. 2003. When agreement gets trigger-happy. In Dunstan Brown, Greville Corbett and Carole Tiberius (eds.) *Agreement: a typological perspective*. Special issue of *Transactions of the Philological Society* 101(2). 313–337. Oxford: Blackwell.

Comrie, Bernard. 2005. Grammatical gender and personification. In Dorit Diskin Ravid and Hava Bat-Zeev Shyldkrot (eds.) *Perspectives on Language and Language Development: Essays in Honor of Ruth A. Berman*. 105–114. Dordrecht: Kluwer.

Corbett, Greville G. 1991. *Gender*. Cambridge: Cambridge University Press

Corbett, Greville G. 2003. Agreement: Canonical instances and the extent of the phenomenon. In Geert Booij, Janet DeCesaris, Angela Ralli and Sergio Scalise (eds.) *Topics in Morphology: Selected papers from the Third Mediterranean Morphology Meeting (Barcelona, September 20–22, 2001)*. 109–128. Barcelona: Universitat Pompeu Fabra.

Corbett, Greville G. 2005. The canonical approach in typology. In Zygmunt Frajzyngier, Adam Hodges and David S. Rood (eds.) *Linguistic Diversity and Language Theories* (Studies in Language Companion Series 72). 25–49. Amsterdam: John Benjamins.

Corbett, Greville G. 2006. *Agreement*. Cambridge: Cambridge University Press

Corbett, Greville G. 2007a. Canonical typology, suppletion and possible words. *Language* 83. 8–42.

Corbett, Greville G. 2007b. Gender and noun classes. In Timothy Shopen (ed.) *Language Typology and Syntactic Description: III: Grammatical categories and the lexicon, second edition*, 241–279. Cambridge: Cambridge University Press.

Corbett, Greville G. 2009. Canonical inflectional classes. In Fabio Montermini, Gilles Boyé and Jesse Tseng (eds.) *Selected Proceedings of the 6th Décembrettes: Morphology in Bordeaux*. 1–11. Somerville, MA: Cascadilla Proceedings Project. Available at: http://www.lingref.com/cpp/decemb/6/abstract2231.html

Corbett, Greville G. 2011. The penumbra of morphosyntactic feature systems. *Morphology* 21. (= Jonathan Bobaljik, Uli Sauerland and Andrew Nevins (eds.) *Markedness and Underspecification in the Morphology and Semantics of Agreement*) 445–480.

Cowell, Mark W. 1964. *A Reference Grammar of Syrian Arabic (based on the dialect of Damascus)* (Arabic series 7). Washington, DC: Georgetown University Press.
De Vos, Lien and Gunther De Vogelaar. 2011. Dutch gender and the locus of morphological regularization. *Folia Linguistica* 45. 245–281.
Demuth, Katherine and Sara Weschler. 2012. The acquisition of Sesotho nominal agreement. *Morphology* 22. 67–88.
Dešeriev, Ju. D. 1953. *Bacbijskij jazyk: fonetika, morfologija, sintaksis, leksika.* Moscow: AN SSSR.
Dixon, R. M. W. 1972. *The Dyirbal Language of North Queensland.* Cambridge: Cambridge University Press.
Dixon, R. M. W. 1982. *Where Have All the Adjectives Gone? and other essays in Semantics and Syntax.* Berlin: Mouton.
Dol, Philomena. 2007. *A Grammar of Maybrat: a language of the Bird's Head Penisula, Papua Province, Indonesia* (Pacific Linguistics, 586). Canberra: Pacific Linguistics, Research School of Pacific and Asian Studies, Australian National University.
Donohue, Mark. 2001. Animacy, class and gender in Burmeso. In Andrew Pawley, Malcolm Ross and Darrell Tryon (eds.) *The boy from Bundaberg: Studies in Melanesian linguistics in honour of Tom Dutton* (Pacific linguistics 514). 97–115. Canberra: Pacific Linguistics.
Enger, Hans-Olav. 2009. The role of core and non-core semantic rules in gender assignment. *Lingua* 119. 1281–1299.
Evans, Nicholas. 2003. Typologies of agreement: some problems from Kayardild. In Dunstan Brown, Greville G. Corbett and Carole Tiberius (eds.) *Agreement: a typological perspective* (Special issue of Transactions of the Philological Society 101(2)). 203–234. Oxford: Blackwell.
Evans, Nicholas, Dunstan Brown and Greville G. Corbett. 2002. The semantics of gender in Mayali: Partially parallel systems and formal implementation. *Language* 78. 111-155.
Fedden, Sebastian. 2011. *A Grammar of Mian.* Berlin: De Gruyter Mouton.
Fortin, Antonio. 2011. *The Morphology and Semantics of Expressive Affixes.* Unpublished DPhil thesis, University of Oxford.
Goddard, Cliff. 1982. Case systems and case marking in Australian languages: a new interpretation. *Australian Journal of Linguistics* 2. 167–196.
Hardison, Debra M. 1992. Gender assignment to nonwords in French: Implications for the role of the final syllable in lexical processing and organization of the mental lexicon. In *Indiana Linguistics Club Twenty-Fifth Anniversary Volume.* 13–25. Bloomington, Indiana: Indiana University Linguistics Club.
Harmer, L. C. and F. J. Norton. 1957. *A Manual of Modern Spanish.* London: University Tutorial Press. [2nd edition, 1st edition 1935]
Haviland, John. 1979. Guugu Yimidhirr. In R. M. W. Dixon and Barry J. Blake (eds.), *Handbook of Australian languages*, 27–180. Canberra: Australian National University Press.
Heuvel, Wilco van den. 2006. Biak: *Description of an Austronesian language of Papua.* PhD thesis, Vrije Universiteit Amsterdam. Available at: http://www.lotpublications.nl/index3.html.
Hockett, Charles F. 1958. *A Course in Modern Linguistics.* New York: Macmillan.
Holisky, Dee Ann and Rusudan Gagua. 1994. Tsova–Tush (Batsbi). In Rieks Smeets (ed.) *Indigenous Languages of the Caucasus IV: The North East Caucasian Languages, Part 2.* 147–212. Delmar, NY: Caravan Books.
Hosokawa, Komei. 1996. 'My face am burning!': quasi-passive, body parts and related issues in Yawuru grammar and cultural concepts. In Hillary Chappell and William McGregor

(eds.) *The grammar of inalienability: a typological perspective on body part terms and the part-whole relation*. 155–192. Berlin: Mouton de Gruyter.
Hyman, Larry M. 2009. How (not) to do phonological typology: the case of pitch-accent. *Language Sciences* 3. (= Michael J. Kenstowicz (ed.) *Data and Theory: Papers in Phonology in Celebration of Charles W. Kisseberth*) 213–128. Amsterdam: Elsevier.
Hyman, Larry M. 2011. *In defense of prosodic typology: A response to Beckman and Venditti*. UC Berkeley Phonology Lab Annual Report. 200–235.
Igartua, Iván. 2006. Genus alternans in Indo-European. *Indogermanische Forschungen* 111. 56–70.
Jensen, Hans. 1959. *Altarmenische Grammatik*. Heidelberg: Carl Winter.
Karatsareas, Petros. 2009. The loss of grammatical gender in Cappadocian Greek. *Transactions of the Philological Society* 107. 196–230.
Kibrik, Aleksandr E. 1977. *Opyt strukturnogo opisanija arčinskogo jazyka: II: Taksonomičeskaja grammatika*. Publikacii otdelenija strukturnoj i prikladnoj lingvistiki 12. Moscow: Izdatel'stvo Moskovskogo universiteta.
Kibrik, Aleksandr E. 1998. Archi (Caucasian – Daghestanian). In Andrew Spencer and Arnold M. Zwicky (eds.) *The Handbook of Morphology*. 455–476. Oxford: Blackwell.
Kibrik, Aleksandr E. (ed.). 2001. *Bagvalinskij jazyk: Grammatika: Teksty: Slovari*. Moscow: Nasledie. [co-editors K. I. Kazenin, E. A. Ljutikova and S. G. Tatevosov.]
Kibrik, A. E., S. V. Kodzasov, I. P. Olovjannikova and D. S. Samedov. 1977. *Arčinskij jazyk: Teksty i slovari*. Publikacii otdelenija strukturnoj i prikladnoj lingvistiki 14. Moscow: Izdatel'stvo Moskovskogo universiteta.
Klein, Jared. 2007. Classical Armenian morphology. In Alan B. Kaye (ed.) *Morphologies of Asia and Africa II*. 1051–1086. Winona Lake, IN: Eisenbrauns.
Lakoff, George. 1987. *Women, Fire, and Dangerous Things: What Categories reveal about the Mind*. Chicago: University of Chicago Press.
Leger, Rudolf. 1998. Grammatical gender in some Southern Bole-Tangale languages – Kwami, Kupto, Kushi and Piya. In I. V. Sledzevskij and D. M. Bondarenko (eds.) *Afrika: Obščestva, kul'tury, jazyki*. 204–216. Moscow: Institute of African Studies.
Lindström, Eva. 2002. *Topics in the grammar of Kuot: a non-Austronesian language of New Ireland, Papua New Guinea*. PhD dissertation: Stockholm University.
Loporcaro, Michele and Tania Paciaroni. 2011. Four-gender systems in Indo-European. *Folia Linguistica* 45. 389–433.
Maiden, Martin. 2011. Morphophonological persistence. In Martin Maiden, John Charles Smith and Adam Ledgeway (eds.) *The Cambridge History of the Romance Languages: I: Structures*. 155–215. Cambridge: Cambridge University Press.
Matasović, Ranko. 2004. *Gender in Indo-European*. Heidelberg: Winter.
Mel'čuk, Igor. 1986. Toward a definition of case. In Richard D. Brecht and James Levine (eds.) *Case in Slavic*. 35–85. Columbus, OH: Slavica. [Revised version in: Igor Mel'čuk. 2006. *Aspects of the Theory of Morphology*, edited by David Beck. 110–179. Berlin: Mouton de Gruyter.]
Modi, Bharati. 2003. Gender in Gujarati. In Ritva Laury, Gerald McMenamin, Shigeko Okamoto, Vida Samiian and K.V. Subbarao (eds.). *Perspectives in Linguistics: Papers in Honor of P.J. Mistry*. 247–259. New Delhi: Indian Institute of Language Studies.
Nedelcu, Isabela. 2013. Three genders: masculine, feminine and neuter. In Gabriela Pană Dindelegan (ed.) *The Grammar of Romanian*. Oxford: Oxford University Press.

Nikolaeva, Irina and Andrew Spencer. 2008. *Nouns as adjectives and adjectives as nouns*. Unpublished manuscript.
Parker, E. M. and R. J. Hayward. 1985. *An Afar-English-French Dictionary (with Grammatical Notes in English)*. London: SOAS, University of London.
Plaster, Keith and Maria Polinsky. 2010. Features in categorization, or a new look at an old problem. In Anna Kibort and Greville G. Corbett (eds.) *Features: Perspectives on a Key Notion in Linguistics*. 109–142. Oxford: Oxford University Press.
Plaster, Keith, Maria Polinsky and Boris Harizanov. In press. *Noun classes grow on trees: Noun classification in the North-East Caucasus*. To appear in a Festschrift. Amsterdam: John Benjamins.
Polinsky, Maria. 2003. Non-canonical agreement is canonical. In Dunstan Brown, Greville Corbett and Carole Tiberius (eds.) *Agreement: A Typological Perspective* (special issue of *Transactions of the Philological Society* 101(2)). 279–312. Oxford: Blackwell.
Polinsky, Maria. 2008. Gender under incomplete acquisition: heritage speakers' knowledge of noun categorization. *Heritage Language Journal* 6. 40–71.
Polinsky, Maria. and Ezra Van Everbroeck, E. 2003. Development of gender classifications: Modeling the historical change from Latin to French. *Language* 79. 356–390.
Reid, Nicholas. 1997. Class and classifier in Ngan'gityemerri. In Mark Harvey and Nicholas Reid (eds.) *Nominal Classification in Aboriginal Australia* (Studies in Language Companion Series 37). 165–228. Amsterdam: John Benjamins.
Rodina, Yulia. 2007. *Semantics and Morphology: The Acquisition of Grammatical Gender in Russian*. PhD thesis. University of Tromsø.
Rovai, Francesco. 2012. Between feminine singular and neuter plural: re-analysis patterns. *Transactions of the Philological Society* 110. 94–121
Sagot, Benoît and Géraldine Walther. 2011. Non-canonical inflection: Data, formalization and complexity measures. In Cerstin Mahlow and Michael Piotrowski (eds.) *Communications in Computer and Information Science* 100. 23–45. Berlin: Springer.
Sansò, Andrea. 2009. Men, women, and birds. An embryonic system of noun classification in Ancient Greek. *Folia Linguistica* 43. 95–133.
Schapper, Antoinette. 2010. Neuter gender in eastern Indonesia. *Oceanic Linguistics* 49. 407–435.
Seifart, Frank. 2005. *The Structure and Use of Shape-based Noun Classes in Miraña (North West Amazon)*. PhD thesis, Radboud University, Nijmegen.
Singer, Ruth. 2010. Creativity in the use of gender agreement in Mawng: How the discourse functions of a gender system can approach those of a classifier system. *Studies in Language* 34. 382–416.
Spencer, Andrew. 2005. Towards a typology of 'mixed categories'. In C. Orhan Orgun and Peter Sells (eds.) *Morphology and the Web of Grammar: Essays in Memory of Steven G. Lapointe (Stanford Studies in Morphology and the Lexicon)*. 95–138. Stanford: CSLI Publications.
Staden, Miriam van. 2000. *Tidore: A Linguistic Description of a Language of the North Moluccas*. PhD thesis, Leiden University.
Stein, David E. S. Forthcoming. Gender representation in Biblical Hebrew. To appear in Geoffrey Khan (ed.) *Encyclopedia of Hebrew Language and Linguistics*. Leiden: Brill.
Stolz, Christel. 2009. A different kind of gender problem: Maltese loanword gender from a typological perspective. In Bernard Comrie, Ray Fabri, Elizabeth Hume, Manwel Mifsud, Thomas Stolz and Martine Vanhov (eds.) *Introducing Maltese Linguistics: Selected papers from the 1st International Conference on Maltese Linguistics, Bremen, 18–20 October, 2007* (Studies in Language Companion Series 113). 321–353. Amsterdam: John Benjamins.

Strom, Clay. 1992. *Retuarã Syntax* (Studies in the Languages of Colombia 3). Dallas, TX: Summer Institute of Linguistics and The University of Texas at Arlington.

Stump, Gregory T. 2005. Word-formation and inflectional morphology. In Pavol Štekauer and Rochelle Lieber (eds) *Handbook of Word-formation* (Studies in Natural Language and Linguistic Theory 64), 49–71. Dordrecht: Springer.

Stump, Gregory T. 2006. Heteroclisis and paradigm linkage. *Language* 82. 279–322.

Stump, Gregory T. and Raphael Finkel. 2008. *Stem alternations and principal parts in French verb inflection*. Paper presented at Décembrettes 6: Colloque International de Morphologie, "Morphologie et classes flexionnelles". December 4–5. 2008. Université de Bordeaux, France.

Suthar, Babubhai Kohyabhai. 2006. *Agreement in Gujarati*. PhD Dissertation, University of Pennsylvania.

Terrill, Angela. 2002. Systems of nominal classification in East Papuan languages. *Oceanic Linguistics* 41. 63–88.

Terrill, Angela. 2003. *A Grammar of Lavukaleve* (Mouton Grammar Library 30). Berlin: Mouton de Gruyter.

Thornton, Anna M. 2009. Constraining gender assignment rules. *Language Sciences* 31. 14–32.

Thornton, Anna M. 2011. Overabundance (multiple forms realizing the same cell): a non-canonical phenomenon in Italian verb morphology. In Maria Goldbach, Marc-Olivier Hinzelin, Martin Maiden and John Charles Smith (eds.) *Morphological Autonomy: Perspectives from Romance Inflectional Morphology*. 358–381. Oxford: Oxford University Press.

Thornton, Anna M., Claudio Iacobini, and Cristina Burani. 1997. *BDVDB: Una base di dati per il vocabolario di base della lingua italiana*, 2nd edition. Rome: Bulzoni.

Tucker, G. Richard, Wallace E. Lambert, and André Rigault, A. A. 1977. *The French speaker's skill with grammatical gender: An example of rule-governed behavior*. The Hague: Mouton.

Visser, Willem. 2011. Historical gender change in West Frisian. *Morphology* 21. 31–56.

Wegener, Claudia. 2008. *A grammar of Savosavo: a Papuan language of the Solomon Islands*. (MPI series in psycholinguistics). PhD thesis, Radboud University, Nijmegen.

Zaliznjak, Andrej A. 1964. K voprosu o grammatičeskix kategorijax roda i oduševlennosti v sovremennom russkom jazyke. *Voprosy jazykoznanija* 4. 25–40.

Zaliznjak, Andrej A. 1973. O ponimanii termina 'padež' v lingvističeskix opisanijax. In Andrej A. Zaliznjak (ed.) *Problemy grammatičeskogo modelirovanija*. 53–87. Moscow: Nauka. [Reprinted in: Andrej A. Zaliznjak. 2002. *Russkoe imennoe slovoizmenenie: s priloženiem izbrannyx rabot po sovremennomu russkomu jazyku i obščemu jazykoznaniju*. 613–647. Moscow: Jazyki slavjanskoj kul'tury.]

Marianne Mithun
Gender and culture

1 Language and culture

It is now generally recognized that grammatical categories develop in languages through use. Distinctions made most often by speakers as they speak tend to become routinized over time in grammatical markers. Many grammatical categories recur in language after language, no doubt because they reflect common human interests. Most languages have grammatical causative constructions, for example, and many have tense systems. But other grammatical markers reflect more specific environmental or cultural interests. Central Alaskan Yup'ik, for example, contains a suffix *-ir-* 'have cold N'. Added to the noun root 'ear', it forms the stem *ciuta-ir-* 'have cold ears', as in the verb *ciuta-ir-tua* 'my ears are cold' (George Charles, speaker p.c.). It is probably no accident that this language is spoken in the Arctic. Central Pomo, a language indigenous to California, has a prefix *č^h-* 'by gambling'. Prefixed to the verb *ley* 'exhaust, die off', it yields the verb *č^h-léy* 'to lose everything in gambling' (Frances Jack, speaker p.c.). California peoples are known for their long traditions of gaming.

Grammatical gender systems appear in languages distributed throughout the world. They show many similarities cross-linguistically, but there are also interesting differences. Comparisons among them raise questions about the extent to which grammatical gender reflects cognitive universals versus cultural specificity.

1.1 Mohawk

Mohawk, an Iroquoian language indigenous to northeastern North America, shows a grammatical gender system that at first looks much like those of more familiar European systems. Nouns contain gender prefixes.[1]

---

[1] Examples are presented here in the official orthography in use in the Mohawk communities. Vowels *i, e, a, o* have approximately IPA values. Nasalized vowels are represented by digraphs: *en* [ʌ] and *on* [ų]. Glottal stop is represented by an apostrophe '. The letter *i* represents a glide [j] before vowels. Vowel length is represented by a colon :. Stress with rising tone is indicated with an acute accent *ó*; stress with falling tone is indicated with a grave accent *ò*.

(1)   Noun prefixes
        Masculine   *ra*-ksà:'a   'boy'
        Feminine   *e*-ksà:'a   'girl'
        Neuter   *ka*-ièn:kwire'   'arrow'

1.2 Agreement

It has been proposed that a fundamental feature of grammatical gender systems is the presence of agreement. Hockett defined gender in just this way: "Genders are classes of nouns reflected in the behavior of associated words." (1958: 231, cited in Corbett 1991: 1). Corbett concurs. "While nouns may be classified in various ways, only one type of classification counts as a gender system; it is one which is reflected beyond the nouns themselves in modifications required of 'associated words'" (1991: 4). The Mohawk examples in (2) indicate that the language does show grammatical gender in the strict sense.

(2)   Mohawk matching prefixes (examples constructed for comparison)
        a. **Ra**-ká:we-hs   ne   **ra**-ksà:='a.
            3M.SG.AGT-paddle-HAB   the   M.SG-child=DIM
            'The boy is paddling.'

        b. **Ie**-ká:we-hs   ne   **e**-ksà:='a.
            3F.SG.AGT-paddle-HAB   the   F.SG-child=DIM
            'The girl is paddling.'

        c. **Ka**-ká:we-hs   ne   **kén**-tsion.
            3N.SG.AGT-paddle-HAB   the   N-fish
            'The fish is paddling.'

        d. **Rati**-ká:we-hs   ne   **rati**-ksa'=okòn:'a.
            3M.PL.AGT-paddle-HAB   the   M.PL-child=DISTR
            'The boys are paddling.'

(By regular rule, the vowel of the Neuter prefix *ka*- fuses with the vowel *i* of a following stem, yielding the nasal vowel *en: ka-itsion > kéntsion* 'fish'.)

The verbal prefix system goes a step further. Verb prefixes represent both arguments of a transitive clause. In some cases, the components corresponding to the two arguments can still be discerned, but for the most part these prefixes are highly fused forms.

(3) Mohawk prefixes in transitives (constructed for comparison)²
    a. **Ronwa**-*nòn:we'-s*   ne   **ra**-*ksà:='a.*
        3F.SG>3M.SG-like-HAB   the   **M.SG**-child=DIM
        'She likes the boy.'

    b. **Iontate**-*nòn:we'-s*   ne   **e**-*ksà:='a.*
        3F.SG>3F.SG-like-HAB   the   **F.SG**-child=DIM
        'She likes the girl.'   or   'The girl likes her.'

    c. *Konwa*-*nòn:we'-s*   ne   **kén**-*tsion.*
        3F.SG>3N.SG-like-HAB   the   **N**-fish
        'She likes the fish.'

    d. **Ronwati**-*nòn:we'-s*   ne   **rati**-*ksa'=okòn:'a.*
        3F.SG>3M.PL-like-HAB   the   **M.PL**-child=DIM
        'She likes the boys.'

Overt lexical nominals or free pronouns need not be present in every clause. Reference can be clear from the verbal prefixes.

2 Males

Not surprisingly, Masculine gender markers are used for all male persons and certain animals whose gender is salient, such as bulls and roosters. Masculine forms are used on occasion for other male animals as well, such as pet dogs or

---

2 The abbreviations used for grammatical terms are the following.

AGT	Grammatical Agent	INS	Instrumental applicative
AUG	Augmentative	LK	Linker
CISLOC	Cislocative	M	Masculine
CONTR	Contrastive	N	Neuter
DIM	Diminutive	NS	Noun Suffix
DISTR	Distributive	PAT	Grammatical Patient
DU	Dual	PFV	Perfective
DV	Duplicative	PL	Plural
F	Feminine	PROG	Progressive
FACT	Factual	PRT	Partitive
FI	Feminine-Indefinite	REP	Repetitive
FUT	Future	REV	Reversive
FZ	Feminine-Zoic	SG	Singular
HAB	Habitual aspect	TRLOC	Translocative
INCH	Inchoative		

other significant individuals, particularly large ones. The excerpt in example (4) is a free translation of a Mohawk account of an encounter with a polar bear. The bolded English pronouns reflect the gender distinguished by the verb prefixes.

(4) Encounter with a polar bear: Josephine Kaieríthon Horne, speaker, p.c.
'The bear (**he**) stood up. **He** was about twelve feet tall. When **he** opened his mouth, the inside of it looked like a ball of fire next to **his** huge white teeth. It took several shots to kill (**him**) the bear. The two brothers were all excited. They quickly went back to camp and happily reported that they had killed (**it**) a bear. But by the time they got back to the spot where (**it**) the bear had been killed, **it** was nowhere to be found.'

The speaker used Masculine forms while the bear was alive, but Neuter forms once he was dead.

Masculine dual and plural prefixes are also used for mixed groups of male and female persons.

3 Objects and animals

Neuter forms are generally used for objects and animals. The most common Neuter prefixes are *ka-/ken-* and *o-*, though there are a few others, and phonological processes can obscure some forms. The kinds of nouns that occur with these prefixes are not surprising: *kèn-reks* 'wildcat, mountain lion', *ka-henta'kéha* 'meadowlark', *ka-nó:tsot* 'muskie (fish)', *ka-ríhton* 'red oak', *ká-hi* 'fruit, berry', *kahén:ta* 'field, meadow', *ka-honwé:ia* 'boat', *ká-tshe* 'bottle, jug, can', *ka-nhóha* 'door' ; *o-hkwá:ri* 'bear', *o-hriò:ken* 'chipmunk', *o-tsí:non* 'flea, louse', *o-tsi'tèn:'a* 'bird', *o-hkwé:sen* 'partridge', *o-iahè:ta'* 'perch (fish)', *otsi'eróhta'* 'crab', *ó-se'* 'willow', *ó-honte'* 'grass', *otsì:tsa'* 'flower', *o-hnennà:ta'* 'potato', *ó'-:iente'* 'wood', *o-'kèn:ra'* 'dust, soil', *o-nén:ia'* 'rock', etc.

For the most part, animals and inanimate objects are represented by the same prefixes. Distinctions can be seen in a few contexts, however. Number is distinguished for animates in verb prefixes, but not for inanimates.

(5) Number distinction for animates: Rita Konwatsi'tsaién:ni Phillips, speaker p.c.
    a. *Awenhniserakwé:kon*   *en-**ka**-hón:take'.*
       all day long   **it** will grass eat
       'All day long **it** (a cow) would graze.'

b. *Awenhniserakwé:kon* en-**konti**-*hón:take'*.
all day long **they** (ZOIC.PL) will grass eat
'All day long **they** (cows) would graze.'

(6) No number distinction for inanimates: Josephine Kaieríthon Horne, speaker p.c.
a. *Kanákta'* **ka**-*kè:ron*.
place **it** is laid out
'A place was laid out (at the table).'

b. *Kanakta'shòn:'a* **ka**-*kè:ron*.
place here and there **it** is laid out
'Places were laid out (at the table).'

Such a pattern is not uncommon cross-linguistically (Corbett 1991: 267–269, Enfield 2007: 78, and many others). Distinctions between animate Neuters (termed Zoic in Iroquoian linguistics) and inanimate Neuters appear in a few other contexts to be described later.

Not surprisingly, inanimate objects are sometimes personified, such as in ceremonial contexts. In (7) the earth is categorized as Feminine, and in (8), the medicines are categorized as Masculine.

(7) Thanksgiving address: Enos Williams, speaker
*Wa'**tiethi**nonhwerá:ton'* ne tsi
we hereby raise thanks to **her** the where
iohwentsiatátie'.
it earth extends along
'We thank **her**, the earth.' ...
*Te**iethi**nòn:weron* *ahsonthenhnéhkha'* *wenhnì:tare'*.
we thank **her** nighttime it moon shines
'We greet **her**, the nighttime moon.'

(8) Oratory: Frank Tekaronhió:ken Jacobs Jr., speaker
***Ietshi**iatahónhsatat* ne *ononhkwa'shòn:'a,*
you all listen to **them** the various medicines
'Listen to the medicines,
tsi *nahò:ten'* ***rón**:ton*.
as such it is a kind **they** (M.PL) are saying
to what **they** (M.PL) are saying.'

4 Female persons

So far, the Mohawk system looks much like those of European languages. It differs in some intriguing ways, however. One is that the prefixes used for female persons are also used as generics 'one, they, people', for persons of unspecified sex, and indefinites. One domain in which generics show up routinely is in terms for tools and other devices. Morphological verbs are often used as referring expressions, and are often lexicalized as such. (The forms below are not restricted to utensils typically used by women.)

(9) Feminine and generic usage
    a. *ie-hiá:tonhs*   '**she, one** writes'
        ie-hiatónhkhwa'   '**she, one** writes with it' = 'pen, pencil'

    b. *ie-kòn:reks*   '**she, one** pounds'
        ie-konhrékstha'   '**she, one** pounds with it' = 'hammer'

Additional examples of generic uses of these forms are in (10), all from spontaneous speech.

(10) Generic usage in speech
    a. *Ieióhe   na-**ie**-nenhstaienthó:ko'.*
        it is time   **one** should unplant the corn
        'It is time to harvest the corn.'

    b. *A**hshako**ié:na'   ne   **iaka**onkwe'táksen*
        he would catch **one**   the   **one** is a bad person
        'He would catch bad people.'

    c. *Ónhka'   **iako**tohetstonhátie'   a**iakhi**nontará:nonte'.*
        someone   **one** is passing by   we would soup feed **one**
        'We would give soup to any strangers who might come our way.'

    d. *Iah   ónhka'   te**iako**tahonhsatá:ton.*
        not   someone   not has **one** pricked one's ears
        'No one listened.'

    e. *Iohsnó:re'   sahón:newe'   tsi   nón:*
        it is fast   they arrived back   to   place
        ***ie**-nakerénion'   nón:kwe.*
        one lives here and there   the person
        'They soon returned to civilization.'

In combination with an indefinite pronoun such as *ónhka'k* 'someone', the same forms are used as indefinites.

(11) Indefinite usage in speech
 Ónhka'k wa-**hshakó**:-ken' ta**iak**awenonhátie'.
 someone he saw **one** **one** is coming along
 'He saw **someone** coming.' (Sex as yet undetermined)

This pronominal category is termed Feminine-Indefinite by Iroquoianists, abbreviated FI.

The use of the same forms for female persons, generics, and indefinites suggests a link between grammar and culture. Iroquoian culture is characterized by longstanding matrilineal and matrilocal traditions. Clan membership is inherited through the mother. Land was traditionally passed down from mothers to daughters. Women have always been highly respected, and they serve important community roles. Chiefs were traditionally men, but they were appointed (and potentially recalled) by the clan mothers. It is perhaps no surprise that generic persons should be represented by Feminine gender forms.

5 Not so fast

In fact the picture is more interesting. Feminine-Indefinite (FI) prefixes are indeed often used in reference to female persons. Just as often, however, a different set of prefixes is used, the same Zoic prefixes used for animals. (This category is accordingly termed Feminine-Zoic (FZ) by Iroquoianists.)

The use of two categories for female persons immediately raises the question of the difference between the two. Speakers are usually surprised when it is brought to their attention. Some are horrified to realize that they are using the same forms for women and animals. They report that they never thought about it, and that "No one notices". The difference in usage between the Feminine-Indefinite and Feminine-Zoic is in fact subtle and intriguing, and subject to variation across communities, families, and even individuals.

5.1 Feminine-Indefinite

When speakers become interested in the difference between the two genders used for women, and ask others to reflect on their own usage, they typically pose questions in terms of the emphatic/contrastive pronouns, *akaónha* 'she, one' (Feminine-

Indefinite) and *aónha* 'she, it' (Feminine-Zoic): "Would you use *akaónha* or *aónha* for X?" A point on which all speakers immediately agree is that *akaónha* (FI) is used for grandmothers and mothers. This principle is often characterized in terms of respect. One speaker generalized the principle as follows: "The baseline is to refer to older relatives as *akaónha* (FI), younger as *aónha* (FZ), but this can change according to personality". An elderly lady noted, "The older you get, the more respect people have for you, so you'll hear less and less *aónha* (FZ)." Many volunteered that *akaónha* (FI) is used "for refined, delicate, lady-like persons". One speaker related usage to the speaker: "*Akáonha* (FI) is used by people who are gentler."

The Feminine-Indefinite is used not just for older women, however. One speaker reported that she would use *akaónha* (FI) "always for little girls, but I know some who would go by personality". Another reported that she used *akaónha* (FI) "for all my daughters, but I know some would do it differently". Several volunteered that Feminine-Indefinite forms have a "diminutive sense" and indicate "endearment". There are, for example, two forms translatable as 'my daughter'. Speakers agree that "Both are definitely acceptable, and both are used all the time." Some noted a slight difference in connotation, however.

(12)   Daughters
       kheièn:'a   'my daughter'   FI   "more loving"
       tièn:'a   'my daughter'   FZ   "more frivolous"

Often mothers are initially shocked to realize that they use different gender prefixes for different daughters. After some reflection, one observed, "Often the firstborn girl is *aónha* (FZ), then succeeding girls are *akaónha* (FI)."

5.2 Feminine-Zoic

Speakers often remark that *aónha* (FZ) is used for "louder, more powerful, more assertive, more aggressive women". Those referred to with *aónha* (FZ) forms are characterized as "tough women", with "an outgoing nature". The speaker cited above who remarked that *akaónha* (FI) forms are used by gentler speakers also noted that *aónha* (FZ) forms would be "used more by someone who is really rough". Another speaker volunteered interesting comments on the two forms in (12).

(13)   Pretty women
       ie-ksa'tí:io   'she is pretty'   FI   "a bit more ladylike"
       ka-ksa'tí:io   'she is pretty'   FZ   "the one he'd like to go out with"

The forms in (12) could suggest a difference in degree of respect, and one speaker made such an observation: "*Aónha* (FZ) would be used for someone you don't respect: an animal or a stranger". These forms are indeed common for non-Mohawk women. The terms for 'nun' and 'queen' are both Feminine-Zoic.

(14) Non-Mohawk women
      io-*ia'tatokénhti*   'nun'   FZ   (literally 'she FZ is bodily holy')
      ka-*kwí:n*   'the Queen'   FZ   (Queen Elizabeth)

Speakers are quick to assert, however, that the forms "do not necessarily indicate a lack of respect". One woman noted, "I wouldn't be insulted if someone used *aónha* (FZ) for me. It would mean they just don't know me well. I do the same with others." Another volunteered, "This is not about respect, but about distance." Still another was quick to say that Feminine-Zoic forms "are not rude, never felt to be rude." One explained these forms as appropriate for "someone we don't know, who is not an elder".

A slightly different angle was suggested by another speaker, and her comment was met with unanimous agreement. "*Aónha* (FZ) might be used for someone you don't like, though the form itself doesn't say that". It was explained that use of Feminine-Zoic forms might convey dislike only if the speaker had always used Feminine-Indefinite forms for an individual before.

Age is mentioned in discussions about *aónha* (FZ) forms as well. Several women have noted that *aónha* (FZ) is used for "contemporaries, women your own age", and their own usage corresponds to their observations. The *aónha* (FZ) forms are used for good friends. They add that "older or younger women could be either". These assessments highlight the subtlety of the distinction, when they are contrasted with the tone of endearment felt in the Feminine-Indefinite daughter terms seen in (11).

Speakers also observe that use of the two categories is very much a family matter. When one woman first became conscious of the grammatical distinction, she asked herself, "Why do I say *aónha* (FZ) for my aunt?" She then realized, "Ah, I'm just imitating my mother." Another noted that "A and her sisters use *aónha* (FZ) forms for each other, with no disrespect." One hypothesized that "The mother decides for a baby girl, and that categorization usually stays for life." Thinking about her own family, she made the following observations. "I am the oldest daughter, so I am *aónha* (FZ). My sisters are *akaónha* (FI). They always use *aónha* for me, and I use *akaónha* for them. I always refer to all my aunts as *aónha* (FZ). But that may be because my mother was the youngest and has always been *akaónha* (FI)."

Usage also differs from one community to the next. Men in Kahnawà:ke generally refer to their wives as *akaónha* (FI), interpreted as a sign of respect. Men in Ahkwesáhsne, however, approximately 50 miles upriver, generally refer to their wives as *aónha* (FZ), interpreted as a sign of affection. One speaker recounted a story from the time she was being courted. Her family was originally from the Ahkwesáhsne community. When she was a teenager, they moved downriver to the Kahnawà:ke community. One day a young man came to the door, asking her mother whether her daughter was at home, using Feminine-Indefinite forms. The mother was perplexed, having no idea who he could be asking for. The daughter he was interested in, the firstborn, had always been referred to with Feminine-Zoic forms. Her younger sisters, referred to with Feminine-Indefinite forms, were much too young to be courted.

The FI/FZ distinction is thus intriguing but far from straightforward. The frequently-cited features of age, respect, and familiarity first evoke European *tu/vous* distinctions, but with closer scrutiny, it becomes clear that the distinctions are not isomorphic. The Mohawk distinction is of course marked in third-person rather than second. It also includes features not commonly associated with the European categories, such as daintiness versus brashness. Feminine-Indefinite forms signal endearment toward family members, but Feminine-Zoic forms signal familiarity among close friends. The Feminine-Indefinite forms are said to mark respect, but it is the Feminine-Zoic forms that are used for people one does not know well. Nevertheless, like the European distinction, and more complex systems like that of Lao described by Enfield (2007: 77–84), usage is a social and cultural matter, one subject to subtle variation across communities, families, and individuals.

6 The real story

The associations between language and culture suggested by use of one category for women and generics on the one hand, and a separate category for some women and animals on the other, are not as direct as might be assumed. In fact the Feminine-Indefinite category did not emerge from a view of women as quintessential or prototypical human beings, and the Feminine-Zoic category did not develop from a view of women as akin to animals. The relationship between grammar and culture here is more complex. This can be seen by examining the successive stages of development of the two grammatical categories over time. Though there are no ancient written records of the Iroquoian languages in which these stages are directly attested, paths of development over time can be traced both from comparisons of the systems of modern related languages and from internal clues within each language.

6.1 Comparative evidence

Relationships among the modern Iroquoian languages for which we have substantial documentation are shown schematically in Figure 1.

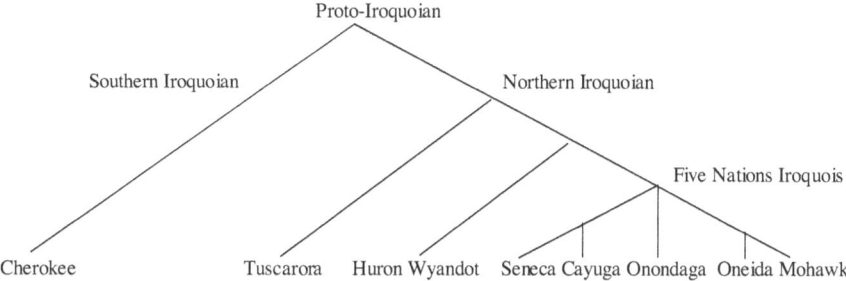

Figure 1: The Iroquoian Language Family

The family first separated into two major branches, Southern Iroquoian and Northern Iroquoian, several thousand years ago. The only known member of the Southern branch is Cherokee, spoken at first contact with Europeans in the 17th century in the North American Southeast, over parts of what is now North Carolina, Virginia, South Carolina, Georgia, and Alabama. The next split occurred within the Northern branch, when the ancestors of modern Tuscarora speakers separated from the main group. The Tuscarora lived until the early 18th century in what is now eastern North Carolina. After the Tuscarora Wars of 1711–1713, they began moving north, eventually settling near the Five Nations groups in western New York and southern Ontario. The Huron language was spoken in the 17th century in what is now Ontario. After epidemics and wars with the Five Nations Iroquois between 1647 and 1649, they were scattered. Some joined other Iroquoian bands in the area and moved west and then south, ultimately settling in Oklahoma, where they are now known as the Wyandot. Others, now known as the Wendat, moved east toward their present location near Quebec City. The Five Nations Iroquois groups lived, at the time of first contacts with Europeans in the early 17th century, in communities extending across what is now New York State. Their villages were located in the configuration shown in Figure 1, with the Seneca at the western edge and the Mohawk at the eastern edge.

It is possible to reconstruct stages in development of the gender categories by comparing the modern languages. Traits found in both branches of the family, Southern Iroquoian (Cherokee) and Northern Iroquoian, can be hypothesized to have been present in their common ancestor, Proto-Iroquoian. On this basis it appears that Proto-Iroquoian had one basic third person category with no gender distinction, and one Indefinite category used only for generic and indefinite humans. Number distinctions were made for all animates in the basic third person category. This system has survived intact in modern Cherokee, where basic third person prefixes are cognate with Mohawk *ka-* and *o-*, and the Indefinite prefix is cognate with Mohawk *ie-*. Traces of this system remain in all of the other languages.

Proto-Northern-Iroquoian shows the introduction of a new Masculine category, present in all of the modern Northern Iroquoian languages (Chafe 1977). The original basic third person category shrank accordingly to apply to just objects, animals, and female persons. The original Indefinite category was still used only for generics and indefinite persons. This system is preserved in modern Wendat (Huron) and Wyandot.

Proto-Five-Nations shows the beginning of another change, still in progress in some of the languages. Speakers began using Indefinite forms not just as generics and indefinites, but also as a sign of respect for certain female persons. This change further diminished the range of the original basic third person markers to just objects, animals, and other female persons. It is thus a residual category, what is left of the original basic third person category after the removal of males to the new Masculine category and some females to the Indefinite category. This is essentially the situation found in modern Onondaga, Oneida, and Mohawk. Chafe (p.c.) reports that in Onondaga, the Feminine-Indefinite category can signal empathy, while the Feminine-Zoic can signal detachment. Abbott (1984) provides a detailed description of the Oneida system. It largely parallels the Mohawk one, with comparable variation across dialects and speakers, but it also shows subtle differences. In his 1953 grammatical sketch of Oneida, Lounsbury reported that age is the principal basis for the distinction, with a tendency among speakers to restrict Feminine-Zoic forms to 'adult, active, female persons' (1953: 51). Abbott noted that several decades later, some speakers, mainly male, concurred: Oneida Feminine-Zoic forms signal greater age than Feminine-Indefinite forms, "with the dividing line somewhat vaguely around adolescence" (1984: 128). He also found, however that other speakers strongly disagreed about the overriding importance of age. As in Mohawk, close relatives tend to be referred to with Feminine-Indefinite forms, but close friends with Feminine-Zoic forms. Abbott concludes that the choice seems to 'be based on age, size, gracefulness, kin relation, or even empathy' (1984: 128).

The extension of Indefinite forms to women has proceeded further in the western Five Nations languages. In modern Seneca and Cayuga, they are now used for all female persons. It is difficult to know precisely when these last developments occurred, and the extent to which they were driven by language contact. The Five Nations groups constituted a strong political alliance, the League of the Iroquois, and it is known that the members of the bands did interact and intermarry to some extent. After the Tuscarora arrived in the area, they too were brought into the League. Modern Tuscarora shows the same system as its immediate Seneca neighbors: reflexes of the original Indefinite forms are now used for all female persons.

6.2 Internal evidence

There is also internal evidence within each of the Northern Iroquoian languages of the extension of original Indefinite forms to female persons.

One indication is the form of traditional personal names. Naming practices follow ancient, pre-contact traditions. Names were the property of clans, traditionally bestowed by the clan mother or some other knowledgeable elder. Often a baby was given the name of a deceased relative of the same clan, but only one person at a time could bear a traditional name. The names are old, so not all are still interpretable, but most are still transparent. Some examples of traditional Mohawk names are in (15).

(15) Some traditional Mohawk women's names
Ka-ia'tanó:ron   'She is body-precious'
Ka-nerahtenhá:wi 'She is carrying leaves'
Ka-heráwaks   'She shakes the cornstalk'

What is significant is that in all of the Five Nations communities and among the Tuscarora as well, traditional names for women may contain Zoic or Neuter prefixes (*Ka-*, *W-*), but never Indefinite prefixes, no matter who the bearer. This is true even in communities where all women are now referred to with Feminine-Indefinite forms. The names predate the extension of the Indefinite gender forms to women.

A second indication of the direction of development of the gender categories involves kinship terms. The kinship terms are based on morphological verbs. As noted earlier, verbal prefixes may be intransitive or transitive. They distinguish three persons, three numbers, three genders, and two roles, grammatical Agent and Patient. Where the relationship is reciprocal, as for cousins, intransitive reciprocal forms are used with dual or plural prefixes ('we two are cousins to each other' = 'my cousin'). Where the relationship is asymmetrical, transitive prefixes are used, with the senior kinsman marked by forms similar to grammatical Agents in regular verbs, and the junior kinsmen marked like grammatical Patients.

(16) Transitive verbs and kinterms
    a. Verb
       rák-ken-hs
       3M.SG/1SG-see-HAB
       '**he** sees **me**.'

    b. Kinterm
       rak-hsót=ha
       3M.SG/1SG-be.grandparent.to=DIM
       '**he** is grandparent to **me**' = 'my grandfather'

Most kinterms for female relatives have both Feminine-Indefinite and Feminine-Zoic forms.

(17) 'My younger sister'
    a. ***khe-'kèn:'=a***
       1SG/3FI-be.older.sibling.to=DIM
       'I am older sibling to **her** (FI)' = 'my younger sister'   FI

    b. ***ke-'kèn:'=a***
       1SG/3FZ.SG-be.older.sibling.to=DIM
       'I am older sibling to **her** (FZ)' = 'my younger sister'   FZ

But not all kinship terms for women have two forms. For grandmothers and mothers, there are only Zoic forms.

(18) Feminine-Zoic only
    a. <u>*ak*</u>*-hsót=ha*
       3FZ.SG/1SG-BE.grandparent.to=DIM
       '**she** (FZ) is grandparent to **me**' = 'my grandmother'   FZ

    b. <u>*ake*</u>*-'nistén=ha*
       3FZ.SG/1SG-be.mother.to=DIM
       '**she** (FZ) is mother to **me**' = 'my mother'   FZ

What is surprising is that these are the very individuals speakers unanimously agree should be referred to with Feminine-Indefinite verbal prefixes and independent pronouns. The gaps begin to make sense when it is recognized that the use of Indefinite forms as a sign of respect for elders is an innovation. Words for 'my grandmother' and 'my mother' are among the earliest kinship terms learned by children and the most frequently used. They are thus the most resistant to change.

The extension of Indefinite forms to certain women is only gradually making its way through the regular verbal and kinship prefix paradigms. It is more advanced in the verbal paradigms, but certainly not complete. There are, for example, no separate Feminine-Indefinite dual or plural verb prefixes. Forms used for referring to more than one woman are descended from the original basic third person forms. The kinship prefix paradigms are even less advanced. The progress of the innovation can be traced in Table 1. For each relationship ('my grandmother', 'your grandmother', etc.) the table shows whether the innovative Feminine-Indefinite form yet exists (FI) or not (–), and whether the original Feminine-Zoic form still persists (FZ) or not (–).

Table 1: Gradual extension of Indefinite forms to female kinsmen

	'my'		'your'		'her'		'his'	
'grandmother'	FZ	–	FZ	–	FZ	–	FZ	–
'mother'	FZ	–	FZ	–	FZ	–	FZ	–
'older sister'	FZ	–	FZ	–	FZ	FI	FZ	FI
'younger sister'	FZ	FI	FZ	FI	FZ	FI	FZ	FI
'daughter'	FZ	FI	FZ	FI	FZ	FI	FZ	FI
'stepdaughter'	FZ	FI	FZ	FI	FZ	FI	FZ	FI
'sister-in-law'	FZ	FI	FZ	FI	FZ	FI	FZ	FI
'daughter-in-law'	FZ	FI	FZ	FI	FZ	FI	FZ	FI
'niece'	FZ	FI	FZ	FI	FZ	FI	FZ	FI
'granddaughter'	FZ	FI	FZ	FI	FZ	FI	FZ	FI
'stepmother'	–	FI	–	FI	–	FI	FZ	FI
'mother-in-law'	–	FI	–	FI	–	FI	–	FI

The earliest learned, most frequently-used terms have been the most resistant to change. The innovation has not yet reached any of the terms for grandmothers and mothers, nor those for 'my older sister' or 'your older sister'. There are now, however, Indefinite forms for 'her older sister' or 'his older sister'. On the other hand, for the terms which are probably the last to be learned and used, the terms denoting those relationships in which it is most important to show respect, the Feminine-Zoic forms have disappeared entirely. There are only Indefinite forms for all mothers-in-law as well as 'my stepmother', 'your stepmother', and 'her stepmother'. A Feminine-Zoic term still persists for 'his stepmother'. (Additional developments in the pronominal system are discussed in Mithun 2010.)

7 Agreement reconsidered

The difference in rates of development between the regular verbal prefix paradigms and the kinship prefix paradigms has lead to prefix mismatches within clauses. Grandmothers and mothers, for example, can be referred to only with Feminine-Zoic kinship terms, but only with Feminine-Indefinite verb prefixes.

(19) Grandmother mismatches: Josephine Kaieríthon Horne, speaker p.c.
    a. *Akhsótha*   *eni**e**nenhstóhare'*
        ak-hsot=ha   en-**ie**-nenhst-ohar-E'
        3FZ/1SG-be.grandparent.to=DIM   FUT-**FI.AGT**-corn-wash-PFV
        my grandmother (**FZ**)   she (**FI**) will corn wash

        tánon'
        tanon'
        and
        and
        'My grandmother (**FZ**) would wash (**FI**) the corn and

    b. *eni**e**the'serón:ni'*   *ohén:ton*
        en-**ie**-the'ser-onni-'   o-hent-on
        FUT-**3FI.AGT**-meal-make-PFV   N-lead-STATIVE
        she (**FI**) will grind   before
        grind (**FI**) it before

        tsi nió:re'
        tsi ni-io-r-e'
        SO PRT-3N.PAT-extend-STATIVE
        so it is far

    c. *kana'tarokhón:we*
        ka-na'tar-o-k=honwe
        N-bread-be.in.water-CONT=genuine
        traditional cornbread
        she (**FI**) made cornbread.'

        *eni**e**na'tarísa'.*
        en-**ie**-na'tar-is-'a-'
        FUT-**3FI.AGT**-bread-finish-PFV
        she (**FI**) will bread finish

It could be argued that this is typical of agreement systems in general. In many languages, the gender markers that appear on different lexical items, such as verbs, nouns, adjectives, demonstratives etc. need not have identical forms; they must simply encode the same categories. But these Mohawk mismatches cannot be generalized by lexical category. Other kinship terms for women have both Zoic and Indefinite forms, and the prefix categories on these terms normally match those on associated verbs.

(20) Zoic daughter: Sha'tekenhátie' Marian Phillips, speaker
Tanon' **konwaièn:'a** *skaià:ta*
tanon' **konwa**-ien'=ah s-**ka**-ia't-at
and **3FI/3FZ.SG**-have.as.offspring REP-**3FZ.SG**-body-be.one
and she (FI) has her(FZ) as child one (FZ) body

Kahentinéhson'
ka-hent-ine-hson'
3FZ.SG.AGT-field-lead-DISTR
she (FZ) leads the field
'And her (FI) one (FZ) daughter (FZ), Kahentinéhson' (FZ)

è:neken' *nenkwá:* *she's* *kanákere'*.
è:neken' nenkwa she's **ka**-naker-e'
up that.side formerly **3FZ.SG.AGT**-reside-STATIVE
up that side formerly she (FZ) resides
used to live (FZ) up there.'

The terms for 'grandmother' and 'mother' could still be accommodated in various ways theoretically. They could be listed as morphologically Zoic but syntactically Indefinite, for example. They could be likened to the Latin *agricola* 'farmer', which appears to have a Feminine ending formally but is categorized as Masculine for purposes of agreement.

These are not the only cases of mismatches. It was seen earlier that Zoic prefixes on verbs distinguish number, while the usually similar Neuter prefixes do not.

(21) Number distinctions
    a. Zoic verbal prefixes
        ka- SG.AGENT *io-* SG.PATIENT
        keni- DU.AGENT
        konti- PL.AGENT *ioti-* DUOPLURAL PATIENT

b. Neuter verbal prefixes
   ka- NEUTER.AGENT (SG/DU/PL)   *io-* NEUTER.PATIENT (SG/DU/PL)

(All of the prefixes exhibit considerable allomorphy.)
    The prefixes on Zoic nouns, however, do not usually distinguish number. The result is again mismatches between the nouns and verbs that are supposed to agree.

(22)   Bug mismatch? Dorothy Karihwénhawe Lazore, speaker p.c.
Kaniataratátie'   *enkontohétstake'*
ka-niatar-at-atie'   en-**konti**-ohetsts-akE'
N-river-extend-PROG   FUT-**3Z.PL.AGT**-pass-CONT
along the river   **they** will pass by

katsi'niowá:nen's   (...)
ka-tsi'non-owan-en-'s
N-bug-be.large-STATIVE-DISTR
it is bug large variously
'Insects (**NEUTER**) will pass by (**ZOIC.PL**) along the river (that you have never seen),

ok   *ò:ni'*   *ne*   *karonhia'kéhshon'*   *enkontítie',*
ok   ohni'   ne   ka-ronhi-a'ke=hshon   en-**kont**-itie-'
and   also   the   N-sky-place=DISTR   FUT-**3Z.PL.AGT**-fly-PFV
and   also   the   through the skies   **they** will fly
and they will also fly (**ZOIC.PL**) through the skies

seken   *ne*   *katsi'niowá:nen's.*
seken   ne   **ka**-tsi'non-owan-en-'s
also   the   3N-bug-be.large-STATIVE-DISTR
also   the   **it** is bug large variously
as well, those insects (**NEUTER**).'

This example reflects a common Mohawk pattern: many terms for animals contain a Neuter prefix that does not distinguish number, but they co-occur with verbs containing Zoic prefixes that do. The term for 'cow(s)' is literally 'it jowl protrudes doubly', no matter how many cows are under discussion. The form of the noun prefix does not change with number, but the form of the verb prefix does.

(23) Cow mismatch: Rita Konwatsi'tsaién:ni Phillips, speaker p.c.
Ísi'   nónhskwati   she's   niió:re'
yonder   bridge beyond   formerly   so it is far

niekonnéhtha'   ne
n-ie-**konn**-e-ht-ha'   ne
PRT-TRLOC-**3Z.PL.AGT**-go.with-HAB   the
there **they (ZOIC.PL)** habitually go   the

teionhónhskwaron.
te-**io**-nhonhskwar-ont
DV-**3N.PAT**-jowl-be.attached
it (**NEUTER**) doubly jowl protrudes
'The cows used to pasture way over on the other side of the bridge.'

(The Duplicative prefix te- (DV) here reflects the fact that two jowls are involved.)

An obvious explanation might be that number is not marked in the noun prefix morphology but it is marked in the verb prefix morphology. Singular, dual, and plural Zoic prefixes on nouns have the same form, but those on verbs are distinct. This hypothesis soon runs into exceptions, however. The term for 'sheep' has a Zoic plural prefix, no matter how many sheep are involved.

(24) Plural prefix on noun 'sheep'
teiotina'karontòn:'a
te-**ioti**-na'kar-ont=on'a
DV-**3Z.PL.PAT**-horn-be.attached=DISTR
'they are doubly horn attached' = 'sheep' (any number)

The number of sheep under discussion is specified only in associated predicates elsewhere in the clause. It is possible to specify that there is just one sheep, but in a larger phrase. Even here the noun for sheep still contains the Zoic plural prefix ioti-.

(25) 'one sheep'
skaià:ta   teiotina'karontòn:'a
s-ka-ia't-at   te-**ioti**-na'kar-ont-on'a
REP-NEUTER-body-be.one   DV-**3Z.PL.PAT**-horn-be.attached=DISTR
one body   sheep

It is interesting to note that in the eastern Mohawk communities, where the first language contact was with French, there is an alternate term for 'sheep': timotón. This word is a transparent copy of a French term, but it is the plural form *des moutons*. Sheep are animals that usually appear in groups (flocks). The unmarked number for sheep is plural. Such cases could be likened to the 'unproblematic mismatches' discussed by Corbett in his work on agreement, mismatches 'which arise because the controller lacks forms which would guarantee matching' (2006: 144).

These mismatches between noun prefixes and the number of referents actually suggest a more general principle, that gender is not a syntactically active property of nouns synchronically. In the account of the encounter with the polar bear seen earlier, the noun for 'bear' retained its Neuter form *o-hkwá:ri*, whether it was categorized in the verbal prefix as Zoic or Masculine.

(26) Masculine polar bear: Josephine Kaieríthon Horne, speaker p.c.
Wa'thá:ta'ne'   *kí:ken*   *ohkwá:ri.*
wa'-t-**ha**-ta-'n-E'   kiken   **o**-ahkwari
FACT-DV-**3M.SG.AGT**-stand-INCH-PFV   this   **NEUTER**-bear
he stood up   this   bear
'The bear (**he**) stood up.'

(27) Zoic polar bear: Josephine Kaieríthon Horne, speaker p.c.
Óksa'k   *sahiathrorià:na'*
oksa'k   sa-hi-at-hrori-ahna-'
immediately   REP-3M.DU.AGT-tell-MIDDLE-ANDATIVE-PFV
immediately   they went back to tell
'They quickly returned to camp to report

tsi   *wa'**konwá**rio'*   *ohkwá:ri.*
tsi   wa'-**konwa**-rio-'   **o**-ahkwari
that   FAC-**3DP/3Z.SG**-kill-PFV   **NEUTER**-bear
that   they killed **it ZOIC**   bear
that they had killed (**it**) a bear.'

It should be noted that this account was related by an excellent speaker. Other speakers agree that these are appropriate forms.

Similarly, in the ceremonial speeches seen earlier where otherwise inanimate objects are personified, it is only the verbal prefixes that show a category shift.

(28) Oratory: Frank Tekaronhió:ken Jacobs Jr., speaker

Ietshiiatahónhsatat	ne	ononhkwa'shòn:'a,
ietshii-at-ahonts-atat	ne	**o**-nonhkw-a'=shon'a
2PL/3HU.PL-MIDDLE-ear-prick	the	NEUTER-medicine-NS=DISTR
you all listen to **them**	the	various medicines

'Listen to the medicines (**NEUTER**)

tsi	nahò:ten'	**rón**:ton.
tsi	n-a-h-o'ten-'	**ron**-aton
at	PRT-FACT-N.-be.a.kind.of -PFV	3M.PL.AGT-say
as	such it is a kind	**they** (M.PL) are saying

to what **they** (M.PL) are saying.'

It should be noted that the prefix *o-* on 'medicines' has approximately the same form as the Neuter Patient prefix that appears on verbs, but the medicines are not functioning as grammatical Agents here, as can be seen in the prefix 'they' on the verb 'they are saying'. The noun 'medicine' always begins with the prefix *o-* no matter what its grammatical role in the clause.

Zoic forms differ from general Neuters not only in showing number distinctions, but also in certain transitive prefix combinations. Basic neuters are not represented unless they are the only core argument of the clause. The Masculine plural agent prefix in intransitive verbs, for example is *rati-/-hati-*, as in: *wa-**hati**-ká:we'* '**they** paddled'. The same form is used in transitives with Neuter patients '**they**/it or them'. Different forms are used in transitives with Zoic patients: *konwa-* '**they/ it** or **her**' and *konwati-* '**they/them**'.

(29) Zoics and Neuters
   a. Zoic (animate) patients
       *Sa-**konwa**-ia'tisákha'*.
       '**They** went back out to look for **it** (a cow).'

       *Sa-**konwati**-ia'tisákha'*.
       '**They** went back out to look for **them** (cows).'

   b. Neuter (inanimate) patients
       *Sa**hati**sákha'*. '**They** went back out to look for (it/them).'

But the agreement patterns are not always as might be expected. The choice of Zoic or Neuter gender prefixes in the verb does not always depend on the referent. The sentences in the next four examples come from an account of the history of the old church bell at Kahnawà:ke, Quebec. The bell was sent by ship at the beginning of the 18th century as a gift from the King of France. It was wartime, however, and the ship was captured and taken to Salem, Massachusetts. The cargo was sold, and the bell was purchased by the town of Deerfield. When news of the sale reached the Mohawks, they set out for Deerfield. They managed to find the bell, take it down from the church steeple there, and fasten it to a beam to carry it back home. It was wintertime, however, and after struggling some way through the deep snow, they decided to bury the bell and return for it in the spring.

In the first clause in sentence (30), the ship was categorized in the verbal prefix *konwa-* as Zoic. This is perhaps not surprising; many English speakers refer to ships as 'she'. But this same ship was categorized by the same speaker as Neuter in the second clause of the same sentence.

(30) Zoic and Neuter ship: Josephine Kaieríthon Horne, speaker p.c.

Wa'konwaié:na' ne *kahonweia'kó:wa,*
wa'-**konwa**-iena-' ne **ka**-honweia'=kowa
FACT-**3PL/3Z**-catch-PFV the **N**-boat=AUG
they caught it (**ZOIC**) the ship (**NEUTER**)
'They captured **it** (**ZOIC**) the ship

iahatíhawe' *wastonhronòn:ke*
i-a-hati-haw-E' waston=hronon'=ke
TRLOC-FACT-3M.PL.AGT-take-PFV Boston=resident=place
they took it (**NEUTER**) United States
and took it (**NEUTER**) to the United States.'

Perhaps even more surprising is the categorization of the town of Deerfield as Zoic in (31).

(31) Zoic town: Josephine Kaieríthon Horne, speaker p.c.

Deerfield *t**konwá**:iats,* tsi *nón:*
Deerfield t-**konwa**-iat-s tsi ne=onwe
Deerfield CISLOC-3FI/**3Z.SG**-call-HAB at the=place
Deerfield they call it (**ZOIC**) at the place

tioia'totarhè:'on.
t-io-ia't-otarhe'-on
CISLOC-**3N.PAT**-bodily-hook-ST
there it (**NEUTER**) was seized
'It was seized at a place called (**ZOIC**) Deerfield.'

In (32) the bell was Neuter, as would be expected.

(32) Neuter bell: Josephine Kaieríthon Horne, speaker p.c.
Karontà:ke   *wahatihwánerenke'.*
ka-ront-=a'ke   wa-hati-hwanerenk-E'
NEUTER-log=place.at   FACT-3M.PL.AGT-tie-PFV
log place   they tied it (**NEUTER**)
'They fastened it (**NEUTER**) to a beam.

Wahonnenhsà:ren' ...
wa-hon-nenhs-a-hren-'
FACT-3M.PL.AGT-shoulder-LK-set.on-PFV
They carried it (**NEUTER**) on their shoulders ... '

But in (33), this same bell was referred to as Zoic.

(33) Zoic bell: Josephine Kaieríthon Horne, speaker p.c.
*En**konwa**ia'táta'*   *ne*   *iehwista'ékstha'.*
en-**konwa**-ia't-at'a-'   ne   ie-hwist-a-'ek-hst-ha'
FUT-**3.PL/3Z.SG**-body-insert-P   the   3FI.AGT-metal-LK-hit-INS-HAB
they will bodily insert it (**ZOIC**)   the   one metal strikes with it
'[They decided] they would bury (it **ZOIC**) the bell.'

This is not a matter of stylistic options. Speakers agree that these prefixes are the only acceptable ones in these sentences.

Similar alternations can be seen in the verbal prefixes associated with corn. In (34) corn is Neuter, as would be expected.

(34) Corn: Josephine Kaieríthon Horne, speaker p.c.

*Nó:nen   akwé: io*státhen
ne-onen   akwék-on   io-stath-en
the-when   be.all-STATIVE 3N.PAT-be.dry-STATIVE
when   all   it (**NEUTER**) is dry

***nó**:nenhste',   sók*
ne=o-nenhst-E'   sok
the-**NEUTER**-corn-NS   then
the corn   then
'When the corn was completely dry (**NEUTER**),

nòn:wa'   entsakwanenhstarón:ko'
ne=onhwa'   en-ts-iakwa-nenhst-a-ron-ko-'
the=now   FUT-REP-1EXCL.PL.AGT-corn-LK-be.attached-REV-PFV
now   we will corn remove
we would take the kernels off the cob.'

But in (35) the corn is referred to as Zoic. This speaker was commenting on what she had noticed during a drive through the surrounding area.

(35) Corn: Watshenní:ne Sawyer, speaker p.c.

*Ó:nenhste'   ken'k   ni-**konti**-hnenié:son's*
o-nenhst-E'   ken'=ok   ni-**konti**-hneni-es-on's
N-corn-NS   small=just   PRT-**3Z.PL.AGT**-length-be.long-DISTR
corn   small   so **THEY** (**ZOIC.PL**) are long variously
'The corn **are** (**ZOIC**) very short.

tsi   ní:io   nakwé:
tsi   ni-io-ht   ne=akwek-on
as   PRT-N.PAT-be.so the=all-STATIVE
as   so it is   the all

thie-ioti:-ten.
th-ie-***ioti***-ten
CONTR-TOC-**3Z.PL.PAT**-be.poor
they (**ZOIC.PL**) are just poor there
They all seem to be doing poorly (**ZOIC**).'

Other speakers concur that only Zoic prefixes could be used here: "'No one would ever say *Ken'k niión:son's* for 'it is short' referring to corn." (Kanerahtenhá:wi Nicholas, p.c.).

The somewhat surprising choices of gender prefixes appear to be controlled by the verb stem. Some additional examples of unexpected verb prefixes are in (36). Verbs for growing and getting frostbitten require Zoic prefixes, which distinguish number. The verb for getting ripe requires a Neuter prefix, with no number distinction. Speakers have no choices here.

(36) Some additional observed verbs
    ioti-ká:ion   'they are growing slowly' (corn)   PL
    ioti-kenhé:ion   'they are slow growing' (corn, berries, potatoes, grass)   PL
    ioti-hniò:'on   'they just grew' (volunteer trees in the woods)   PL
    ioti-iénhton   'they got frosted' (berries)   PL
    ion-atonníson   'they have finished growing, they're ripe' (potatoes)   PL
    io-hiá:ri   'they are ripe' (blackberries)   SG

Relatively few verb stems can be used with either animate or inanimate arguments. It appears that verbs for growing, catching, burying, and having a proper name require grammatically animate patients, that is, they routinely occur with Zoic Patient prefixes. Prototypical scenarios have been routinized to grammatical requirements.

The prefixes on many nominals do not signal gender directly. The original number markers have been frozen in the lexicalized nominals. Basic morphological nouns consist minimally of three parts: a noun prefix, a noun stem, and a noun suffix. Nouns beginning with *o-* (or its allomorphs) are usually Neuter.

(37)   Morphological noun
         ó:nenhste'
         o-nenhst-E'
         NEUTER-corn-NOUN.SUFFIX
         'corn'

A very large number of lexicalized referring expressions are actually morphological verbs, without overt nominalizers. Some were seen earlier. Their prefixes may match the gender category of their referents, as in the case of 'nun', or not, as in the case of 'pencil', literally '**one** writes with it'.

(38) Many syntactic nominals (referring expressions) are morphological verbs.

    a. *ioia'tatokénhti*
       io-ia't-a-tokenht-i
       ZOIC.SG.PAT-body-LK-be.holy-STATIVE
       'she is body holy' = 'nun'

    b. *iehiatónhkhwa'*
       ie-hiaton-hkw-ha'
       INDEFINITE.AGT-write-INS-HAB
       'one writes with it' = 'pen, pencil'

There are in fact very few true morphological human nouns. The terms for 'boy' and 'girl' seen earlier, and for 'man' and 'woman', are ancient, but they are based on the verb roots *-ksa* 'be a child' and *-onkwe-* 'be a person'.

(39) Common nominals

    raksà:'a   *rón:kwe*
    ra-ksa='a   r-onkwe
    M.SG.AGT-**be.a.child**=DIM   M.SG.AGT-**be.a.person**
    'boy'   'man'

    ieksà:'a   *iakón:kwe*
    ie-ksa='a   iak-onkwe
    FI.AGT-**be.a.child**=DIM   FI.AGT-**be.a.person**
    'girl'   'woman'

These roots occur most often in the referring expressions above, but there is ample evidence of their status as verb roots. The sets of noun and verb stems are completely distinct in Mohawk. Only noun stems can serve as the foundation of morphological nouns, and only verb stems can serve as the foundation of morphological verbs. Mohawk shows extensive noun incorporation, whereby a noun stem is compounded with a verb stem to form a new verb stem. Only morphological noun stems can be incorporated. The verb roots *-ksa* 'be a child' and *-onkwe* 'be a person' must be overtly nominalized before they can be incorporated.

(40) Nominalized roots

    a. *ra-ksa-'t-í:io*
       M.SG.AGT-be.a.child-**NOMINALIZER**-be.good
       'He is a good boy.'

b. *r-onkwe-'t-í:io*
M.SG.AGT-be.a.person-**NOMINALIZER**-be.good
'He is a good man.'

The morphological structures of noun and verb words are also completely distinct. The two verb roots 'be a child' and 'be a person' participate in verbal morphological constructions, such as the Coincident.

(41) Coincident construction
Shikeksà:'a, ...
shi-ke-ksa='a
COINCIDENT-1SG.AGT-be.a.child=DIM
'When I was a child ...'

They are negated like other verbs as in (42), rather than like nouns as in (43).

(42) Clausal and verbal negation
Iáh   teskaksà:'a.
iah   te-s-ka-ksa='a
not   NEG-REP-FZ.SG.AGT-be.a.child=DIM
'She is no longer a child.'

(43) Nominal negation
Iáh   ó:nenhste'   tè:ken.
iah   o-nenhst-E'   te'-ka-i
not   N-corn-NS   NEG-3N.AGT-be
not   corn   is it
'It is not corn.'

Other terms for persons are also morphological verbs, such as *akokstèn:ha* 'elderly lady' and *rokstèn:ha* 'elderly man' based on the verb root *-ksten* 'be old'; *nitiakoiòn:ha* 'young woman', and *nithoiòn:ha* 'young man', based on another root *-akaion* 'be old'; *ieià:tase* 'young lady' (literally 'she is new bodied'), and *ranekénhteron* 'young man', a stative verb based on the verb stem *-nekenhter-* 'be a young man'. The same verb stem is used as a syntactic predicate: *kenekénhteron* 'I am a young man'. The word *rohsken'rakéhte'* 'warrior, post-adolescent man', is literally 'he carries a weapon ('he rust-carries'). The word *rahsennowá:nen* 'chief' is a verb meaning literally 'his name is great'. The word *ratsiénhaienhs* 'councillor' is literally 'he lays the (council) fire'. As was seen earlier, kinship terms are based on morphological verbs. Terms that characterize people in terms of their activities or professions are morphological verbs, such as *rató:rats* 'hunter', literally 'he hunts', or *ra'swáhtha* 'fireman', literally 'he extinguishes'. One term, *owirà:'a* 'baby', is a morphological noun based on the noun root 'offspring', but it is marked grammatically as Neuter with its prefix *o-*.

The prefixes on referring expressions do not necessarily classify the referents of those terms directly. Many are simply relics of the original verbal constructions that were their sources. In some cases the sources are still very much alive and alternatives exist: *ra'swáhtha* 'fireman', *ron'swáhtha* 'firemen' ('they extinguish'). In others, the terms have simply become labels, even if speakers can retrieve the sources: *teionhónhskwaron* 'cow(s)'.

8 Conclusions

The material seen in the preceding sections illustrates several points about relations between grammatical gender systems and culture.

The first is that such grammatical systems can be more intricate and interesting than might first appear on the basis of elicited sentences. The sets of constructed Mohawk sentences seen at the outset would, at first, appear to show a typologically prototypical, even European-type gender system, with Masculine, Feminine, and Neuter gender categories marked on nouns and reflected in agreement prefixes on verbs. The Masculine prefixes are used for male persons, the Feminine prefixes for female persons, and the Neuter prefixes for objects and animals. Examination of spontaneous speech quickly shows that the categorization is more complex, however. Within the Neuter category a formal distinction is made between inanimates and animates, with number distinguished only for animates. Such a situation is not uncommon cross-linguistically. Mohawk Masculine and Feminine prefixes are sometimes used for personified objects and animals, again not a rare phenomenon. Somewhat surprising is the fact that the Feminine forms used for certain female persons are also used to refer to unidentified persons or to people in general. Perhaps even more surprising is the fact that the same Neuter (Zoic) forms used for animals are also used for referring to other female persons. The factors governing choices between these two categories, termed Feminine-Indefinite and Feminine-Zoic, are complex and variable across communities, families, and individuals. These gender categories are not isomorphic with others found elsewhere in the world, and the factors underlying their distribution do not match criteria for choice seen among categories elsewhere either. Like gender systems in many other languages, however, they are subject to variation across speakers and communities.

Second, the existence of agreement has often been cited as a fundamental property of grammatical gender systems, and the first set of Mohawk examples would appear to illustrate exactly this property. The nouns and associated verbs in those examples contain similar sets of prefixes reflecting gender and number. A closer look at spontaneous speech shows, however, that standard notions of agreement do not fully capture the relationships between the forms that actually occur. The prefixes on nouns may match the coreferential pronominal prefixes on verbs in gender and number, but they often do not. The noun prefixes are not synchronically active. They are an artifact of their diachronic sources and remain unchanged no matter what their referent or syntactic role in the clause. The forms of the noun prefixes may or may not match the referents of the nouns. Furthermore, the verbal prefixes are actually fully referential bound pronominal forms, which reflect features of their referents, rather than noun classes.

Finally, a reconstruction of the development of the Mohawk gender system shows that though grammatical gender categories may indeed reflect culture, the relationship is not necessarily immediate and direct. The fact that the same gender category is used for women and generic reference to human beings is not a result of a conception of women as prototypical humans. It is, instead, the result of the use of original indefinite forms to refer to certain women as a sign of respect. That extension of the original indefinite category to certain female persons does of course reflect an aspect of culture. The fact that the same gender category is used for animals and certain other women is not a result of the conception of women as akin to animals. That gender category is a residual category, one that originated as a basic third person category undifferentiated for gender but was narrowed in successive steps, first with the introduction of a separate Masculine category for males, and then with the use of the original generic category for certain females.

Relations do indeed exist between grammatical gender categories and culture, but these relations are often more complex and interesting than might be assumed.

9 References

Abbott, Clifford. 1984. Two feminine genders in Oneida. *Anthropological Linguistics* 26(2). 125–137.
Chafe, Wallace. 1977. The evolution of third person verb agreement in the Iroquoian languages. In Charles N. Li (ed.), *Mechanisms of Syntactic Change*. 493–524. Austin: University of Texas Press.
Corbett, Greville. 1991. *Gender*. Cambridge, UK: Cambridge University Press.
Corbett, Greville. 2006. *Agreement*. Cambridge, UK: Cambridge University Press.

Enfield, Nick. J. 2007. *A Grammar of Lao*. (Mouton Grammar Library.) Berlin: Mouton de Gruyter.
Hockett, Charles F. 1958. *A Course in Modern Linguistics*. New York: Macmillan.
Lounsbury, Floyd. 1953. *Oneida Verb Morphology*. New Haven: Yale University Press.
Mithun, Marianne. 2010. The search for regularity in irregularity: Defectiveness and its implications for our knowledge of words. In Matthew Baerman, Greville Corbett, and Dunstan Brown (eds.), *Defective paradigms: Missing forms and what they tell us*. Oxford, UK: British Academy and Oxford University Press. 125–149.

Niels O. Schiller
Psycholinguistic approaches to the investigation of grammatical gender

1 Psycholinguistic approaches to the investigation of grammatical gender in speech production: An overview and new data

In some languages, the selection of grammatical features, such as number, case, or gender (Corbett 1991) is mandatory to establish grammatical agreement in noun phrase (NP) production. Grammatical gender is a morphosyntactic feature that occurs in many languages of the world (see Corbett, this volume). It has been shown in the past that grammatical gender may impact linguistic processing in gender-marking languages. For instance, in Germanic languages like Dutch and German, native speakers are faster to name an object in the presence of a distractor word with the same gender as the name of the object than when the distractor has a different gender (Finocchiaro et al. 2011; Heim et al. 2009; La Heij et al. 1998; Schiller and Caramazza 2003, 2006; Schiller and Costa 2006; Schriefers 1993; Schriefers and Teruel 2000; Van Berkum 1997).

Schriefers (1993) was the first to observe this so-called *gender congruency effect*. He accounted for the effect in the following way: When a picture has to be named with a determiner(Det)-adjective(Adj) NP in Dutch (e.g., **het** groene $boek_{neu}$ 'the green $book_{neu}$'),[1] participants need to retrieve the necessary grammatical features of the noun to be able to produce the grammatically correct NP because determiners and adjectives are gender-marked in Dutch and their gender-marking has to agree with the gender of the head noun. According to Schriefers (1993), the picture name activates its corresponding gender feature (e.g., neuter). The gender feature has to be selected in order to activate the corresponding form of the definite determiner (*de* or *het* in Dutch). This process may be disturbed by the presence of a distractor word. When the distractor word has a different gender than the target, it activates a different gender feature. The simultaneous activation of two different gender features presumably results in competition. As a consequence, the selection of the gender feature of the target is delayed compared to the situation when both the target and distractor word activate the same

---

[1] In this article, we will use the following abbreviations: *neu* for neuter, *fem* for feminine, *mas* for masculine, and *com* for common gender.

gender feature, thereby boosting its activation and facilitating its selection. The gender congruency effect in Germanic languages such as Dutch (La Heij et al. 1998; Schiller and Caramazza 2003, 2006; Van Berkum 1997) and German (Heim et al. 2009; Schiller and Caramazza 2003; Schiller and Costa 2006; Schriefers and Teruel 2000) is a stable phenomenon that has been replicated many times in different laboratories.

However, Miozzo and Caramazza (1999) failed to replicate this effect with Italian speakers. They noted that in Italian (as well as in other Romance languages) the selection of the determiner during the production of an NP does not only depend on the gender of the noun but also on the immediate phonological context. For instance, the masculine determiner in Italian is *il* as in *il tavolo* ('the table') or *il grande scienziato* ('the great scientist') except when the word following the determiner starts with a vowel, a consonant cluster of the type <s> + consonant or <gn>, or an affricate. If one of the latter conditions holds, the determiner is *lo* as in *lo strano tavolo* ('the strange table') or *lo scienziato* ('the scientist'). Therefore, the selection of determiner forms (e.g., *la, il* or *lo*) in Italian (as well as in other Romance languages) cannot be carried out at the level where gender feature selection occurs but must wait instead until the phonological form of the lexical item that follows the determiner has been selected – a fairly late process in NP production.

Two scenarios for the absence of a gender congruency effect in Italian are possible. One possibility is that the selection of grammatical features is a competitive process but a competition effect is masked by the late selection of the determiner form in Italian. By the time the determiner is selected, any competition may have been resolved. The other possibility is that grammatical feature selection is not a competitive process, but an automatic consequence of lexical node selection. Selection competition, on this view, is restricted to the selection of lexical forms, including different forms of determiners. However, because determiners can only be selected relatively late during NP production in Italian, the effects of a distractor word are not visible at the level of determiner selection in this language. This latter hypothesis is in accordance with the results of a study by Costa et al. (1999) who were not able to replicate the gender congruency effect in two other Romance languages, namely Spanish and Catalan, which have similar characteristics with respect to determiner selection as Italian. Moreover, Alario and Caramazza (2002) failed to obtain the effect with determiners in French, another language in which determiner selection is affected by phonological context.

In Germanic languages like Dutch or German, however, the form of a determiner exclusively depends on the gender of the noun. As soon as the noun's gender information becomes available (along with information about "definiteness" and number), a determiner can be selected. We will refer to Romance and

Germanic languages as "late" versus "early selection languages", respectively, to emphasize the observed differences concerning the point at which determiner selection can take place.

Costa et al. (2003) found the gender congruency effect in Croatian, another early selection language. Since Croatian is a Slavic language and does not have determiners, they asked participants in their experiments to name objects with a verb phrase (VP) including a gender-marked pronoun ('I see it$_{mas/fem}$') and found a gender congruency effect with pronouns, i.e. free-standing gender-marked morphemes. However, they did not find a gender congruency effect when participants were asked to produce gender-marked (possessive) Adj NPs ('my$_{mas/fem}$ <object name>$_{mas/fem}$'). What could be the reason for the contrasting results? Costa et al. (2003) considered two possibilities, both based on the fact that the gender-marked items in the pronoun and Adj NP conditions differed in a crucial respect: gender agreement for adjectives, but not for (clitic) pronouns, involves the affixation of a bound morpheme. This means that the initial part of the adjective, i.e. the stem, in an Adj NP is the same for different genders (e.g., *moj*$_{mas}$ *krevet*$_{mas}$ 'my bed' vs. *moja*$_{fem}$ *truba*$_{fem}$ 'my trumpet'). One possible implication of this fact is that since gender-suffixed variants of an adjective differ at the end of the word, any effects of competition in the selection of affixes are not measurable with the currently used paradigms. Perhaps participants prepare for production of the adjective stem and begin speaking as soon as they have enough information about the noun, thereby masking any effects of competition that may occur in the selection of the gender-marked suffix. The other possibility is that the selection of morphophonological features, unlike that of free-standing morphemes and stems, is not a competitive process but an automatic consequence of specific grammatical properties.

However, before we can further consider these possibilities, we must first confirm the reliability and generalizability of the results reported in Costa et al. (2003) for Croatian. This is important because Schriefers (1993) found a gender congruency effect with Adj NPs in Dutch (*groen*$_{neu}$ *boek*$_{neu}$ 'green book' vs. *groene*$_{com}$ *tafel*$_{com}$ 'green table'). The difference in results between the two studies remains unresolved, and it could reflect differences between languages – Croatian versus Dutch. It is important therefore to first investigate whether or not the gender congruency effect is also found in the production of NPs in which the gender-marked elements are purely inflectional features and not free-standing morphemes or stems. We addressed this issue with three experiments in German and Dutch. From earlier research (Heim et al. 2009; La Heij et al. 1998; Schiller and Caramazza 2003, 2006; Schiller and Costa 2006; Schriefers 1993; Schriefers and Teruel 2000; Van Berkum 1997) we know that the gender congruency effect with free-standing morphemes is a stable phenomenon in these languages during the production of Det (Adj) NPs. Therefore, these languages are particularly appropriate to test whether the selection of free-standing and bound morphemes are subject to different processing constraints.

The method we use in all experiments of this study is the picture-word interference paradigm. In this paradigm, participants are presented with a picture that must be named as fast as possible while ignoring a concurrently displayed distractor word. This task is a variant of the Stroop (1935) task and it has been widely used to investigate various aspects of speech production including lexical access (for reviews see Glaser 1992 and MacLeod 1991). It has been shown, for instance, that picture naming latencies are affected by specific properties of the distractor word (Glaser and Düngelhoff 1984; Glaser and Glaser 1989; Lupker 1979, 1982; Schriefers, Meyer, and Levelt 1990; Starreveld and La Heij 1995, 1996). In this study, we manipulated the gender of the target picture name and the distractor word.

2 Experiment 1: Indefinite Det NP production in German

In the first experiment, we tested (indefinite) determiner NPs. German distinguishes three grammatical genders – masculine, feminine, and neuter. Masculine and neuter are marked by the indefinite determiner *ein* 'a(n)' (e.g., *ein*$_{mas}$ *Tisch*$_{mas}$ 'a table' or *ein*$_{neu}$ *Buch*$_{neu}$ 'a book'), the feminine form is *eine* (e.g., *eine*$_{fem}$ *Tür*$_{fem}$ 'a door'). Participants were asked to name objects using an indefinite Det NP while a gender-congruent or a gender-incongruent distractor word was visually presented. Schriefers' gender feature competition hypothesis predicts a gender congruency effect in this situation. However, depending on whether *ein/eine* are treated as morphologically simple or complex, different expectations may follow. In the former case, we may expect a gender congruency effect because different gender-marked morphemes compete for selection. In the latter case, however, we may not necessarily expect such an effect because if *ein/eine* are derived from the same stem *ein*, followed by affixation, the situation would be formally similar to the case of *moj/moja* in Croatian (see above).

2.1 Method

2.1.1 Participants

Twenty native German speakers participated in the study. Most of them were students at the University of Münster in Germany. Participants were paid for their participation in the experiment.

2.1.2 Materials

Ninety pictures corresponding to monomorphemic German nouns (30 masculine, 30 feminine, and 30 neuter) were selected as targets for the experiment. They were matched for frequency of occurrence (CELEX: Baayen, Piepenbrock and Gulikers 1995) and word length (all F's < 1). In addition, an equal number of gender-congruent distractor words were chosen (again, all F's < 1). Care was taken to ensure that targets and distractors were not semantically or phonologically related. For each gender, the target items of the other two genders served as gender-incongruent distractors. The complete list of target pictures and distractor words can be found in Appendix A.

Pictures were black line drawings of everyday objects presented on a white background. They were taken from the pool of pictures of the Max Planck Institute for Psycholinguistics in Nijmegen. Distractor words were displayed in their singular form in black characters (font type and size: Geneva, 30 pts.) inside or across the pictures. Pictures fitted into a 7 cm x 7 cm frame and appeared in the center of the screen with the distractor words appearing around fixation.

2.1.3 Procedure

Participants were tested individually in a dimly lit testing room. They sat in front of a computer screen at a viewing distance of approximately 80 cm. The experimenter sat in the same room to score potential errors. On each trial, a fixation point appeared for 500 ms followed by the picture and the distractor word. Participants were instructed to fixate the fixation point and to name the target picture as quickly and as accurately as possible *with the appropriate indefinite determiner* in German. At picture onset, a voice key connected to a microphone (Sennheiser HME 25–1) was activated to measure the naming latencies. As soon as a response was given and the voice key was triggered, picture and distractor word disappeared from the screen and after a short pause of one second the next trial started.

If no response was recorded within two seconds, the next trial started automatically. The presentation of the trial sequences was controlled by NESU (Nijmegen Experimental Set-Up). A response was considered invalid when it exceeded the response deadline of two seconds, when it included a speech error, when a wrong determiner or picture name was produced, or when the voice key was triggered incorrectly. Invalid responses were excluded from the reaction time analyses.

2.1.4 Design

The experiment consisted of three parts. First, participants were engaged in a familiarization phase. They saw each picture once on the computer screen to become familiar with the pictures and learn the designated picture names (in case alternative names were preferred by the participants). Each picture appeared on the screen as a black-on-white line drawing and after two seconds the designated name was added below the picture. Both remained in view for another three seconds. Participants were asked to use the designated name for each picture. After the familiarization phase, participants were engaged in a practice phase during which each picture was presented once in the center of the screen preceded by a fixation point. Participants' task was to name the picture as quickly and as accurately as possible using the appropriate *definite* determiner and picture name, e.g., *der Tisch* ('the table'). This procedure was adopted to ensure that participants knew the gender of all target picture names. After completion of the practice phase, the experimenter corrected participants if they did not use the designated name for a given picture. Then a second practice block consisting of 30 randomly chosen trials was administered together with distractor words. Participants were requested to name those pictures in the same way as in the first practice block.

The naming phase proper began immediately after the practice phase. Stimuli were presented in three blocks of 90 trials each. The stimulus-onset-asynchrony (SOA) between target and distractor was 0 ms.

Three additional trials included at the beginning of each block served as warm-up trials and were not included in the analyses. In each block, targets and distractors of the three grammatical genders were represented approximately equally often. Each target appeared once with a distractor word from each gender (90 pictures x 3 genders = 270 trials + warm-up trials). Blocks were randomized individually for each participant with the following constraints: (a) Before the same object was presented again, at least four other objects appeared in-between; and (b) targets could have the same gender on no more than two consecutive trials. Finally, the order of the blocks was varied across participants. The experiment lasted approximately one hour.

2.2 Results

The data of two participants had to be excluded due to excessive error rates (> 15%). Naming latencies shorter than 350 ms and longer than 1,500 ms were counted as outliers (3.4% of the data). The mean naming latencies and error rates are summarized in Table 1. Analyses of variance were run with Gender Condition (congruent or incongruent) and Gender of Target (masculine, feminine, or neuter) as independent variables. Separate analyses were carried out with participants (F_1) and items (F_2) as random variables.

Table 1: Mean naming latencies (in ms) and percentage errors (in parentheses) in Experiment 1.

	Gender of Distractor			
	Masculine	Feminine	Neuter	Mean
Gender of Target				
Masculine	613 (4.8)	602 (3.5)	621 (4.1)	612 (4.1)
Feminine	618 (5.4)	622 (6.5)	615 (6.5)	618 (6.1)
Neuter	610 (4.8)	611 (5.2)	617 (3.7)	613 (4.6)

2.2.1 Naming latencies

Picture naming latencies were 4 ms faster in the gender-incongruent condition (613 ms) than in the gender-congruent condition (617 ms). The effect of Gender Condition was not significant ($F_1(1,17) = 1.43$, $MS_e = 147.85$, ns; $F_2(1,89) = 1.49$, $MS_e = 605.25$, ns). Masculine targets were named fastest (612 ms), followed by neuter (613 ms) and feminine targets (618 ms), but the effect of Gender of Target was not significant ($F_1(2,34) < 1$; $F_2(1,87) = 1.47$, $MS_e = 616.22$, ns) nor was the interaction between Gender Condition and Gender of Target significant ($F_1(2,34) = 3.23$, $MS_e = 221.06$, ns; $F_2(2,87) < 1$).

2.3 Discussion

There was no difference in naming latencies between the gender-congruent and the gender-incongruent condition. The gender feature competition hypothesis predicted a gender congruency effect because the production of gender-marked indefinite NPs makes the retrieval of gender features necessary. However, in this experiment, we found no effect of Gender Condition (congruent vs. incongruent). Note, that this result replicates an earlier finding using partially distinct materials by Schiller and Costa (2006). Is there an explanation for the absence of a gender congruency effect in this task? As noted in the introduction, one possibility is that gender congruency effects are only found in the production of utterances where the gender-marked item is a free-standing, morphologically simple morpheme (see also Janssen, Schiller and Alario in press). Note that the gender-marked indefinite articles in German, *ein*$_{mas/neu}$ and *eine*$_{fem}$, are structurally similar to the possessive adjectives in Croatian, *moj*$_{mas}$ and *moja*$_{fem}$ (see above), where no gender congruency effect was found (Costa et al., 2003). Therefore, although *ein/eine* are formally determiners, they seem to behave like adjectives with respect to the way in which they are selected for production. That is, perhaps *ein/eine* share a stem – *ein* – and differ only in the suffix, i.e. – ø (zero morpheme) versus – *e*. Moreover, if we assumed that the process of stem retrieval is faster than affix retrieval (plus subsequent affixation), or articulation of the stem can start before affix retrieval and affixation have been completed, any gender congruency effect would be masked, just as in Croatian. Alternatively, if we assumed that morphophonological processes, such as affixation, are not selected competitively but automatically, we would similarly not expect to find a gender congruency effect in the production of phrases with the indefinite determiners *ein/eine*. On either account, we should not find a gender congruency effect with Adj NPs in German, even though, as already noted, Schriefers (1993) found such an effect in Dutch.

The absence of a gender congruency effect has been demonstrated in an Adj NP experiment in German (Experiment 1b reported in Schiller and Caramazza 2003). The inflectional gender system in German is similar to its determiner system: Adjectives take different suffixes in the singular to establish gender agreement with the noun referent (e.g., *grüne Tür* ('green door', fem), *grüner Tisch* ('green table', mas), or *grünes Buch* ('green book', neu)), but not in the plural (e.g., the same suffix -*e* is used for all three genders – *grüne Türen* ('green doors', fem), *grüne Tische* ('green tables', mas), or *grüne Bücher* ('green books', neu)). If the gender congruency effect only occurs when a free-standing morphologically marked word form (like a gender-marked definite determiner) has to be selected, then no such effect should be found when the gender-marked morpheme is bound to a word stem such as an adjective. Therefore, in a task in which participants were asked to produce Adj NPs, we expected that in both singular and plural conditions there would be no gender congruency effects. If, however, the effect occured also for bound morphemes such as gender-marked suffixes (as reported by Schriefers, 1993), it should have been observable in singular Adj NPs in German. However, we found no sign of a gender congruency effect in Adj NP naming in German, neither in the singular nor in the plural.

3 Experiment 2: Indefinite Det NP production in Dutch

The second experiment of this study is a replication of Experiment 1 in Dutch. As mentioned above, Dutch distinguishes two genders, common and neuter. The definite determiners for common and neuter gender are *de* and *het*, respectively. However, there is only one indefinite determiner for both genders – *een*. According to the hypothesis that gender congruency effects reflect competition between free-standing phonological forms (Caramazza et al. 2001; Miozzo and Caramazza 1999; Schiller and Caramazza 2003, 2006), no interference effect is expected because the same determiner form is produced for both genders. However, the gender feature competition hypothesis (Schriefers 1993) predicts a gender congruency effect.

It may be argued that gender is not accessed at all in such a situation, i.e. indefinite Det NP naming in Dutch. For instance, Levelt, Roelofs, and Meyer (1999) proposed that gender features are only selected when they are necessary for the encoding of an utterance. This assumption was made to account for the absence of the gender congruency effect in bare noun naming in Dutch (La Heij et al. 1998). Levelt, Roelofs, and Meyer (1999) argued that the reason for the absence of the effect in this situation was that bare nouns could be named without the selection of their gender features in Dutch. Hence, no gender congruency effect occurred. This argument could also be applied to the indefinite determiner NP case in Dutch. Since the indefinite determiner is invariably *een*, the production system does not have to select the corresponding gender feature of the noun.

From different research, however, we know that this argument does not hold: When German participants produced bare nouns in the singular and in the plural, they showed a significant cost from singular to plural production for masculine and neuter nouns (*Tisch* 'table' – *Tische* 'tables' and *Buch* 'book' – *Bücher* 'books', respectively), whereas for feminine nouns (*Tür* 'door' – *Türen* 'doors') no such cost occurred (Schiller and Caramazza 2003). This shows that even when a plural NP is produced and the selection of the gender feature is not logically necessary, the gender of the noun is selected and the corresponding singular determiner is activated. This leads to a competition effect in the case of masculine and neuter nouns where the determiners are different in the singular and in the plural (*der – die* and *das – die*, respectively), whereas in the case of feminine nouns the two determiners are identical (*die – die*) and hence there cannot be form competition. Janssen and Caramazza (2003) obtained similar findings for Dutch diminutive and plural NPs and Schriefers, Jescheniak, and Hantsch (2002) for German plural NPs.

As in the original study by Schriefers (1993), different SOAs were included in Experiment 2 because it is possible that the gender congruency effect is contingent on SOA. When the distractor word is presented too early with respect to picture onset, the activation of an incongruent gender feature may have already decayed and thus would be too weak to influence the selection of the target's gender node. When the distractor is presented too late, the gender of the target word may have already been selected and therefore immune to the activation of an incongruent gender feature. Indeed, Schriefers (1993) obtained the largest gender congruency effect at SOA 0 ms. The effect was only half as large at SOA –200 ms in his Experiment 1, and at SOA +450 ms no significant congruency effect was found. In his Experiment 2, the gender congruency effect was only significant at SOA 0 ms. Since this is the SOA at which the semantic interference effect is usually obtained, this was taken as evidence that the gender congruency effect occurs at the same level as the semantic interference effect, i.e. the lexical node level (but see Schriefers and Teruel 2000). We tested three SOAs in this experiment, namely –100 ms, 0 ms, and +100 ms, in order to maximize the probability of getting a gender congruency effect. The motivation for this manipulation was to ensure that the distractor word's gender feature was activated near the point in time at which the target word's gender feature was being selected.

3.1 Method

3.1.1 Participants

Sixteen native Dutch participants from the pool of participants of the Max Planck Institute for Psycholinguistics in Nijmegen took part in Experiment 2 in exchange for pay.

3.1.2 Materials

Twenty-two target pictures corresponding to monomorphemic Dutch nouns were selected for naming. Half of them had common gender; the other half had neuter gender. The target pictures overlapped for the most part with the materials used by Schriefers (1993) and La Heij et al. (1998). Each target picture was paired with a gender-congruent, a gender-incongruent, a phonologically, and a semantically related distractor word (see Appendix 8.2 for a complete list of target pictures and distractor words). The reason for including the semantic and phonological distractors was to obtain evidence for processing of the distractors in the potential absence of a gender congruency effect. In addition, there was a set of 32 filler pictures paired with gender-congruent, phonologically and semantically unrelated distractors. Pictures were simple black line drawings of everyday objects presented on white background. They were taken from the picture database of the Max Planck Institute for Psycholinguistics in Nijmegen. Distractor words were displayed as black characters (font type and size: Geneva, 30 pts) inside or across the pictures. Pictures were presented in the center of the screen with the distractor words appearing around fixation.

3.1.3 Procedure

The procedure was the same as in the previous experiment.

3.1.4 Design

Again, there was a familiarization phase, a practice phase, and a naming phase. The familiarization phase was as before. During the practice phase, participants had to name each object with the appropriate definite determiner to make sure participants knew the correct gender. The naming phase consisted of three blocks (one for each SOA) of 120 trials. Except for the filler pictures, all pictures were tested in all conditions (22 pictures x 4 conditions x 3 SOAs equals 264 trials + 32 filler pictures x 3 SOAs equals 360 trials altogether). There was a short break between each naming block. The order of blocks was varied across participants and the blocks were randomized individually for each participant with the same constraints as in the first experiment. The whole experiment lasted approximately 45 minutes.

3.2 Results

Naming latencies shorter than 350 ms and longer than 1,500 ms were counted as outliers (3.4% of the data). The mean naming latencies and error rates are summarized in Table 2. Analyses of variance were carried out with Condition (gender-congruent, gender-incongruent, semantically related, or phonologically related) and SOA (−100 ms, 0 ms, or +100 ms) as independent variables. Separate analyses were carried out with participants (F_1) and items (F_2) as random variables.

Table 2: Mean naming latencies (in ms) and percentage errors (in parentheses) in Experiment 2.

SOA	Condition	Gender of Target		
		Common	Neuter	Mean
−100 ms				
	Congruent	620 (8.5)	617 (10.2)	618 (9.4)
	Incongruent	635 (17.1)	625 (10.2)	630 (8.8)
	Semantically related	647 (13.6)	634 (13.6)	640 (13.6)
	Phonologically related	622 (6.8)	625 (11.4)	623 (9.1)
0 ms				
	Congruent	659 (11.4)	634 (8.5)	647 (9.9)
	Incongruent	638 (10.2)	646 (9.1)	642 (9.7)
	Semantically related	684 (17.0)	654 (24.4)	670 (20.7)
	Phonologically related	659 (11.9)	638 (17.6)	649 (14.8)
+100 ms				
	Congruent	686 (6.3)	675 (8.0)	681 (7.1)
	Incongruent	684 (8.0)	677 (9.7)	681 (8.8)
	Semantically related	663 (20.5)	680 (21.0)	672 (20.7)
	Phonologically related	641 (11.9)	643 (9.7)	642 (10.8)

3.2.1 Naming latencies

The main effect of Condition was marginally significant ($F_1(3,45) = 2.57$, $MSE = 1,106.59$, $p = .07$; $F_2(3,63) = 4.28$, $MSE = 2,511.12$, $p < .01$). Pictures were named fastest in the phonologically related condition (638 ms), followed by the gender-congruent (649 ms) and the gender-incongruent (651 ms) conditions; the semantically related condition was slowest (660 ms). Considering the gender-congruent condition as baseline, t-tests revealed that no condition was significantly different from the gender-congruent one (all p's > .07). Furthermore, pictures were named fastest at SOA − 100 ms (628 ms) followed by SOA 0 ms (651 ms), and slowest at SOA +100 ms (669 ms). This effect was significant ($F_1(2,30) = 7.79$, $MSE = 3,576.75$, $p < .01$; $F_2(2,42) = 32.13$, $MSE = 1,240.21$, $p < .01$) as was the interaction between Condition and SOA ($F_1(6,90) = 2.16$, $MSE = 751.70$, $p = .05$, $F_2(6,126) = 2.62$, $MSE = 1,402.83$, $p < .05$). Analyses of simple effects showed that Condition yielded a significant result only at SOA +100 ms ($F_1(3,45) = 3.96$, $MSE = 1,057.08$, $p < .05$; $F_2(3,63) = 4.18$, $MSE = 1,908.85$, $p < .01$), but not at SOA − 100 ms ($F_1(3,45) = 2.09$, $MSE = 458.22$, ns; $F_2(3,63) = 2.61$, $MSE = 1,211.95$, $p = .06$) nor at SOA 0 ms ($F_1(3,45) < 1$; $F_2(3,63) = 3.17$, $MSE = 2,195.97$, $p < .05$) – at least not in the analyses by participants. Although the simple effects were not significant at SOAs − 100 ms and 0 ms, we conducted pair-wise comparisons between the individual condition means. The difference between the gender-congruent and the gender-incongruent condition was not significant at any SOA, but the difference between the gender-congruent and the phonologically-related condition was significant at SOA +100 ms ($t_1(15) = 2.82$, $SD = 48.02$, $p < .05$, $t_2(21) = 3.63$, $SD = 49.55$, $p < .01$). The difference between the gender-congruent and the semantically related condition was marginally significant at SOA − 100 ms ($t_1(15) = 1.94$, $SD = 36.19$, $p = .07$; $t_2(21) = 2.63$, $SD = 50.16$, $p < .05$). These semantic and phonological effects showed that the distractor words were processed and influenced naming in the absence of any gender congruency effects.

3.3 Discussion

As predicted by the gender-marked free-standing morpheme congruency hypothesis, there were no gender congruency effects at any SOA. This result is in contrast with the gender feature selection hypothesis which predicted an effect – at least at SOA 0 ms, the SOA at which Schriefers (1993) also found his gender congruency effect. We can be sure, however, that participants processed the distractor words because we found effects of phonological facilitation (at SOA +100 ms) and semantic interference effects (though only marginally significant in the subject analysis at SOA − 100 ms).

This result parallels the absence of a gender congruency effect obtained with indefinite Det NP naming in German. In Dutch, just like in German, there is no effect of a gender-incongruent distractor word on the naming of an object when an indefinite Det NP is used. However, gender congruency effects have been found with similar materials when a slightly different task, i.e. definite Det NP production, was used (Schiller and Caramazza 2003, 2006). The reason for the absence of a gender congruency effect is likely the absence of a difference in form (een_{com} vs. een_{neu}). Reliable effects of gender congruency have been found in Dutch, German, Croatian, and recently in Italian (Finocchiaro (2013)) whenever

4 Experiment 3: Possessive Adj NP production in Dutch

The third experiment of this study is a replication of Experiment 2 using a different utterance format. In Dutch, the form of the possessive adjective *mijn* ('my') is invariable, i.e. independent of the gender of the noun referent. That is, it behaves similarly to the indefinite article *een* ('a') tested in the previous experiment. For instance, in Dutch one can say *mijn tafel*$_{com}$ ('my table$_{com}$') or *mijn boek*$_{neu}$ ('my book$_{neu}$') – the possessive adjective *mijn* has the same form for both genders. Therefore, the predictions for a picture-word interference experiment are the same as in the previous experiment: According to the gender feature competition hypothesis (Schriefers 1993), a gender congruency effect is predicted. The alternative hypothesis, however, predicts that gender congruency effects are due to the competition for selection between free-standing phonological forms (Caramazza et al. 2001). Consequently, no gender congruency effect is expected according to this latter view because the same form of the possessive adjective is used for both common and neuter gender nouns. As in the previous experiment, we tested the same stimuli under the same three SOAs, namely –100 ms, 0 ms, and +100 ms, in order to maximize the probability of obtaining a gender congruency effect. The motivation for this manipulation was to make sure that the distractor word's gender feature was activated near the point in time at which the target word's gender feature was being selected.

4.1 Method

4.1.1 Participants

Twenty-two native Dutch participants from the pool of participants of the Max Planck Institute for Psycholinguistics in Nijmegen took part in Experiment 3 in exchange for pay.

4.1.2 Materials, Procedure, and Design

Materials, Procedure, and Design were the same as in the previous experiment, except that participants were requested to name each picture using a possessive adjective NP of the format *mijn* ('my') + <picture name>.

4.2 Results

Naming latencies shorter than 350 ms and longer than 1,500 ms were counted as outliers (4.2% of the data). The mean naming latencies and error rates are summarized in Table 3. Analyses of variance were carried out with Condition (gender-congruent, gender-incongruent, semantically related, or phonologically related) and SOA (–100 ms, 0 ms, or +100 ms) as independent variables. Separate analyses were carried out with participants (F_1) and items (F_2) as random variables.

Table 3: Mean naming latencies (in ms) and percentage errors (in parentheses) in Experiment 3.

		Gender of Target		
SOA	Condition	Common	Neuter	Mean
–100 ms				
	Congruent	506 (11.6)	502 (9.5)	504 (10.5)
	Incongruent	491 (12.0)	503 (9.1)	497 (10.5)
	Semantically related	519 (11.6)	512 (9.1)	516 (10.3)
	Phonologically related	509 (14.5)	507 (12.0)	508 (13.2)
0 ms				
	Congruent	520 (10.3)	505 (9.9)	513 (10.1)
	Incongruent	518 (9.5)	519 (9.1)	519 (9.3)
	Semantically related	524 (14.0)	520 (9.9)	522 (12.0)
	Phonologically related	505 (10.3)	503 (10.7)	504 (10.5)
+100 ms				
	Congruent	524 (9.5)	515 (8.3)	520 (8.9)
	Incongruent	521 (11.2)	533 (9.5)	527 (10.3)
	Semantically related	528 (15.3)	516 (9.1)	522 (12.2)
	Phonologically related	522 (7.4)	519 (6.6)	514 (7.0)

4.2.1 Naming latencies

The main effect of Condition was significant ($F_1(3,63) = 3.19$, $MSE = 1,321.67$, $p < .05$; $F_2(3,63) = 3.41$, $MSE = 1,610.23$, $p < .05$). Pictures were named fastest in the phonologically related condition (508 ms), followed by the gender-congruent (512 ms) and the gender-incongruent (514 ms) conditions; the semantically related condition was slowest (520 ms). Considering the gender-congruent condition as baseline, t-tests revealed that only the phonologically-related condition was significantly different from the gender-congruent one by subjects, but not by items ($t_1(21) = 2.69$, $SD = 14.68$, $p < .05$; $t_2(21) = 1.74$, $SD = 22.47$, $p < .10$). Furthermore, pictures were named fastest at SOA − 100 ms (506 ms) followed by SOA 0 ms (514 ms), and slowest at SOA +100 ms (521 ms). This effect was only significant in the items analysis ($F_1(2,42) = 1.76$, $MSE = 5,158.86$, ns; $F_2(2,42) = 10.75$, $MSE = 4,702.96$, $p < .01$) but the interaction between Condition and SOA was significant by both subjects and items ($F_1(6,126) = 2.14$, $MSE = 769.00$, $p = .05$; $F_2(6,126) = 2.19$, $MSE = 940.26$, $p < .05$). Analyses of simple effects showed that Condition yielded a marginally significant result at SOA 0 ms ($F_1(3,63) = 2.56$, $MSE = 1,363.28$, $p = .06$; $F_2(3,63) = 3.17$, $MSE = 1,483.41$, $p < .05$) and a significant effect at SOA − 100 ms ($F_1(3,63) = 4.25$, $MSE = 911.82$, $p < .01$; $F_2(3,63) = 5.33$, $MSE = 1,417.49$, $p < .01$), but not at SOA +100 ms ($F_1(3,63) = 1.51$, $MSE = 584.59$, ns; $F_2(3,63) < 1$).

Although the simple effects were not always significant, we conducted pairwise comparisons between all the individual condition means for each SOA. The difference between the gender-congruent and the gender-incongruent condition was not significant at any SOA, but the difference between the gender-congruent and the phonologically-related condition was significant at SOA 0 ms by subjects but not by items ($t_1(21) = 2.42$, $SD = 20.28$, $p < .05$; $t_2(21) = 1.36$, $SD = 27.74$, ns). The difference between the gender-congruent and the semantically related condition reached significance at SOA − 100 ms ($t_1(21) = 2.10$, $SD = 24.87$, $p < .05$; $t_2(21) = 3.03$, $SD = 19.83$, $p < .01$). The semantic and the phonological effect (though the latter only significant by subjects) showed that the distractor words were processed and influenced naming in the absence of any gender congruency effects.

4.3 Discussion

As predicted by the gender-marked free-standing morpheme congruency hypothesis, there were no gender congruency effects at any SOA. This result is in contrast with the gender feature selection hypothesis which predicts an effect – at least at SOA 0 ms, the SOA at which Schriefers (1993) also found his effect. We can be relatively confident, however, that participants processed the distractor words in Experiment 3 (as in the previous experiments) because we found effects of phonological facilitation (at SOA +100 ms, though only significant in the subjects analysis) and effects of semantic interference (at SOA − 100 ms).

This result parallels the absence of a gender congruency effect obtained with indefinite Det NP naming in German (Experiment 1) and in Dutch (Experiment 2). In Dutch, furthermore, there is no effect of a gender-incongruent distractor word on the naming of an object when an Adj NP is used. However, gender congruency effects have been found with similar materials when a slightly different task was used, i.e. definite Det NP production (Schiller and Caramazza 2003, 2006). The reason for the absence of a gender congruency effect is likely the absence of a difference in form ($mijn_{com}$ vs. $mijn_{neu}$). Reliable effects of gender congruency have been found in Dutch, German, Croatian, and Italian whenever free-standing gender-marked morphemes, such as definite determiners or clitic pronouns, were produced.

5 General Discussion

In three experiments reported above, we investigated the gender congruency effect to further specify the circumstances under which this effect can be obtained. In Experiment 1, German participants were asked to produce gender-marked indefinite determiner NPs such as *ein Tisch* 'a table' or *eine Tür* 'a door' while gender-congruent or gender-incongruent distractor words were displayed visually. No effect of gender congruency was obtained. Experiment 2 involved the production of indefinite determiner NPs in Dutch. Again, there were no signs of a gender congruency effect. Finally, Experiment 3 tested possessive adjective NPs in Dutch, again without yielding a gender congruency effect. However, effects of semantic and phonological relatedness in Experiments 2 and 3 demonstrated that distractor words were being processed in the current study.

According to the gender feature competition hypothesis (Schriefers 1993), we should have observed gender congruency effects in all three experiments. This is because in each case gender has to be selected for the production of NPs and the presence of a gender-incongruent distractor word should have interfered with the selection of the target gender feature. As already noted, Schriefers (1993) obtained results consistent with that hypothesis: He found that participants were faster in Det+Adj and Adj NPs with gender congruent than incongruent distractors. However, the results reported here and other results in the literature converge in support of an alternative hypothesis. There are three sets of data that are relevant: the results on Romance languages, the results on plural NP production in Germanic languages, and the results on Adj NPs in Germanic languages and in Croatian.

In a series of experiments that investigated the gender congruency effect in various Romance languages, Caramazza and collaborators systematically failed to observe a gender congruency effect in Italian (Miozzo and Caramazza 1999; Miozzo, Costa, and Caramazza 2002), Spanish and Catalan (Costa et al. 1999), and French (Alario and Caramazza 2002). The failure to obtain a gender congruency effect in these languages occurred in the context of experiments that manipulated SOA, and had sufficient statistical power to reveal reliably semantic interference and phonological facilitation effects. Recently, Finocchiaro (2013) reported a gender congruency effect for Italian clitic pronouns demonstrating that the visibility of the effect does not depend on the language *per se*, but on the selection properties of the specific condition.

Although various explanations could be entertained for the contrasting results between Germanic and Romance languages, Caramazza and collaborators (2001) proposed that the gender congruency effect is really a determiner congruency effect that is observed only in early selection languages like German and Dutch. That is, the effect does not reflect competition in the selection of gender features but rather competition in the selection of determiners. The latter effects are visible in experiments with early selection languages where the activation of a competing determiner is sufficiently strong to be detectable in picture-word interference experiments. Converging evidence for the determiner competition hypothesis comes from experiments that directly compared the two hypotheses.

Schiller and Caramazza (2003, 2006; Schiller and Costa 2006) have shown that a gender congruency effect is found in NP production experiments with German and Dutch speakers only when the determiners associated with gender incongruent nouns are phonologically distinct. In Dutch and German, plural Det (Adj) NPs employ the same determiner for all genders (e.g., Dutch: ***de** tafels*$_{com}$ 'the tables' – ***de** boeken*$_{neu}$ 'the books' – ***de rode** tafels*$_{com}$ 'the red tables' – ***de rode** boeken*$_{neu}$ 'the red books'; and German: ***die** Tische*$_{mas}$ 'the tables' – ***die** Türen*$_{fem}$ 'the doors' – ***die** Bücher*$_{neu}$ 'the books' – ***die roten** Tische*$_{mas}$ 'the red tables' – ***die roten** Türen*$_{fem}$ 'the red doors' – ***die roten** Bücher*$_{neu}$ 'the red books'). As predicted by the hypothesis that the gender congruency effect only occurs when different determiner forms are associated with the target and distractor nouns, a gender congruency effect was found for singular NPs but not plural NPs in German as well as in Dutch (as evidenced in Experiments 1c and 4b of that study). Note that this result is consistent with the results of our present Experiment 2 where no gender congruency effect was found in the production of indefinite determiner NPs in Dutch. In the latter case, as in the case of plural NPs in Dutch and German, a single determiner form is used for both genders, precluding the possibility of determiner selection competition. Thus, the results from plural NP production in German and Dutch and the results from indefinite determiner NP production reported above support the view that the gender congruency effect is not due to competition during the selection of grammatical features but due to competition during the selection of gender-marked free-standing morphemes.

The third set of results, which is relevant for specifying the constraints on the occurrence of a gender congruency effect, concerns the case of Adj NPs. Schriefers (1993) reported a gender congruency effect with Dutch Adj NPs. Schiller and Caramazza (2003) showed that they could not replicate this result in Dutch nor in German. Furthermore, Costa et al. (2003) also failed to obtain a gender congruency effect for Adj NPs (e.g., moj_{mas} $krevet_{mas}$ 'my bed' or $moja_{fem}$ $truba_{fem}$ 'my trumpet') in Croatian. As already noted, Croatian can be classified as an early selection language and this was confirmed by the fact that Costa et al. (2003) obtained a clear gender congruency effect when participants were required to produce utterances in which the gender-marked item was a free-standing morpheme (e.g., $vidim$ ga_{mas} 'I see it$_{mas}$' [picture: $krevet_{mas}$ 'bed'] or $vidim$ je_{fem} 'I see it$_{fem}$' [picture: $truba_{fem}$ 'trumpet']). Thus, the bulk of the evidence would seem to favor the empirical generalization that the gender congruency effect is not obtained in the production of Adj NPs that involve the "selection" of a gender-marked, bound morpheme.

The pattern of results that has emerged provides a coherent picture of the gender congruency effect: the effect is obtained in the production of NPs with gender-marked free-standing morphemes for those languages where the selection of the latter morphemes can occur immediately after the selection of their controlling nouns. Definite NPs in Dutch and German are prototypical exemplars of these conditions. The effect is not obtained for late selection languages (e.g., Romance languages; but see Finocchiaro (2013) for an exception) or utterances in which the gender-marked items are bound morphemes (e.g., Adj NPs in Croatian and German). This pattern of constraints is most naturally explained by assuming that gender feature selection is an automatic (non-competitive) consequence of noun selection and that the gender congruency effect reflects competition at the level of gender-marked, free-standing morpheme selection (Caramazza et al. 2001). This formulation of the hypothesis is more general than the previous proposal by Caramazza et al. who had stated it in terms of competition between determiners in NPs (the only evidence available at the time concerned determiners). The more general formulation is made necessary by the results reported by Costa et al. (2003) who found a gender congruency effect in the production of utterances in which the gender-marked item was a pronoun. In other words, it seems that the congruency effect depends on selection competition between gender-marked, free-standing morphemes.

There are two issues that are closely connected to the question of grammatical gender processing but which go beyond the limits of the current chapter, i.e. gender congruency effects in bare noun naming and selection mechanisms in closed- vs. open-class words. The first issue, i.e. bare noun naming, has been briefly mentioned above and for more information we refer the interested reader to the literature (Cubelli et al. 2005; Finocchiaro et al. 2011; Paolieri et al. 2010a, 2010b). The second issue, i.e. selection mechanisms in closed- vs. open-class words, has recently gained a lot of attention following Schriefers, Jescheniak, and Hantsch (2002; see also Schriefers, Jescheniak, and Hantsch 2005; but see Costa et al. 2003 and Schiller and Costa 2006) who claimed that different selection mechanisms are at play for these two types of words. More recently, Lemhöfer, Schriefers, and Jescheniak, (2006; see also Jescheniak, Lemhöfer, and Schriefers, in press) claimed that two types of closed-class items, i.e. free-standing determiners as well as bound inflectional morphemes, are both selected by a competitive lexical selection mechanism. However, see Janssen, Schiller, and Alario (in press) for a reassessment of the evidence.

Finally, let us have a look at data from different paradigms. In a recent study by Heim and colleagues (Heim et al. 2009), not only behavioral effects of Det NP production in German are reported, but also the neurocognitive correlates of potential competition processes. Using functional magnetic resonance imaging (fMRI), these authors found a steeper slope in the haemodynamic response function (HRF) for picture naming (vs. rest) in the left Brodmann area (BA) 44 in the gender-congruent relative to the incongruent condition. These data suggest the involvement of BA 44 in the selection of determiner forms for language production.

Using electroencephalography (EEG), Ganushchak, Verdonschot, and Schiller (2011) demonstrated neurocognitive effects in a gender classification task. Error-negativity (ERN) responses of Dutch-English bilinguals were significantly higher not only in Dutch (L1) gender classification, but also in English (L2). This result was interpreted as electrophysiological support for grammatical gender transfer. Interestingly, this effect was demonstrated even though the L2, English in this case, does not have grammatical gender in its nominal system.

One issue still remains unresolved. Why is it that we failed to find a gender congruency effect for indefinite determiner NPs in German (Experiment 1; see also Schiller and Costa 2006, Experiment 1A)? That is, why do German indefinite determiners behave like adjectives and not like definite determiners in our experiments? Does this result imply that the selection of the phonological form of an indefinite determiner in German involves some type of morphophonological transformation just like adjectives? This is an intriguing possibility that will have to wait further experimental and theoretical investigation before it can be resolved.

In conclusion, the results reported in this study together with earlier results (Alario and Caramazza 2002; Caramazza et al. 2001; Costa et al. 1999, 2003; Heim et al. 2009; La Heij et al. 1998; Miozzo and Caramazza 1999; Schiller and Caramazza 2003, 2006; Schiller and Costa 2006; Van Berkum 1997) suggest that the selection of grammatical features is an automatic, non-competitive process. The selection of lexical nodes, however, is a competitive process. The current study qualifies this last statement: a competition effect between lexical nodes is only observed when these nodes correspond to free-standing morphemes.

6 Acknowledgements

The author would like to thank Pienie Zwitserlood and Jens Bölte (both University of Münster, Germany) for support in conducting Experiment 1, and Suzan Kroezen, Frouke Hermens, Anne Jacobs, and Janneke van Elferen (formerly Max Planck Institute for Psycholinguistics, Nijmegen, The Netherlands) for running participants of Experiments 2 and 3. A slightly different version of this chapter was read at the Workshop "The Expression of Gender", Max Planck Institute for Psycholinguistics, Nijmegen, 4 March 2011. The author would like to thank the audience of this workshop for their comments.

7 References

Alario, François-Xavier and Alfonso Caramazza. 2002. The production of determiners: Evidence from French. *Cognition* 82. 179–223.
Baayen, R. Harald, Richard Piepenbrock, and L. Gulikers. 1995. The CELEX lexical database (CD-ROM). *Linguistic Data Consortium*, University of Pensylvania, Philadelphia, PA.
Caramazza, Alfonso, Michele Miozzo, Albert Costa, Niels O. Schiller, and François-Xavier Alario. 2001. A cross-linguistic investigation of determiner production. In Emanuel Dupoux (ed.), *Language, Brain, and Cognitive Development: Essays in Honor of Jacques Mehler*, 209–226. Cambridge, MA: MIT Press.
Corbett, Greville G. 1991. *Gender*. Cambridge: Cambridge University Press.
Corbett, Greville G. 2013. Gender Typology. In Greville G. Corbett (ed.), *The Expression of Gender*, 87–130. Berlin/New York: Mouton de Gruyter.
Costa, Albert, Núria Sebastián-Gallés, Michele Miozzo, and Alfonso Caramazza. 1999. The gender congruity effect: Evidence from Spanish and Catalan. *Language and Cognitive Processes* 14: 381–391.
Costa, Albert, D. Kovacic, E. Fedorenko, and Alfonso Caramazza. 2003. The gender-congruency effect and the selection of freestanding and bound morphemes: Evidence from Croatian. *Journal of Experimental Psychology: Learning, Memory, and Cognition* 29. 1270–1282.

Cubelli, Roberto, L. Lotto, Daniela Paolieri, M. Girelli, and Remo Job. 2005. Grammatical gender is selected in bare noun production: Evidence from the picture-word interference paradigm. *Journal of Memory and Language* 53. 42–59.

Finocchiaro, Chiara. 2013. Facilitation effects of gender-congruency in the production of Italian clitic pronouns. *Journal of Cognitive Psychology* 25. 24–29.

Finocchiaro, Chiara, François-Xavier Alario, Niels O. Schiller, Albert Costa, Michele Miozzo, and Alfonso Caramazza. 2011. Gender congruency goes Europe: A cross-linguistic study of the gender congruency effect in Romance and Germanic languages. *Italian Journal of Linguistics* 23. 161–198.

Ganushchak, Lesya Y., Rinus G. Verdonschot, and Niels O. Schiller. 2011. When leaf becomes neuter: event-related potential evidence for grammatical gender transfer in bilingualism. *NeuroReport* 22. 106–110.

Glaser, W. R. 1992. Picture naming. *Cognition* 42. 61–105.

Glaser, W. R. and F.-J. Düngelhoff. 1984. The time course of picture-word interference. *Journal of Experimental Psychology: Human Perception and Performance* 10. 640–654.

Glaser, W. R. and M. O. Glaser. 1989. Context effects in Stroop-like word and picture processing. *Journal of Experimental Psychology: General* 118. 13–42.

Heim, Stefan, Angela D. Friederici, Niels O. Schiller, Shirley-Ann Rüschemeyer, and Katrin Amunts. 2009. The determiner congruency effect in language production investigated with functional MRI. *Human Brain Mapping* 30. 928–940.

Janssen, Niels and Alfonso Caramazza. 2003. Determiner selection in diminutive and plural noun phrases in Dutch. *Journal of Memory and Language* 48. 635–652.

Janssen, Niels, Niels O. Schiller, and François-Xavier Alario. in press. The selection of closed-class elements during language production: A reassessment of the evidence and a new look on new data. *Language and Cognitive Processes*.

Jescheniak, Jörg D., Herbert Schriefers, and Kristin Lemhöfer. in press. Selection of freestanding and bound gender-marking morphemes in speech production – A review. *Language and Cognitive Processes*.

La Heij, Wido, Pim Mak, J. Sander, and E. Willeboordse. 1998. The gender-congruency effect in picture-word tasks. *Psychological Research* 61. 209–219.

Lemhöfer, Kristin, Herbert Schriefers, and Jörg D. Jescheniak. 2006. The processing of free and bound gender-marked morphemes in speech production: Evidence from Dutch. *Journal of Experimental Psychology: Learning, Memory, and Cognition* 32. 437–442.

Levelt, Willem J. M., Ardi Roelofs, and Antje S. Meyer. 1999. A theory of lexical access in speech production. *Behavioral and Brain Sciences* 22. 1–75.

Lupker, Stephen J. 1979. The semantic nature of response competition in the picture-word interference task. *Memory & Cognition* 7. 485–495.

Lupker, Stephen J. 1982. The role of phonetic and orthographic similarity in picture-word interference. *Canadian Journal of Psychology* 36. 349–367.

MacLeod, Colin M. 1991. Half a century of research on the Stroop effect: An integrative review. *Psychological Bulletin* 109. 163–203.

Miozzo, Michele and Alfonso Caramazza. 1999. The selection of determiners in noun phrase production. *Journal of Experimental Psychology: Learning, Memory, and Cognition* 25. 907–922.

Miozzo, Michele, Albert Costa, and Alfonso Caramazza. 2002. The absence of a gender congruency effect in Romance languages: A matter of stimulus onset asynchrony? *Journal of Experimental Psychology: Learning, Memory and Cognition* 28. 388–391.

Paolieri, Daniela, L. Lotto, L. Morales, Teresa Bajo, Roberto Cubelli, and Remo Job. 2010a. Grammatical gender processing in Romance languages: Evidence from bare noun naming in Italian and Spanish. *European Journal of Cognitive Psychology* 22. 335–347.

Paolieri, Daniela, L. Lotto, D. Leoncini, Roberto Cubelli, and Remo Job. 2010b. Differential effects of grammatical gender and gender inflection in bare noun production. *British Journal of Psychology* 102. 19–36.

Schiller, Niels O. and Alfonso Caramazza. 2003. Grammatical feature selection in noun phrase production: Evidence from German and Dutch. *Journal of Memory and Language* 48. 169–194.

Schiller, Niels O. and Alfonso Caramazza. 2006. Grammatical gender selection and the representation of morphemes: The production of Dutch diminutives. *Language and Cognitive Processes* 21. 945–973.

Schiller, Niels O. and Albert Costa. 2006. Different selection principles of free-standing and bound morphemes in language production. *Journal of Experimental Psychology: Learning, Memory, and Cognition* 32. 1201–1207.

Schriefers, Herbert. 1993. Syntactic processes in the production of noun phrases. *Journal of Experimental Psychology: Learning, Memory, and Cognition* 19. 841–850.

Schriefers, Herbert, Jörg D. Jescheniak and Ansgar Hantsch. 2002. Determiner selection in noun phrase production. *Journal of Experimental Psychology: Learning, Memory, and Cognition* 28. 941–950.

Schriefers, Herbert, Jörg D. Jescheniak, and Ansgar Hantsch. 2005. Selection of gender marked morphemes in speech production. *Journal of Experimental Psychology: Learning, Memory, and Cognition* 31. 159–168.

Schriefers, Herbert, Antje S. Meyer, and Willem J. M. Levelt. 1990. Exploring the time course of lexical access in language-production: Picture-word interference studies. *Journal of Memory and Language* 29. 86–102.

Schriefers, Herbert and E. Teruel. 2000. Grammatical gender in noun phrase production: The gender interference effect in German. *Journal of Experimental Psychology: Learning, Memory, and Cognition* 26. 1368–1377.

Starreveld, Peter A. and Wido La Heij. 1995. Semantic interference, orthographic facilitation, and their interaction in naming tasks. *Journal of Experimental Psychology: Learning, Memory, and Cognition* 21. 686–698.

Starreveld, Peter A. and Wido La Heij. 1996. Time-course analysis of semantic and orthographic context effects in picture naming. *Journal of Experimental Psychology: Learning, Memory, and Cognition* 22. 896–918.

Stroop, J. Ridley. 1935. Studies of interference in serial verbal reactions. *Journal of Experimental Psychology* 28. 643–662.

Van Berkum, Jos J. A. 1997. Syntactic processes in speech production: The retrieval of grammatical gender. *Cognition* 64. 115–152.

8 Appendices

8.1 Stimulus materials in Experiment 1

Target picture name	Gender	Distractor word condition		
		Congruent	Incongruent (mas)	Incongruent (neu)
Tür ('door')	feminine	Glocke ('bell')	Fuß ('foot')	Krokodil ('crocodile')
Sonne ('sun')	feminine	Feder ('feather')	Koffer ('suitcase')	Faß ('barrel')
Schlange ('snake')	feminine	Banane ('banana')	Mund ('mouth')	Klavier ('piano')
Gans ('goose')	feminine	Palme ('palm tree')	Schuh ('shoe')	Lasso ('lasso')
Kerze ('candle')	feminine	Sonne ('sun')	Besen ('groom')	Pferd ('horse')
Leiter ('ladder')	feminine	Kasse ('cash register')	Knopf ('button')	Herz ('heart')
Bombe ('bomb')	feminine	Ente ('duck')	Tisch ('table')	Regal ('shelf')
Hose ('pants')	feminine	Tür ('door')	Teller ('plate')	Sofa ('couch')
Birne ('pear')	feminine	Pfeife ('pipe')	Frosch ('frog')	Zebra ('zebra')
Palme ('palm tree')	feminine	Tasse ('cup')	Magnet ('magnet')	Kreuz ('cross')
Pfeife ('pipe')	feminine	Gabel ('fork')	Affe ('monkey')	Schwein ('pig')
Nase ('nose')	feminine	Lupe ('magnifying glass')	Stern ('star')	Bett ('bed')
Gabel ('fork')	feminine	Hose ('pants')	Baum ('tree')	Kissen ('pillow')
Brille ('glasses')	feminine	Leiter ('ladder')	Finger ('finger')	Schaf ('sheep')
Flasche ('bottle')	feminine	Birne ('pear')	Helm ('helmet')	Blatt ('bottle')
Vase ('vase')	feminine	Brille ('glasses')	Zahn ('tooth')	Messer ('knife')
Banane ('banana')	feminine	Tasche ('bag')	Kamm ('comb')	Kamel ('camel')
Blume ('flower')	feminine	Schlange ('snake')	Löffel ('spoon')	Kanu ('canoe')
Ente ('duck')	feminine	Kette ('chain')	Rock ('skirt')	Ruder ('oar')
Feder ('feather')	feminine	Ziege ('goat')	Korb ('basket')	Zelt ('tent')
Glocke ('bell')	feminine	Puppe ('puppet')	Hammer ('hammer')	Fenster ('window')
Kasse ('cash register')	feminine	Flasche ('bottle')	Hund ('dog')	Brot ('bread')
Kette ('chain')	feminine	Gans ('goose')	Schlitten ('sled')	Floß ('raft')
Lupe ('magnifying glass')	feminine	Mauer ('wall')	Tiger ('tiger')	Kabel ('cable')
Mauer ('wall')	feminine	Trommel ('drum')	Schrank ('closet')	Glas ('glass')
Puppe ('puppet')	feminine	Blume ('flower')	Vogel ('bird')	Auto ('car')
Tasche ('bag')	feminine	Vase ('vase')	Stuhl ('chair')	Rad ('wheel')
Tasse ('cup')	feminine	Nase ('nose')	Kreis ('circle')	Schiff ('boat')
Trommel ('drum')	feminine	Bombe ('bomb')	Sattel ('saddle')	Bein ('leg')
Ziege ('goat')	feminine	Kerze ('candle')	Ofen ('stove')	Schwert ('sword')
Schlitten ('sled')	masculine	Zahn ('tooth')	Gabel ('fork')	Kanu ('canoe')
Knopf ('button')	masculine	Vogel ('bird')	Palme ('palm tree')	Lasso ('lasso')
Teller ('plate')	masculine	Föhn ('hair dryer')	Leiter ('ladder')	Schiff ('boat')
Fuß ('foot')	masculine	Hammer ('hammer')	Puppe ('puppet')	Blatt ('leaf')

Target picture name	Gender	Distractor word condition		
		Congruent	Incongruent (mas)	Incongruent (neu)
Tisch ('table')	masculine	Fuß ('foot')	Glocke ('bell')	Krokodil ('crocodile')
Affe ('monkey')	masculine	Kamm ('comb')	Tasche ('bag')	Brot ('bread')
Frosch ('frog')	masculine	Baum ('tree')	Mauer ('wall')	Kissen ('pillow')
Hund ('dog')	masculine	Teller ('plate')	Birne ('pear')	Faß ('barrel')
Helm ('helmet')	masculine	Korb ('basket')	Sonne ('sun')	Zelt ('tent')
Hammer ('hammer')	masculine	Rock ('skirt')	Tür ('door')	Ruder ('oar')
Schuh ('shoe')	masculine	Mund ('mouth')	Banane ('banana')	Klavier ('piano')
Koffer ('suitcase')	masculine	Helm ('helmet')	Brille ('glasses')	Sofa ('couch')
Löffel ('spoon')	masculine	Schlitten ('sled')	Gans ('goose')	Floß ('raft')
Magnet ('magnet')	masculine	Knopf ('button')	Kasse ('cash register')	Herz ('heart')
Kamm ('comb')	masculine	Löffel ('spoon')	Hose ('pants')	Schaf ('sheep')
Korb ('basket')	masculine	Hund ('dog')	Flasche ('bottle')	Schwein ('pig')
Ofen ('stove')	masculine	Schuh ('shoe')	Trommel ('drum')	Fenster ('window')
Schrank ('closet')	masculine	Affe ('monkey')	Blume ('flower')	Auto ('car')
Stuhl ('chair')	masculine	Tiger ('tiger')	Vase ('vase')	Messer ('knife')
Rock ('skirt')	masculine	Stern ('star')	Tasse ('cup')	Bett ('bed')
Baum ('tree')	masculine	Finger ('finger')	Pfeife ('pipe')	Zebra ('zebra')
Besen ('broom')	masculine	Frosch ('frog')	Schlange ('snake')	Kamel ('camel')
Finger ('finger')	masculine	Tisch ('table')	Ente ('duck')	Regal ('shelf')
Kreis ('circle')	masculine	Besen ('groom')	Ziege ('goat')	Pferd ('horse')
Mund ('mouth')	masculine	Stuhl ('chair')	Kette ('chain')	Kabel ('cable')
Sattel ('saddle')	masculine	Magnet ('magnet')	Lupe ('magnifying glass')	Kreuz ('cross')
Stern ('star')	masculine	Koffer ('suitcase')	Feder ('feather')	Rad ('wheel')
Tiger ('tiger')	masculine	Sattel ('saddle')	Bombe ('bomb')	Bein ('leg')
Vogel ('bird')	masculine	Kreis ('circle')	Nase ('nose')	Glas ('glass')
Zahn ('tooth')	masculine	Ofen ('stove')	Kerze ('candle')	Schwert ('sword')
Brot ('bread')	neuter	Schaf ('sheep')	Leiter ('ladder')	Finger ('finger')
Bein ('leg')	neuter	Zebra ('zebra')	Pfeife ('pipe')	Frosch ('frog')
Zebra ('zebra')	neuter	Glas ('glass')	Nase ('nose')	Stuhl ('chair')
Schaf ('sheep')	neuter	Kabel ('cable')	Feder ('feather')	Koffer ('suitcase')
Messer ('knife')	neuter	Bett ('bed')	Bombe ('bomb')	Stern ('star')
Bett ('bed')	neuter	Faß ('barrel')	Schlange ('snake')	Hammer ('hammer')
Pferd ('horse')	neuter	Kreuz ('cross')	Lupe ('magnifying glass ')	Magnet ('magnet')
Kamel ('camel')	neuter	Sofa ('couch')	Brille ('glasses')	Helm ('helmet')
Schiff ('ship')	neuter	Rad ('wheel')	Vase ('vase')	Tiger ('tiger')
Zelt ('tent')	neuter	Schwert ('sword')	Kerze ('candle')	Ofen ('stove')
Lasso ('lasso')	neuter	Fenster ('window')	Tür ('door')	Schrank ('closet')
Faß ('barrel')	neuter	Blatt ('leaf')	Puppe ('puppet')	Baum ('tree')

Target picture name	Gender	Distractor word condition		
		Congruent	Incongruent (mas)	Incongruent (neu)
Klavier ('piano')	neuter	Floß ('raft')	Gans ('goose')	Schlitten ('sled')
Glas ('glass')	neuter	Brot ('bread')	Birne ('pear')	Knopf ('button')
Regal ('shelf')	neuter	Auto ('car')	Blume ('flower')	Affe ('monkey')
Kissen ('pillow')	neuter	Pferd ('horse')	Ziege ('goat')	Besen ('broom')
Auto ('car')	neuter	Kamel ('camel')	Tasche ('bag')	Kamm ('comb')
Blatt ('leaf')	neuter	Regal ('shelf')	Ente ('duck')	Tisch ('table')
Fenster ('window')	neuter	Ruder ('oar')	Kette ('chain')	Rock ('skirt')
Floß ('raft')	neuter	Zelt ('tent')	Sonne ('sun')	Korb ('basket')
Herz ('heart')	neuter	Kissen ('pillow')	Kasse ('cash register')	Kamm ('comb')
Kabel ('cable')	neuter	Schiff ('boat')	Palme ('palm tree')	Schuh ('shoe')
Kanu ('canoe')	neuter	Schwein ('pig')	Flasche ('bottle')	Hund ('dog')
Kreuz ('cross')	neuter	Herz ('heart')	Hose ('pants')	Teller ('plate')
Krokodil ('crocodile')	neuter	Lasso ('lasso')	Mauer ('wall')	Sattel ('saddle')
Rad ('wheel')	neuter	Kanu ('canoe')	Gabel ('fork')	Zahn ('tooth')
Ruder ('oar')	neuter	Klavier ('piano')	Banane ('banana')	Mund ('mouth')
Schwein ('pig')	neuter	Messer ('knife')	Trommel ('drum')	Kreis ('circle')
Schwert ('sword')	neuter	Bein ('leg')	Tasse ('cup')	Vogel ('bird')
Sofa ('couch')	neuter	Krokodil ('crocodile')	Glocke ('bell')	Fuß ('foot')

8.2 Stimulus materials in Experiments 2 and 3

Target picture name	Gender	Distractor word condition			
		Congruent	Gender	Incongruent	Gender
poes ('cat')	common	kerk ('church')	common	blad ('leaf')	neuter
wortel ('carrot')	common	muis ('mouse')	common	stuur ('wheel')	neuter
stoel ('chair')	common	jas ('jacket')	common	plein ('square')	neuter
vork ('fork')	common	zoon ('son')	common	touw ('rope')	neuter
mond ('mouth')	common	zeep ('soap')	common	nest ('nest')	neuter
tafel ('table')	common	kers ('cherry')	common	glas ('glass')	neuter
gitaar ('guitar')	common	ladder ('ladder')	common	strand ('beach')	neuter
zaag ('saw')	common	klap ('bang')	common	papier ('paper')	neuter
trein ('train')	common	schoen ('shoe')	common	hoofd ('head')	neuter
taart ('cake')	common	auto ('car')	common	bureau ('desk')	neuter
fles ('bottle')	common	staart ('tail')	common	wiel ('wheel')	neuter
konijn ('rabbit')	neuter	stuur ('wheel')	neuter	kerk ('church')	common
kasteel ('castle')	neuter	blad ('leaf')	neuter	jas ('jacket')	common
hemd ('shirt')	neuter	wiel ('wheel')	neuter	muis ('mouse')	common
been ('leg')	neuter	strand ('beach')	neuter	auto ('car')	common
geweer ('rifle')	neuter	bureau ('desk')	neuter	staart ('tail')	common
schaap ('sheep')	neuter	nest ('nest')	neuter	kers ('cherry')	common
schip ('ship')	neuter	glas ('glass')	neuter	zeep ('soap')	common
brood ('bread')	neuter	plein ('square')	neuter	klap ('bang')	common
paard ('horse')	neuter	touw ('rope')	neuter	zoon ('son')	common
bed ('bed')	neuter	papier ('paper')	neuter	ladder ('ladder')	common
raam ('window')	neuter	hoofd ('head')	neuter	schoen ('shoe')	common
poes ('cat')	common	hamster ('hamster')	common	poets ('trick')	common
wortel ('carrot')	common	asperge ('asparagus')	common	worm ('worm')	common
stoel ('chair')	common	bank ('couch')	common	stoep ('pavement')	common
vork ('fork')	common	lepel ('spoon')	common	vonk ('spark')	common
mond ('mouth')	common	neus ('nose')	common	monnik ('monk')	common
tafel ('table')	common	kast ('cupboard')	common	tabak ('tobacco')	common
gitaar ('guitar')	common	cello ('cello')	common	giraf ('giraffe')	common
zaag ('saw')	common	hamer ('hammer')	common	zaak ('thing')	common
trein ('train')	common	bus ('bus')	common	trede ('step')	common
taart ('cake')	common	koek ('cake')	common	taal ('language')	common
fles ('bottle')	common	kan ('jug')	common	fluit ('flute')	common
konijn ('rabbit')	neuter	lam ('lamb')	neuter	koren ('corn')	neuter
kasteel ('castle')	neuter	huis ('house')	neuter	katoen ('cotton')	neuter
hemd ('shirt')	neuter	pak ('suit')	neuter	hek ('fence')	neuter
been ('leg')	neuter	oor ('ear')	neuter	beeld ('statue')	neuter
geweer ('rifle')	neuter	kanon ('gun')	neuter	gewicht ('weight')	neuter
schaap ('sheep')	neuter	hert ('deer')	neuter	schaak ('chess')	neuter

Target picture name	Gender	Distractor word condition			
		Congruent	Gender	Incongruent	Gender
schip ('ship')	neuter	veer ('ferry')	neuter	schild ('shield')	neuter
brood ('bread')	neuter	ei ('egg')	neuter	brein ('brain')	neuter
paard ('horse')	neuter	varken ('pig')	neuter	paleis ('palace')	neuter
bed ('bed')	neuter	rek ('rack')	neuter	beest ('animal')	neuter
raam ('window')	neuter	luik ('hatch')	neuter	rag ('cobweb')	neuter

8.3 Stimulus materials in Experiments 2 and 3 (continued)

Filler picture name	Gender	Distractor word	Gender
bijl ('axe')	common	haan ('rooster')	common
bril ('glasses')	common	kwast ('brush')	common
eend ('duck')	common	jurk ('dress')	common
fiets ('bike')	common	tand ('tooth')	common
hoed ('hat')	common	bal ('ball')	common
schaar ('scissors')	common	tijger ('tiger')	common
vis ('vis')	common	klomp ('clog')	common
hand ('hand')	common	zon ('sun')	common
klok ('clock')	common	schaats ('skate')	common
bloem ('flower')	common	maan ('moon')	common
tent ('tent')	common	noot ('nut')	common
trompet ('trumpet')	common	kaart ('card')	common
kaars ('candle')	common	trui ('sweater')	common
aap ('monkey')	common	emmer ('bucket')	common
peer ('pear')	common	wolk ('cloud')	common
kleed ('carpet')	neuter	circus ('circus')	neuter
masker ('mask')	neuter	bord ('plate')	neuter
mes ('knife')	neuter	dak ('roof')	neuter
net ('net')	neuter	blik ('can')	neuter
oog ('eye')	neuter	web ('web')	neuter
penseel ('brush')	neuter	geld ('money')	neuter
spook ('ghost')	neuter	lint ('ribbon')	neuter
zwaard ('sword')	neuter	blok ('block')	neuter
harp ('harp')	neuter	robot ('robot')	neuter
bot ('bone')	neuter	laken ('sheet')	neuter
kruis ('cross')	neuter	schort ('apron')	neuter
slot ('lock')	neuter	kalf ('calf')	neuter
fornuis ('stove')	neuter	vest ('vest')	neuter
potlood ('pencil')	neuter	monster ('monster')	neuter
anker ('anchor')	neuter	zadel ('saddle')	neuter
boek ('book')	neuter	spel ('game')	neuter
hart ('heart')	neuter	orgel ('organ')	neuter

Mulugeta T. Tsegaye, Maarten Mous and Niels O. Schiller
Plural as a value of Cushitic gender: Evidence from gender congruency effect experiments in Konso (Cushitic)

1 Introduction

The grammatical features gender and number are related in a complex way in Cushitic languages (see Hayward 1979; Corbett and Hayward 1987; Mous 2008). The relation between gender and number becomes apparent in the so-called "plural" gender nouns. Interestingly and arguably, a third value of grammatical gender in addition to masculine and feminine has been identified for some Cushitic languages (Hayward 1979; Mous 2008). In contrast to other languages that have three-way gender distinction systems, this third value is not neuter in Cushitic. In terms of agreement, this third gender value requires the same agreement pattern as the third person plural. As a result, it is called "plural" gender in many studies of Cushitic languages. In order to avoid confusion, the term "plural" is used to refer to this gender value and "multiple reference" to refer to the multiplicity of number, with the abbreviations (m), (f) and (p) to stand for masculine, feminine and plural gender values in that order, and (m.r.) and (s.r.) to represent multiple reference and singular reference nouns, respectively, throughout this chapter, after Hayward (1984) and Mous (2008). We also used the term "feature" to refer to gender and number constructs, and "values" for sets of values within these features (e.g. masculine, feminine and plural for gender) following Corbett (see Corbett's chapter in this volume). This complex interrelatedness between grammatical gender and number sometimes paves ways to different, often conflicting analyses of these features in different Cushitic languages.

Two conflicting hypotheses have been put forward to analyze the gender systems of Cushitic languages. The first one comes from Corbett and Hayward (1987), in which only two gender values are recognized and the third value is analyzed as part of the number feature. This analysis is applied to Bayso, a Lowland East Cushitic language. The argument is that this value has a small membership and should be analyzed with features indicating irregularity in number agreement, marked as irregular nouns taking plural agreement (Corbett and Hayward 1987). Corbett (2012: 223–233) explains that taking the value plural from the number system as a value in the gender system as well runs counter to the general principle of exclusiveness that one value belongs to just one feature. This principle is at the basis of both typology and theoretical studies. A language system in which plural operates as a value for gender undermines this central claim and any alternative analysis of such a gender and number system should be scrutinized. This is exactly what Corbett (2012: 224–233) does for Bayso in great clarity and detail. The proposed analysis for Bayso has the added advantage that it explains anomalies in the system at the cost of marking only a limited number of nouns with lexical features for exceptional behaviour. If we can show that the plural value of the gender feature is like the masculine and feminine value of this feature in terms of psycholinguistic relevance, this poses an important challenge to the general principle that a value can only belong to one feature, provided that the plural values for gender and number are indeed instances of the same value.

The second one is the position taken in most descriptive studies on Cushitic languages (Hayward 1979 for Bayso, Pillinger and Galboran 1999 for Rendille, Savà 2005 for Ts'amakko, and Orkaydo 2013 for Konso) and argued for in Mous (2008). The argument is that gender and number are two independent agreement systems and adjectives show agreement for both features independently (Mous 2008). If the third value of gender is taken to be plural [multiple reference], a situation can arise in which adjectives show conflicting values for number and gender agreement with one and the same head noun. For instance, a word in Iraqw that is of multiple reference and plural in gender has two different agreement markers on the adjective. One agreement system (gender) has low tone on the final syllable for (f) and (p) head nouns and high tone for (m) head nouns irrespective of number; the second agreement system has a different form of the adjective for multiple reference nouns (for examples, see Mous 2008: 156).

The analysis that Corbett (2012) proposes for Bayso introduces extra challenges when applied to Konso. First of all, in the case of Konso the number of underived (p) gender nouns is much larger than in Bayso. Based on a count of the appendix of nouns in Orkaydo's (2013) grammar of Konso, 96 underived nouns are (p), against 135 (f) and 245 (m). It becomes less satisfactory to treat all (p) nouns as exceptional. Secondly, in Konso, gender and number display two separate agreement systems. An adjective agrees in number with the head noun by initial reduplication and in gender by a final suffix, for example *filaa-sini' poor-aa* /comb-def.p [sg]black-p/'the black comb' against *orra-si' ka-kapp-a* /people-def.m/f pl-fat-m/f/ 'the fat people' Orkaydo (2013: 79). If this (p) head noun were analysed as not having a gender value but showing plural number agreement, the morphological analysis would be /comb-def.pl [sg]black-pl/ with competing values of number on the two agreement slots of the adjective. Moreover the agreement on the definite marker and the final suffix of the adjective would be according to gender for one set of nouns but according to number for another set of nouns – note that multiple reference words like 'people' can be masculine in gender. The Cushitic languages that are mentioned in Corbett (2012: 233) do not have these additional challenges because they do not show independent number agreement (Bayso, Kambaata), or do not have a (p) gender value (Sidamo, Kambaata). The analysis for Bayso taking certain nouns as exceptional and similar to pluralia tantum nouns had the added advantage of explaining anomalies in the system. The analysis of (p) as a value for gender has the disadvantage of downplaying a number of anomalies of the Konso gender and number system. Nouns that are derived for number have predictable gender properties: singulatives are either masculine or feminine (depending on the formative, not on the gender of the base as is the case in Bayso) and never (p) in gender; pluratives, derived plural nouns, are all (p) in gender; there are seven different plural formations in Konso and all impose (p) gender (Orkaydo 2013: 94–99). Thus, there is ample indication in Konso for an association of (p) words and plurality in number.

This chapter aims at providing experimental, psycholinguistic evidence to shed light on the processing of grammatical gender in Cushitic languages and possibly decide whether the third value (plural gender) is a proper gender value or rather belongs to the number system in Cushitic languages that have this value. We employed the picture-word interference paradigm, a commonly used paradigm in the study of lexical access. In this paradigm, participants are asked to name a picture while ignoring a distractor word presented with it. It has been shown that the naming time of the picture is affected by the relationship between the to-be-named and the to-be-ignored words. When the words are semantically related, for example, interference appears (slower naming times), however, facilitation (faster naming times) occurs when the two words are phonologically related. Whereas the interference effect is due to competition at the level of lexical node selection, the facilitation effect is due to the priming at the level of the phonological form activation (Levelt et al., 1999). In the same way, the so-called gender congruency effect, i.e. naming times of a picture are faster when the to-be-named and the to-be-ignored words have the same gender compared to when they have a different gender, has been proposed for gender processing mechanisms (see Schiller's chapter in this volume for a detailed discussion of psycholinguistic work on gender).

The discussions of the gender congruency effect in psycholinguistic research have begun after 1993 following Schriefers' work. Schriefers (1993) found faster reaction times (RTs) when the target picture and the distractor word had the same gender compared to when they had a different gender in Dutch noun phrase (NP) production. He interpreted the effect as demonstrating the competition for selection of a word's syntactic features (in this case gender).

According to Bordag and Pechmann (2008), many features inhibit the gender congruency effect and its interpretation might be more complicated than suggested by Schriefers (1993). They point out that the gender congruency effect has been found to be language-specific, which leads to the question of cross-linguistic differences in gender representation and NP production mechanisms. Another point of debate is whether the effect is really a gender congruency effect or rather a determiner congruency effect (Schiller and Caramazza 2002), which leads to the question of whether it reflects competition at the grammatical (abstract gender nodes) or at the phonological level (phonological forms). Finally, Bordag and Pechmann mention the presence of inconsistent evidence in relation to the magnitude of the gender congruency effect. Thus, Schiller and Caramazza (2003) found the effect only when an NP in the form of a free morpheme (article or other determiner) + noun was produced, whereas Schriefers (1993) also obtained the effect in the production of NPs consisting of an adjective ending in a gender-marked inflection (a bound morpheme) + a noun. Moreover, La Heij et al. (1998) observed the effect only when participants named the pictures with gender-marked NPs, but not when bare nouns were produced in Dutch, implying that the gender feature may not be always selected. Cubelli et al. (2005), on the other hand, obtained an interference effect due to gender congruency when bare nouns were produced in Italian.

This chapter, therefore, attempts to contribute to filling the gap of cross-linguistic confirmation from non-western languages in all these areas, specifically on the magnitude of gender congruency effect, that is, whether or not the effect is found in naming bare nouns (Experiment 1), and in naming a noun + a gender-marked inflection (a bound morpheme) (Experiment 2) in addition to addressing the issue of deciding whether or not the third value is a proper gender value in Cushitic languages.

Cushitic languages that arguably have a three-way gender distinction system with the third being plural besides feminine and masculine are Bayso, Konso, Dirayta, Ts'amakko, Rendille, and Boni of the Southern Lowland as well as Iraqw, Alagwa, and Burunge of Southern Cushitic languages (Mous 2008). The language we investigate is Konso, a Lowland East Cushitic language. Konso is spoken in the south-west of Ethiopia by 250,000 people (Central Statistics Agency of Ethiopia 2009), see the map in Figure 1 at the end of the chapter for its location. The language has no standardized writing system, proper dictionary or published grammar book yet. However, Ongaye Oda Orkaydo has recently finished his PhD thesis on the grammar of Konso. Most of the materials for the experiments reported in this chapter are taken from him and his work. Konso was chosen for several reasons: first, it has a relatively large number of underived plural gender nouns; second, an in-depth analysis of the grammar of the language is available (Orkaydo 2013); third, Ongaye Oda Orkaydo, a native-speaker linguist was available to help with the selection of the stimuli; fourth, carrying out experiments is feasible in Konso because the population is large enough and relatively easily accessible.

2 Gender system of Konso

Konso is said to have a three-way gender distinction system, and the third gender, besides feminine and masculine, is plural gender (Orkaydo 2013). According to Orkaydo, for the majority of the nouns neither the form of a noun nor its meaning predicts its gender value. Nouns in Konso can be classified into three gender values on the basis of their agreement on the verb: those nouns that show the same agreement as the third person masculine singular subject (which is not morphologically marked) are masculine; those nouns that show the same agreement as the third person feminine singular subject (marked on the verb by the suffix *–t*) are feminine; and those nouns that show the same agreement as the third person plural subject (marked on the verb by the suffix *–n*) are plural. Note that gender on the verb is realized as long as nouns function as non-focused subjects.

For example, nouns that are semantically masculine, such as *sakoota* 'coward' may have feminine gender agreement on the verb. Similarly, nouns that are semantically feminine, for example *ʔokkatta* 'cow', may have masculine gender agreement on the verb; also, nouns that are semantically singular, *filaa* 'comb' as in (c) of Table 1, may have a plural gender agreement. Likewise, nouns that are semantically undetermined for sex (as feminine or masculine) may have masculine, feminine or plural gender agreement on the verb.

Table 1: Konso subject gender agreement on the verb (Orkaydo p.c.)

(a) sakoota-siʔ   ʔi=ɗey-t-i
     coward.DEF.F/M   3=come-3SF-PF
     'The coward came.'

(b) ʔokkatta-siʔ   ʔi=pat-ay
     cow-DEF.F/M   3=disappear-PF(.M)
     'The cow disappeared.'

(c) filaa-siniʔ   ʔi=pat-i-n
     comb-DEF.P   3=disappear-PF-PL
     'The comb disappeared.'

(d) ʔiskatta-siʔ   parre   ʔi=ɗey-a
     women-DEF.F/M   tomorrow   3=come-IPF.FUT(.M)
     'The women will come tomorrow.'

The examples in Table 2 show that the assignment of definite marking on nouns is determined by the gender of the noun. Thus, nouns that show the same gender agreement as the third person masculine or feminine subject take the singular definite suffix –*siʔ* while those that show the same agreement as the third person plural subject on the verb take the definite suffix -*siniʔ*.

Table 2: Assignment of definite marking on nouns in Konso (Orkaydo 2013: 77–78)

(a) ɖimayta-siʔ   ʔi=kutiʔ-ay
    old.man-DEF.F/M   3=sit.down-PF(.M)
    'The old man sat down.'

(b) ʔalleeta-siʔ   ʔi=piʔ-t-i
    hut-DEF.F/M   3=fall-3SF-PF
    'The hut fell.'

(c) ʔinnaa-siniʔ   ʔi=muk-i-n
    child-DEF.P   3=sleep-PF-PL
    'The child slept.'

(d) lahadɗaa-siniʔ   ʔi=kat-am-a-n
    rams-DEF.P   3=sell-PASS-IPF.FUT-PL
    'The rams will be sold.'

Taken together, there are two divergent ways of analyzing the so-called plural gender in Cushitic languages that are characterized by this value. On the one hand, only two gender values, namely masculine and feminine, are recognized and the third value is analyzed as part of number feature (Corbett and Hayward 1987). On the other hand, three gender values are recognized and the third is treated as a proper gender value (Mous 2008; Savà 2005; Orkaydo 2013). We want to investigate whether words like *ʔinnaa* 'child' which are (p) in gender are represented like words such as *karmaɗaa* 'lions' which are plural in number (supporting Corbett's analysis) or are treated like words such as *furaa* 'key' which are also (p) in gender (supporting Mous' analysis) in Konso.

3 Gender congruency effect experiments in Konso

Two gender congruency effect experiments that measured and compared naming times were conducted in Konso for the first time in the language and in the area. The first experiment was on the production of bare nouns and the second was on the production of definite nouns. Both experiments were carried out at a Konso high school, where the majority of the students speak Konso natively.

3.1 Overview of the experiments

3.1.1 Participants

Forty-six pre-university students, aged between 17 and 25 years, took part in the two experiments. Twenty-two and 24 students participated in the first and in the second experiments, respectively. All participants were native speakers of Konso and they all had normal or corrected-to-normal vision. They were all paid for participating in the study.

3.1.2 Materials

Targets were selected from various semantic categories and were presented as black line drawings on a white background. Names of different gender nouns were equally represented in both target and distractor conditions. Each target picture was presented with gender-congruent and gender-incongruent words as well as with gender-neutral pink noise. The reason to use a neutral distractor condition (pink noise) was to see if participants processed the distractor words. Targets and distractor words were not related in terms of meaning (they did not belong to the same or related semantic categories) and sound (their initial sounds were not the same and they did not share more than three phonemes). The target pictures were presented in the center of a 15.6 inch laptop screen accompanied by one of the distractor words, which was auditorily presented via headphones.

3.1.3 Procedure

Participants were tested individually in a quiet room. They sat in front of a laptop screen at a viewing distance of around 60 cm. Reaction times (RTs) were measured from the onset of the target stimulus to the beginning of the naming response using a voice key. Participants were instructed that they would see a picture and hear a word or pink noise and were asked to name the target picture while ignoring the word/pink noise they heard.

Each trial began with a fixation point (+) presented in the centre of the screen for 500 ms followed by the target picture along with the auditorily presented distractor word until response or for maximally 2,000 ms. Then the asterisk sign (*) in the centre of the screen was shown before the presentation of the next trial. The experimenter registered errors and malfunctioning of the voice key.

The whole experiment was conducted in three phases; familiarization, practice and test. During the familiarization phase, participants were presented with all the target pictures along with their intended names twice so as to encourage the use of the designated picture names of each target. In the practice phase, each picture was put on the laptop screen for 350 ms accompanied by pink noise. Participants were asked to name the picture and corrected when they produced a noun different from the intended one. In the last phase, the test proper, participants were asked to name the picture as quickly and as accurately as possible while ignoring simultaneously presented auditorily distractor words/pink noise. The Stimulus Onset Asynchrony (SOA) was 0 as the target picture and the distractor element were presented at the same time. The stimuli were presented in different blocks with a break between them. Under each block, trials were pseudo-randomized using a Latin square so as to avoid the subsequent appearance of each distractor condition in a row.

3.1.4 Analysis

Responses were excluded from further analyses in light of the following criteria: (a) unintended name for the picture; (b) non-verbal sounds that triggered the voice key; (c) unregistered responses including responses given after 2,000 ms; and (d) reaction times shorter than 250 ms and longer than 1,900 ms. Analyses of Variance (ANOVAs) were conducted on the filtered correct responses based on the aforementioned criteria to compare reaction times in different distractor conditions. The significance level used in both experiments was $p=0.05$. All ANOVAs that are reported in this chapter were performed on the means per subject (F1) and the means per item (F2).

3.2 Experiment 1: Production of bare nouns in Konso

In this experiment, participants were asked to name the picture by producing the noun only (the bare noun). The aim was to be able to decide whether the gender value "plural" (p) is a proper gender value or rather a value inherent to the number feature. The logic behind this experiment was that a picture should be named relatively faster when a word with the same gender is used as a distractor than the use of a word with a different gender. If (p) is a proper gender value in Konso, we should find a gender congruency effect in the production of plural nouns, that is, naming a picture with (p) value should be relatively faster when a gender-congruent distractor word is presented as compared to the presentation of a gender-incongruent distractor word. If it does not show these properties, this may be due to the value (p) not belonging to the gender feature and hence probably belonging to the number feature instead. Such a finding would also have an implication on the analysis of current models of language production (see below).

3.2.1 Materials

A total of 60 target pictures corresponding to underived Konso nouns were selected. Twenty of the nouns were masculine, 20 feminine and 20 plural gender nouns. For each target picture, in addition to neutral pink noise, a gender-congruent and two gender-incongruent (labeled as incongruent I and incongruent II) distractor words were selected. A total of 240 (20 [target pictures] x 3 [target genders] x 4 [distractor conditions] = 240) trials were used in this experiment.

The materials were presented in four blocks of 60 items. In each block, each pictured appeared only once, either with a congruent, one of the two incongruent, or the neutral (pink noise) distractor conditions. Each picture was presented four times to each participant throughout the experiment, once in each condition and in each block.

Table 3: Example of the experimental items used in Experiment 1

Target picture name	Gender	Distractor word conditions*			
		Congruent	Incongruent I	Incongruent II	Neutral
kaawwata 'mirror'	feminine	eetota 'dinner/supper'	muutiya 'worm'	ɲupuraa 'component of a set of weaving'	pink noise
tuyyuuraa 'airplane'	masculine	ammaʔitta 'breakfast'	paakkota 'span (measurement)'	χoffaa 'groin'	pink noise
kupaʔtaa 'tortoise'	plural	marfaa 'hip'	hiparaata 'bat'	hallaka 'fat'	pink noise

* For (m) target, (f) is incongruent I and (p) is incongruent II; for (f) target, (m) is incongruent I and (p) is incongruent II; and for (p) target, (f) is incongruent I and (m) is incongruent II

Table 3 shows the design for the first experiment. Each target picture was presented four times, each time associated with different distractors. For the masculine target *tuyyuura* 'air plane', for example, we had a gender-congruent distractor word *ammayitta* 'breakfast' in one trial, a gender-incongruent feminine word *paakkota* 'span (measurement)' in another trial, another gender-incongruent (incongruent II) plural gender *xoffaa* 'groin' and a neutral 'pink noise' as a control in different trials. The same was true for the other targets as well. The list of items used in Experiment 1 can be found in Appendix A.

3.2.2 Results and discussion

From a total of 5,280 observations, 982 (19%) were discarded from the analysis as they were incorrect responses and 207 (3.92%) were labeled as outliers, RTs shorter than 250 ms and longer than 1,900 ms. Thus, a total of 4,091 (77.48%) data points were included in the statistical analysis.

Table 4: Reaction Times (RTs) in ms and error in percentage (%e)

Distractor conditions	Congruent	Neutral	Incongruent*	Congruency effect
RTs (%e)	1010 (5%)	908 (3%)	1029 (11%)	19 (6%)

* Represents a combined effect of incongruent I and incongruent II conditions

Table 4 shows the mean RTs in the three distractor conditions (congruent, neutral and incongruent). The first overall ANOVA was performed with Distractor Condition (congruent, neutral and incongruent) and Target Gender (masculine, feminine and plural) as independent factors. This analysis showed a significant effect of the factor Distractor Condition in both the subject and the item analyses ($F1(2,42) = 25.098$, $p < .0001$; $F2(2,110) = 45.193$, $p < .0001$). It took the participants slightly more time to produce a noun in the gender-incongruent condition (picture-word pairs having a different gender value) than to produce a noun in the congruent (picture-word pairs having the same gender value) or in the pink noise (neutral) conditions. The fastest RTs in the pink noise condition reveal that participants indeed processed the distractors, as processing words interferes more with naming a picture than processing pink noise. The factor Target Gender reached significance in the subject analysis ($F1 (2,42) = 13.340$, $p < .0001$) but not in the item analysis ($F2 (2,55) = 1.552$, $p < .221$). The interaction between Target Gender and Distractor Condition, however, failed to reach significance in both subject and item analyses ($F1 (4,84) = .858$, $p < .497$; $F2 (4,110) = .586$, $p < .674$).

In the bare noun production, the mean RTs in the gender-congruent condition were 19 ms faster than naming latencies in the incongruent condition. To examine the effect of gender congruency (congruent versus incongruent), a separate ANOVA was performed on the mean reaction times per subject (F1) and per item (F2) with Distractor Condition (congruent and incongruent) and Target Gender (masculine, feminine and plural) as independent factors. This analysis showed a significant effect only on the subject analysis of the factor Target Gender (F1 (2,42) = 12.072, p < .0001) and was close to reaching significance on the subject analysis of the factor Distractor Condition (F1 (1,21) = 3.848, p < .063).

One could speculate, however, that the overall slow RTs, the nature of the language (gender is not marked on the nouns) and methodological issues might be possible causes for the inhibition of the effect in the variables that did not reach significance level. Compare the 982 ms mean RT of our study to that of less than 700 ms in previous studies (e.g. La Heij et al. 1998). Moreover, the comparatively weak performance of participants reflected in the relatively high rate of incorrect responses, i.e. 982 (19%), compared to less than 10% in previous studies. This means that participants of this language require more training than set by the standard, as they are inexperienced in participating in this sort of experiments and working with some of the equipment. Additional experiments with better training of participants ensuring faster and better performance, may give us a better picture of the issue.

The fact that gender is not marked on the nouns themselves in Konso might also inhibit the effect from being revealed. Involving gender-marking elements such as verbs as part of the experiment might help here. Although all possible precautions were taken in the absence of norms in the language to control for factors such as frequency, familiarity, typicality and age of acquisition, it could be the case that our result is inconclusive because of some methodological flaws such as the use of badly selected words in the experiment (see below).

Table 5: Mean RT by target gender and distractor condition

Target gender	Distractor condition			
	Congruent	Incongruent	Neutral	Congruency effect
Masculine	978	998	872	20
Feminine	1047	1048	923	1
Plural	1007	1042	932	35

Table 5 shows that 20 ms congruency effect in masculine noun production and 35 ms in the plural gender noun production but almost nothing in feminine noun production (1 ms). In order to see why we failed to obtain a congruency effect in feminine noun production in the presence of a comparable effect in masculine and plural gender nouns, we conducted item-by-item analysis of both the target and distractor words. Our investigation revealed that participants performed very slowly in naming certain nouns. Table 6 shows that the majority of the nouns that have relatively slow RTs are feminine nouns (6 out of 10) followed by plural gender nouns (3 out of 10) and only one masculine noun had slow RTs. This might be due to semantic interference effects between different targets and the clarity of the pictures used (see Table 6). Only further research will exclude the possibility of the role of methodological flaws for the absence of the congruency effect on feminine noun production.

Table 6: Targets that show relatively slow RTs with possible reasons

	Target	Gender*	Potential reasons for slow RT
1.	*muklaa* 'bangle'	(p)	Less familiar word
2.	*tuuyyata* 'pig'	(f)	Less familiar word and semantic interference with *kaharta* 'ewe' (used as a feminine target)
3.	*hirribaa* 'eyelash'	(p)	Less clear picture
4.	*napahata* 'ear'	(f)	the preferred word is *kurra* (s.r.) (m) 'ear'
5.	*xashitta* 'shoulder'	(f)	Less clear picture and semantic interference with *kessa* 'arm' (used as a masculine target)
6.	*mulaketa* 'frog'	(f)	Less clear picture and semantic interference with *kupataa* 'tortoise' (used as a plural target)
7.	*paala* 'feather'	(m)	
8.	*hiipta* 'lip'	(f)	Semantic interference with *afaa* 'mouth' (used as a plural target)
9.	*loqta* 'leg'	(f)	Semantic interference with *kessa* 'arm' and *xashitta* 'shoulder'
10.	*hashallaa* 'leaf'	(p)	

* 3 (p) words, 6 (f) words and 1 (m) word

Thus, explaining the present result in the light of current models of language production is not straightforward. Recall, however, that La Heij et al. (1998) failed to find a gender congruency effect in bare noun production in Dutch. Moreover, most current models of language production suggest that syntactic properties such as gender are not selected in bare noun naming (Caramazza 1997; Levelt, Roelofs and Meyer 1999).

According to Caramazza's (1997) Independent Network (IN) model, a word's grammatical gender is activated after the selection of the related lexical node and hence its selection is an automatic (non-competitive) process. Although the WEAVER++ model of Levelt et al. (1999) assumes that the activation of a noun's gender takes place before the selection of the lexeme node, it also assumes that the activation of gender has no effect on the activation level of the nodes related to nouns with the same gender. This model, therefore, predicts no gender congruency effect in bare noun naming as the selection of gender is expected only in the production of NPs that involve the selection of gender marked elements such as determiners.

Cubelli et al. (2005), however, found interference effect of grammatical gender in the production of bare nouns with Italian speakers. They interpret the result as showing the obligatory selection of grammatical gender, and thus gender is always selected whenever its noun has to be named, which is in opposition to the prediction of the WEAVER++ model. Moreover, they argue that the selection of the noun's gender is a competitive process in contrast to the assumption of IN model. In order to explain the variation of their data with the assumption of both WEAVER++ and IN models, they came up with the Double Selection model, which assumes the independent and competitive selection of both lexical-semantic and lexical-syntactic information prior to the selection of the phonological form of a word.

In sum, the overall naming latencies in the gender incongruent condition were 19 ms slower than the congruent condition. This result, however, failed to reach significance except in the subject analysis of the factor Target Gender. Moreover, a 35 ms congruency effect observed in naming plural gender nouns could be taken as a sign for recognizing plural as a proper gender value in Konso.

3.3 Experiment 2: Production of definite nouns in Konso

The gender of nouns also determines the assignment of definite marking on nouns in Konso (Orkayda 2013). Plural gender nouns take the definite suffix -*siniʔ* (e.g. *ʔinnaa-siniʔ* 'the child'). Nouns that show the same gender agreement as the third person masculine or feminine subject, however, take the singular definite suffix -*siʔ* (e.g. *ɡímayta-siʔ* 'the old man'). In Experiment 2, we investigated the gender congruency effect in naming nouns with a suffixed definite marker (noun + -*siʔ* [masculine or feminine definite nouns] versus noun + -*siniʔ* [plural gender definite noun]). If (p) is a proper gender value in Konso, we should find a gender congruency effect in the production of plural gender definite nouns.

3.3.1 Materials

Forty target line drawings were selected from Experiment 1, i.e. 20 (noun + -*siniʔ* [plural gender definite noun]) and 20 (noun + -*siʔ* [masculine or feminine] nonplural gender definite nouns). A total of 120 (20 [pictures] x 2 [genders] x 3 [conditions] = 120) trials in three blocks were used in this experiment. The list of items used in Experiment 2 can be found in Appendix B.

Table 7: Examples of the experimental items used in Experiment 2

Target gender	Target picture	Distractor conditions		
		Congruent	Incongruent	Neutral
Plural gender definite noun	*filaasini?* 'the comb'	*oytaasini?* 'the upper part of the compound'	*tuubutasi?* 'the false banana bread'	*pink noise*
Non-plural (m/f) gender definite noun	*kaawwatasi?* 'the glass'	*eetutasi?* 'the dinner'	*pakaannaasini?* 'the root crop'	*pink noise*

3.4 Results and discussion

From a total of 2,880 observations, 491 (17%) were eliminated from the analysis, as they were incorrect responses and 137 (4.76%) were labeled as outliers, RTs outside of 250 to 1,900 ms. Thus, a total of 2,252 (78.19%) data points were included for statistical analysis.

Table 8: Reaction Times (RTs) in ms and error in percentage (%e)

Distractor condition	Congruent	Neutral	Incongruent	Congruency effect
RT (%e)	1210 (7%)	980 (4%)	1223 (6%)	13 (-1%)

Table 8 shows the mean RTs in the three distractor conditions (congruent, neutral and incongruent). An ANOVA was performed with Distractor Condition and Target Gender as independent factors. This analysis showed a significant effect of the factor Distractor Condition in both the subject and the item analyses ($F1 (2,46) = 129.733$, $p < .0001$; $F2 (2,76) = 62.975$, $p < .0001$). It took the participants slightly more time to produce a noun in the gender-incongruent condition than to produce a noun in the gender-congruent and the pink noise condition. The factor Target Gender reached significance only in the item analysis ($F2 (1,38) = 64.489$, $p < .002$). The interaction between Target Gender and Distractor Condition, however, failed to reach significance in both subject and item analyses ($F1 (2,46) = 1.241$, $p < .298$; $F2 (2,76) = .160$, $p < .853$). Although we obtained a 13 ms congruency effect, ANOVAs comparing only the gender-congruent and incongruent conditions did not reach significance for any variable.

To examine the effect of gender congruency between plural-congruent versus plural-incongruent and non-plural congruent versus non-plural incongruent in the distractor conditions, separate ANOVAs were performed on these data. These analyses only showed a significant effect in the subject analysis between plural-congruent versus plural-incongruent (F1 (1,23) = 4.395, p < .047) but not between non-plural congruent versus non-plural incongruent. The congruency effects were 32 ms and −6 ms, respectively, as can be seen in Table 9. Similar to the first experiment that showed no effect of gender congruency in feminine noun productions, the non-plural gender definite nouns (in which half of them are feminine definite nouns taken from Experiment 1) had a non-significant reversed congruency effect.

Table 9: Mean RTs by target gender and distractor condition

Target gender	Distractor conditions			
	Congruent	Incongruent	Neutral	Congruency effect
Plural	1197	1228	977	32
Non-plural	1223	1217	982	−6

Studies investigating the issue of whether the competition for selection hypothesis applies to the retrieval of gender-marked inflections or restricted to only free-standing morphemes like determiners are few and present contradictory results (see Schiller's chapter in this volume).

Schriefers (1993) obtained a congruency effect when participants produced NPs in the form of adjective + noun in Dutch (gender is marked in the adjectives suffixed as bound morphemes, e.g. $groen_{neu}$ $boek_{neu}$ 'green book' versus $groene_{com}$ $tafel_{com}$ 'green table'), suggesting that either the gender features compete for selection, or else there is competition for selection of the bound morphemes associated with the gender inflection of the adjective.

Schiller and Caramazza (2003), however, failed to replicate this result in both German and Dutch (see also Schiller's chapter in this volume). To account for the failure of replicating Schriefers' (1993) result in the production of adjective + noun that involve the selection of a gender-marked bound morpheme, the assumption that the gender congruency effect reflects competition at the level of gender-marked, free-standing morpheme selection is hypothesized (see Schiller's chapter in this volume.

The significant 32 ms congruency effect in plural gender definite noun productions shows the effect could be obtained in gender-marked bound morphemes in Konso. This result is in line with the *gender feature selection hypothesis*

(Schriefers 1993). In light of the present result, one could also argue that the so-called plural gender nouns that take –*sini?* as their definite suffix belong to the proper gender feature in Konso.

4 General discussion

This chapter attempted to address the issue of deciding whether the so-called plural gender is a proper gender value or a value inherent to the number system in Cushitic languages using a picture-word interference paradigm in two experiments. Besides, the psycholinguistic investigations of gender are restricted to a limited number of Germanic and Romance languages. We believe that field-based psycholinguistic investigations in less studied languages are important to provide additional empirical and cross-linguistic evidence as well as to broaden our knowledge of language processing in general and the cognitive representation of gender features in particular. In this regard, we took a new step to fill the gap of cross-linguistic confirmation from non-western languages and to introduce psycholinguistic approaches into the study of Cushitic languages by tackling Konso.

The two experiments reported in this chapter attempted to shed more light on the magnitude of the so-called gender congruency effect in psycholinguistic research, particularly whether or not the effect is obtained in naming bare nouns (Experiment 1), and in naming a noun + a gender-marked inflection (a bound morpheme) (Experiment 2).

In the bare noun production (Experiment 1), we found 35 ms and 20 ms congruency effects for the production of the so-called plural gender nouns and masculine nouns, respectively, though we found no effect of congruency for the feminine nouns. As far as the issue of plural gender in Cushitic is concerned, the 35 ms congruency effect observed in naming plural gender nouns could be taken as a preliminary sign for recognizing plural as a proper gender value in Konso although the 19 ms overall congruency effect is significant only in the subject analysis of the factor Target Gender. Mention was made of the effect in the other factors (that were not significant), which might be masked by the overall slow RTs, lack of overt gender markers on the nouns in the language and methodological issues in relation to the selection of stimuli.

In Experiment 2, we investigated the gender congruency effect in naming nouns with a suffixed definite marker with the prediction that a gender congruency effect in the production of plural gender definite nouns should be observed if (p) is a proper gender value in Konso. We found a significant 32 ms congruency effect in the plural gender definite noun productions. This result provides an indication for the so-called "plural" gender nouns, which take –*sini?* as their definite suffix marker, to belong to the proper gender value in Konso. It also shows that gender congruency effect could be obtained in the production of gender-marked bound morphemes, which confirms the prediction of *gender feature selection hypothesis* (Schriefers 1993).

The non-significant overall 13 ms congruency effect and −6 ms congruency effect in the non-plural gender definite noun production of the present result, however, pose the question whether gender congruency effects are found in a gender-marked bound morpheme production at all. Note that the *gender-marked freestanding morpheme congruency hypothesis* (see Schiller's chapter in this volume) predicts no effect of gender congruency in a gender-marked bound morpheme production. The negative congruency effect observed in the non-plural gender definite nouns might also be due to the overall slow RTs, lack of overt gender marking on the nouns in the language and methodological issues in relation to the selection of stimuli. This is because half of the stimuli in the non-plural gender definite noun group are the feminine nouns that were also used in Experiment 1.

Taken together, the overall results in both experiments fail to reach robust significance levels and hence it is difficult to make any strong generalizations. Parts of the results of the two experiments (i.e. the presence of gender congruency effects in the plural gender nouns in both experiments), however, tend to suggest that the so-called "plural" gender is a proper gender value. Nevertheless, it is emphasized that there is an urgent need for replicating both experiments by giving better trainings to participants, by involving gender marking elements such as verbs as part of the experiment and by replacing part of the stimuli that are identified as problematic with better ones.

5 Acknowledgements

The authors would like to thank Ongaye Orkaydo for his assistance in selecting the materials, and Anto Arkato for recording the experimental stimuli. The authors would also like to express their gratitude to the Leiden University Fund (LUF) for sponsoring Mulugeta's field trip to Ethiopia that was carried out between January and April, 2012. The paper resulted from the project 'Plural as a value of Cushitic gender: a psycholinguistic study', which is part of the Leiden University Center for Linguistics (LUCL) 'Language Diversity in the World' research profile area. Various parts of this paper were presented at the Language and Cognition Group (LACG) meetings, Leiden Institute for Brain and Cognition (LIBC). The authors would like to thank the audience of this group for their valuable comments.

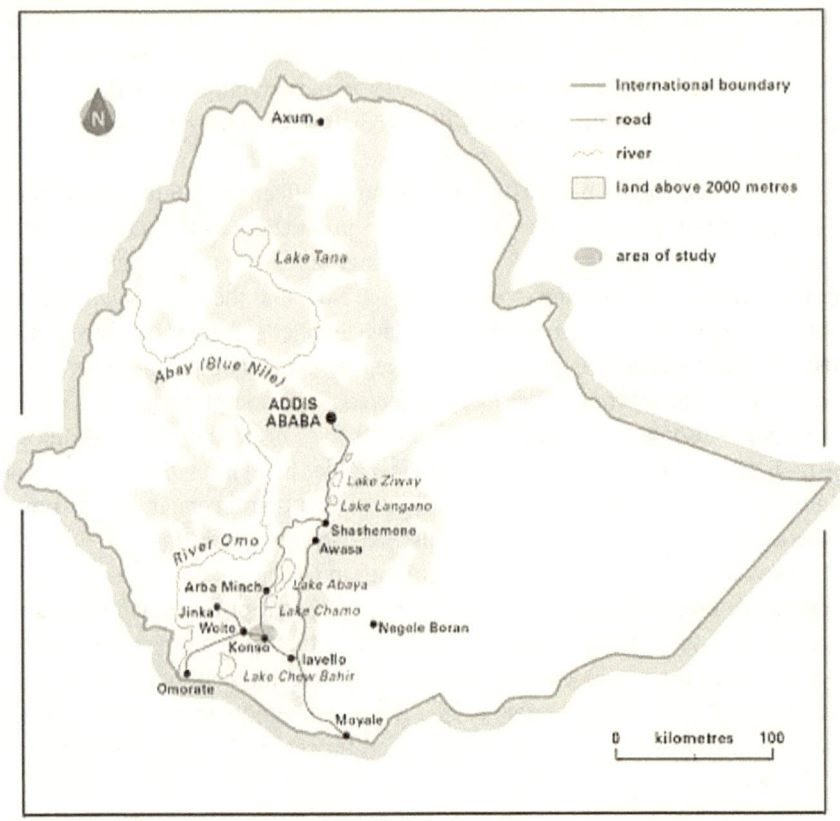

Figure 1: The location of Konso in Ethiopia (map by Ian Agnew: taken, with permission, from http://www.geog.cam.ac.uk/research/projects/konsoethnography/)

6 References

Bordag, Denisa and Thomas Pechmann. 2008. Grammatical gender in speech production: Evidence from Czech. *Journal of Psycholinguistic Research* 37. 69–85.
Caramazza, Alfonso. 1997. How many levels of processing are there in lexical access? *Cognitive Neuropsychology* 14. 177–208.
Central Statistics Agency of Ethiopia (CSA). 2009. Statistical Tables for the 2007 Population and Housing Census of Ethiopia.
Corbett, Greville G. 2012. *Features*. Cambridge: Cambridge University Press.
Corbett, Greville G. 2013. Gender Typology. In Greville G. Corbett (ed.) *The Expression of Gender*. 1–39. Berlin/New York: Mouton de Gruyter.
Corbett, Greville G. and Richard Hayward. 1987. Gender and number in Bayso. *Lingua* 73. 1–28.
Cubelli, Roberto, L. Lotto, Daniela Paolieri, M. Girelli, and Remo Job. 2005. Grammatical gender is selected in bare noun production: Evidence from the picture-word interference paradigm. *Journal of Memory and Language* 53. 42–59.
Hayward, Richard J. 1979. Bayso revisited: Some preliminary linguistic observations II. *BSOAS* 42(1). 101–132.
Hayward, Richard J. 1984. *The Arbore language: A first investigation including a vocabulary* [Kuschitische Sprachstudien 2]. Hamburg: Helmut Buske.
La Heij, Wido, Pim Mak, J. Sander, and E. Willeboordse. 1998. The gender-congruency effect in picture-word tasks. *Psychological Research* 61. 209–219.
Levelt, Willem J. M., Ardi Roelofs, and Antje S. Meyer. 1999. A theory of lexical access in speech production. *Behavioral and Brain Sciences* 22. 1–75.
Mous, Maarten. 2008. Number as an exponent of gender in Cushitic. In Zygmunt Frajzyngier and Erin Shay (eds) *Interaction of Morphology and Syntax: Case Studies in Afroasiatic* (Typological Studies in Language 75), 137–160. Amsterdam: John Benjamins.
Orkaydo, Ongaye Oda. 2013. *A Grammar of Konso*. Utrecht: LOT publications.
Pillinger, Steve and Letiwa Galboran. 1999. *A Rendille dictionary including a grammatical outline and an English-Rendille Index*. Cologne: Rüdiger Köppe.
Savà, Graziano. 2005. *A grammar of Ts'amakko* [Kuschitischen Sprachstudien 22]. Cologne: Rüdiger Köppe.
Schiller, Niels O. and Alfonso Caramazza. 2002. The selection of grammatical features in word production: The case of plural nouns in German. *Brain and Language* 81. 342–357.
Schiller, Niels O. and Alfonso Caramazza. 2003. Grammatical feature selection in noun phrase production: Evidence from German and Dutch. *Journal of Memory and Language* 48. 169–194.
Schiller, Niels O. this volume. Psycholinguistic approaches to the investigation of grammatical gender. In Greville G. Corbett, *The Expression of Gender*. Berlin/New York: Mouton de Gruyter.
Schriefers, Herbert. 1993. Syntactic processes in the production of noun phrases. *Journal of Experimental Psychology: Learning, Memory, and Cognition* 19. 841–850.

7 Appendix

Appendix A: Stimulus materials in Experiment 1

Target picture name	gender	Distractor word conditions*		
		congruent	Incongruent I	Incongruent II
kaawwata 'mirror'	feminine	eetuta 'dinner/supper'	muutiya 'worm'	ɲupuraa 'component of a set of weaving'
lawaʃeeta 'mouse'	feminine	fillayyaata 'flea'	saalpataa 'belt'	pahnaa 'example'
harreeta 'donkey'	feminine	ʃureeta 'dirt'	toma 'bowl'	pakataa 'wide shield'
piirtuta 'sun'	feminine	ʃooɠɠita 'mud'	hoppatta 'guts'	miɗaa 'cabbage leaves'
hiɓta 'lip'	feminine	ʃileeta 'stick used by old women'	kaɓa 'canal for irrigation'	payraa 'type of farm tool'
pottaata 'pumpkin'	feminine	haaruta 'revenge'	hoʃʃa 'cliff'	saaraa 'poem'
ɠapaleeta 'monkey'	feminine	ɗalta 'seed'	xaʔtiya 'fly'	pohaa 'contribution, tribune'
ʃifeeta 'a ring'	feminine	ohta 'cloth (worn in the night)'	kanta 'sub-village'	piʃaa 'water'
napahta 'ear'	feminine	haaɗita 'load, burden'	kasirayta 'tick (parasite)'	paankaa 'machete'
irroota 'mountain'	feminine	hoollata 'sheep skin'	hiiɓa 'meat soup'	peeɠaa 'quarrel'
kaharta 'ewe'	feminine	kaaɓtuta 'farm tool'	hawla 'grave, tomb'	mookkaa 'cassava'
tika 'house'	feminine	koorita 'type of cloth'	sataʔta 'heart'	leɠaa 'a loan (money)'
muukuta 'frog'	feminine	kanaʔta 'palm'	kappaa 'wheat'	teepaa 'rope'
lafta 'bone'	feminine	koromta 'heifer'	karayta 'tributary'	urmalaa 'market'
loɠta 'leg'	feminine	kulleeta 'hood; cap'	ɗaammaa 'flour'	pakaannaa 'root crop'
farta 'horse'	feminine	kusumta 'navel'	ʃenɠera 'hook'	xallaa 'kidney'
tuuyyata 'pig'	feminine	leemmuta 'bubble'	kaasa 'horn'	paarkaalaa 'enemy'
oxinta 'fence'	feminine	kuuɲata 'gnat'	kuuɲata 'gnat'**	dooʃʃaa 'sarcasm'
xampirteeta 'bird'	feminine	kannoota 'calabash to drink from'	ilkitta 'tooth'	koofinaa 'lung'
taaltaallata 'giraffe'	feminine	kawwatta 'terrace'	orritta 'devil'	masaanaa 'autumn'

* For (f) target, (m) is incongruent I and (p) is incongruent II
** Has (f) gender value and also used as a congruent distractor for *oxinta* 'fence' (f)

Appendix A: Stimulus materials in Experiment 1 (continued)

Target picture name	gender	Distractor word conditions*		
		congruent	Incongruent I	Incongruent II
arpa 'elephant'	masculine	hoofa 'hole'	xoraa 'fine, punishment'**	kawlaa 'metal tool for ginning'
kessa 'chest'	masculine	alkitta 'sisal'	mooluta 'bald'	tiraa 'liver'
paala 'feather'	masculine	ekerta 'olive'	noodduta 'bribe'	kolkaa 'food without cabbage'
harka 'arm'	masculine	ɗila 'field'	moonta 'sky'	toorraa 'opposition'
murkuʃaa 'fish'	masculine	falaɠɠitta 'flat stone'	pokkeeta 'short (with pockets)'	tiyyaa 'dispute'
tuyyuuraa 'air plane'	masculine	amma?itta 'breakfast'	paakkuta 'span (measurement)'	xoffaa 'groin'
mottooɠaa 'truck'	masculine	ukkaʃʃa 'husk''	hakayta 'second round harvest'	toʃaa 'water droplet'
sookitta 'salt'	masculine	hallaka 'fat'	paallata 'piece of clay to fetch fire with'	torraa 'speech, talk'
okkatta 'cow'	masculine	urratta 'cloud'	pooyta 'mourning, cry'	ʃaaɓɓaa 'stretcher'
ɠoyra 'tree'	masculine	irɲa 'gum'	poɠoota 'lower jaw'	ilmaamaa 'tears'
tuuma 'onion'	masculine	ʃapara 'rig'	furoota 'type of bead'	sinɗaa 'urine'
lukkalitta 'chicken'	masculine	ditiitaa 'sweat'	ɠaawuta 'coughing'	xapnaa 'forest'
ɠayranta 'leopard'	masculine	ɗa?ta 'butter'	mate?ta 'upper millstone'	xaaʃaa 'reed'
ɠupitta 'finger'	masculine	ʃaɓɓaa 'weed'	ʃaloota 'cotton thread'	kaaʃaa 'money'
kuta 'dog'	masculine	ɗakaa 'stone'	taamta 'branch'	elalaa 'cowrie shell'
oraayta 'hyena'	masculine	ɗapna 'temple'	kala?ta 'spider'	kasaraa 'dreadlocks'
xaʃʃitta 'shoulder'	masculine	ɗamayta 'wind'	talteeta 'she-goat'	ʃaɓɓeernaa 'belt for bullets'
parʃuma 'stool'	masculine	ɗikla 'elbow'	kee?uta 'belching'	eennaa 'vacant homestead'
pora 'road'	masculine	ɠayya 'smoke'	kaankita 'mule'	koottaa 'buttocks'
karmaa 'lion'	masculine	ɗuttana 'belly'	landeeta 'spleen'	ʃiiʃaa 'curse'

* For (m) target, (f) is incongruent I and (p) is incongruent II
** has a (p) gender value

Appendix A: Stimulus materials in Experiment 1 (continued)

Target picture name	gender	Distractor word conditions*		
		congruent	Incongruent I	Incongruent II
innaa 'boy'	plural	hiippaa 'a riddle'	taammata 'desert bee'	hikkitta 'star'
ukukkaa 'egg'	plural	ararsaa 'local beer made for sale'	tampoota 'tobacco'	arrapa 'tongue'
furaa 'key'	plural	aataa 'culture'	tolloʔta 'hump'	kirra 'river'
filaa 'comb'	plural	oytaa 'upper part of the compound'	tuuɓuta 'false banana bread'	kolalta 'acacia'
haaʃʃullaa 'leaf'	plural	makkaa 'sickness'	tulluppaata 'wood boring beetle'	kokaa 'skin, hide'
ɲirfaa 'hair'	plural	aannaa 'milk'	keltoota 'cattle louse'	koɗaa 'work'
uwwaa 'dress'	plural	ellaa 'spirit'	furoota 'type of bead'**	hakalaa 'cabbage'
fulaa 'door'	plural	ikkaamaa 'selected seeds'	χaayyata 'nightmare'	keltayta 'baboon'
rikaa 'a tooth brush'	plural	erkannaa 'message'	yoʔta 'greed'	kawsa 'chin, beard'
timɓaa 'drum'	plural	ipsaa 'light'	χarinta 'horizontally placed fence bar'	ɗankaa 'throat'
siinaa 'nose'	plural	olsaa 'dream'	yaakata 'bead'	karitta 'belly'
χolmaa 'neck'	plural	unɠulaa 'grain store from bamboo'	kaaffata 't'eff'	mura 'forest'
χopaa 'shoe'	plural	ʃorrooɠaa 'eye discharge'	moossuta '(piece of) bread'	leya 'month'
ɲaaɲɲaa 'tomato'	plural	kaariyyaa 'devil (ghost)'	faroota 'luck'	kittayyaa 'bed bug'
kiʔsaa 'cricket'	plural	utaa 'faeces'	aχawuta 'roasted grain'	tokkayta 'porcupine'
afaa 'mouth'	plural	fuuraa 'fear'	puulluta 'fermented dough'	kilpa 'knee'
hirriiɓaa 'eyelash'	plural	ɠolfaa 'bark of trees'	χompalta 'cactus'	fanɠala 'splinter'
akataa 'sugar cane'	plural	ɗarɗaa 'lie, untruth'	ɗuusuta 'fart'	roopa 'rain'
muklaa 'bangle'	plural	hanʃufaa 'saliva'	uffaata 'balloon'	ɗaltayta 'relative'
kupaʔtaa 'tortoise'	plural	marʃaa 'hip'	hiparaata 'bat'	hallaka 'fat'***

* For (p) target, (f) is incongruent I and (m) is incongruent II
** it has also been used as a distractor for the target *tuuma* 'onion' (m)
*** it has also been used as a distractor for the target *sookita* 'salt' (m)

Appendix B: Stimulus materials in Experiment 2

Target picture name	Gender	Distractor word conditions*	
		congruent	Incongruent I
innaasiniʔ 'the boy'	plural	hiippaasiniʔ 'the riddle'	taammatasiʔ 'the desert bee'
ukukkaasiniʔ 'the egg'	plural	ararsaasiniʔ 'the local beer made for sale'	tampootasiʔ 'the tobacco'
furaasiniʔ 'the key'	plural	aataasiniʔ 'the culture'	tolloʔtasiʔ 'the hump'
filaasiniʔ 'the comb'	plural	oytaasiniʔ 'the upper part of the compound'	tuuputasiʔ 'the false banana bread'
haaʃʃullaasiniʔ 'the leaf'	plural	makkaasiniʔ 'sickness'	tulluppaatasiʔ 'the wood boring beetle'
ɲirfaasiniʔ 'the hair'	plural	aannaasiniʔ 'the milk'	keltootasiʔ 'the cattle louse'
uwwaasiniʔ 'the dress'	plural	ellaasiniʔ 'the spirit (e.g. of well)'	furootasiʔ 'the type of bead'
fulaasiniʔ 'the door'	plural	ikkaamaasiniʔ 'the selected seed'	χaayyatasiʔ 'the nightmare'
rikaasiniʔ 'the tooth brush'	plural	erkannaasiniʔ 'the message'	yoʔtasiʔ 'the greed'
timɓaasiniʔ 'the drum'	plural	ipsaasiniʔ 'the light'	χarintasiʔ 'the horizontally placed fence bar'
siinaasiniʔ 'the nose'	plural	olsaasiniʔ 'the dream'	karittasiʔ 'the belly'
χolmaasiniʔ 'the neck'	plural	unɠulaasiniʔ 'the grain store from bamboo'	murasiʔ 'the forest'
χopaasiniʔ 'the shoe'	plural	forrooɠaasiniʔ 'the eye discharge'	leyasiʔ 'the month'
ɲaaɲɲaasiniʔ 'the tomato'	plural	kaariyyaasiniʔ 'the devil (ghost)'	kittayyaasiʔ 'the bed bug'
kiʔsaasiniʔ 'the cricket'	plural	utaasiniʔ 'the faces'	arrapasiʔ 'the tongue'
afaasiniʔ 'the mouth'	plural	fuuraasiniʔ 'the fear'	kilpasiʔ 'the knee'
hirriiɓaasiniʔ 'the eyelash'	plural	ɠolfaasiniʔ 'the bark of trees'	keltaytasiʔ 'the baboon'
akataasiniʔ 'the sugar cane'	plural	ɗarɗaasiniʔ 'the lie'	koɗaasiʔ 'the work'
muklaasiniʔ 'the bangle'	plural	hanʃufaasiniʔ 'the saliva'	kawsasiʔ 'the chin, the beard'
kupataasiniʔ 'the tortoise'	plural	marʃaasiniʔ 'the hip'	ɗankaasiʔ 'the throat'

* Half of the incongruent distractors are masculine and the other half are feminine nouns

Appendix B: Stimulus materials in Experiment 2 (continued)

Target picture name		Gender	Distractor word conditions			
			Congruent		Incongruent	
harreetasiʔ	'the donkey'	feminine	ʃureetasiʔ	'the dirt'	peeɠaasiniʔ	'the quarrel'
hiɓtasiʔ	'the lip'	feminine	ʃileetasiʔ	'the stick used by old women'	pakataasiniʔ	'the wide shield'
irrootasiʔ	'the mountain'	feminine	hoollatasiʔ	'the sheep skin'	midaasiniʔ	'the cabbage leaves'
ʃifeetasiʔ	'the ring'	feminine	ohtasiʔ	'the cloth (worn in the night)'	piʃaasiniʔ	'the water'
kaawwatasiʔ	'the glass'	feminine	eetutasiʔ	'the dinner'	pakaannaasiniʔ	'the root crop'
lawasheetasiʔ	'the mouse'	feminine	fillayyaatasiʔ	'the flea'	saaraasiniʔ	'the poem'
napahtasiʔ	'the ear'	feminine	haaditasiʔ	'the load, burden'	paankaasiniʔ	'the machete'
piirtutasiʔ	'the sun'	feminine	ʃooggitasiʔ	'the mud'	χapnaasiniʔ	'the forest'
pottaatasiʔ	'the pumpkin'	feminine	haarutosiʔ	'the revenge'	kaaʃaasiniʔ	'the money'
ɠapaleetasiʔ	'the monkey'	feminine	daltasiʔ	'the seed'	pohaasiniʔ	'the contribution, the tribune'
arpasiʔ	'the elephant'	masculine	hoofasiʔ	'the hole'	tiraasiniʔ	'the liver'
harkasiʔ	'the arm'	masculine	dilasiʔ	'the field'	pahnaasiniʔ	'the example'
kessasiʔ	'the chest'	masculine	alkittasiʔ	'the sisal'	torraasiniʔ	'the speech, the talk'
mottooɠaasiʔ	'the truck'	masculine	ukkaʃʃasiʔ	'the husk'	toʃaasiniʔ	'the water droplet'
murkuʃaasiʔ	'the fish'	masculine	ʃalaɠɠittasiʔ	'the flat stone'	kawlaasiniʔ	'the metal tool for ginning'
okkattasiʔ	'the cow'	masculine	urrattasiʔ	'the cloud'	ʃaaɓɓaasiniʔ	'the stretcher'
paalasiʔ	'the feather'	masculine	ekertasiʔ	'the olive'	tiyyaasiniʔ	'the dispute'
ɠoyrasiʔ	'the tree'	masculine	irɲasiʔ	'the gum'	χoffaasiniʔ	'the groin'
tuumasiʔ	'the onion'	masculine	ʃaparasiʔ	'the rig'	ɲupuraasiniʔ	'the component of a set of weaving'
tuyyuuraasiʔ	'the air plane'	masculine	ammaʔittasiʔ	'the breakfast'	χaaʃaasiniʔ	'the reed'

Author index

Aalto, Penti 50
Abbott, Clifford 142
Abe, Hideko Nornes 43
Adam, Lucien 60
Adelaar, Willem 60
Adriaen, Monique 12
Alario, François-Xavier 162, 168, 180
Allan, Keith 75
American Dialect Society 20
Annand, Joseph 54
Audring, Jenny 104–105
Austin, Peter 111

Baker, John R. 53
Ballard, William L. 41
Barbin, Hercule 17
Bargh, John A. 79
Baron, Naomi 24
Barrett, Rusty 26
Basilico, David 83
Beardsley, Elizabeth Lane 22
Bell, Eleanor O. 75
Bem, Sandra L. 70
Benor, Sarah B. 73, 76, 83
Bertinetti, Marco 97
Birdsong, David 72–73, 83
Birtalan, Agnes 50
Black, Maria 34
Bloomfield, Leonard 33–34, 36
Bock, J. Kathryn 72
Bodine, Anne 69, 71–72, 84
Bogoras, Waldemar 55
Bordag, Denisa 193–194
Boroditsky, Lera 5
Bradley, John 50–51
Breton, Raymond 58
Brown, Dunstan 112
Brown, Lea 123
Browne, Gerald M. 96
Burani, Cristina 108
Burr, Elisabeth 11–13
Butler, Judith 84

Cabral, Ana Suelly 58
Camden, William G. 53
Cameron, Deborah 17
Campbell, Lyle 58
Caramazza, Alfonso 162, 169–170, 173–174, 176, 178–179, 194, 202, 205
Cassidy, Kimberley 75
Caudwell, Sarah 92
Chafe, Wallace 142
Charlie, Bella 50–51
Chatterjee, Anjan 83
Chumakina, Marina 98, 107–108
Clark, Michael J. 44
Comrie, Bernard 122
Connors, Kathleen 12
Cooper, William E. 69–73, 75–78, 84
Corbett, Greville G. 4, 5, 9, 87, 89, 91, 94, 96, 100–102, 105, 107–109, 112, 117, 124, 135, 150, 161, 191–192
Costa, Albert 162–163, 168, 178–179
Coward, Rosalind 34
Cowell, Mark W. 119n
Cresson, Edith 12
Cubelli, Roberto 194, 203
Curzan, Anne 6–8, 20, 22
Cutler, Anne 81

De Lauretis, Teresa 84
De Vogelaar, Gunther 104
De Vos, Lien 104
Deaux, Kay 77, 79
Demuth, Katherine 118n
Dešeriev, Ju. D. 95
Diekman, Amanda B. 77, 79
Dixon, R. M. W. 105, 115
Dol, Philomena 101
Donohue, Mark 101–104
Drude, Sebastian 61–62
Dryer, Matthew S. 123
Dunn, Michael 54

Eagly, Alice H. 77, 79
Eckert, P. 40
Ekka, Francis 49

Enfield, Nick 135
Enger, Hans-Olaf 118
Evans, Nicholas 112
Everett, Daniel L. 44, 59–60

Fausto-Sterling, Anne 16–17
Fedden, Sebastian 112–113, 123
Fenk-Oczlon, Gertrude 73, 75, 81
Finocchiaro, Chiara 173, 178–179
Fiske, Susan T. 77
Flannery, Regina 56
Fleming, Luke 46
Fletcher, Katie 77
Fortune, David L. 62
Fortune, Gretchen 62
Foucault, Michel 17
François, Alexandre 52
Frank, Francine W. 33

Gagua, Rasudan 96
Ganushchak, Lesya Y. 180
Gelfer, Marylou Pausewang 44
Glück, Helmut 42, 55–56
Goddard, Cliff 101

Haas, Mary R. 42–43, 47, 57
Hall, Kira 17–20
Hantsch, Ansgar 170, 180
Harmer, L. C. 123
Haviland, John 100
Hay, Jennifer 75, 77
Hayward, Richard J. 114, 191–192
Healy, Bernard 26
Hegarty, Peter L. 77–80, 83
Heim, Stefan 180
Henry, Victor 60
Hillenbrand, James M. 44
Hilton, Denis J. 76
Hock, Hans Henrich 47
Hockett, Charles F. 89, 132
Hoff, Berend J. 58
Hoffman, Curt 77
Holisky, Dee Ann 96
Hough, Carole 75
Hurst, Nancy 77

Iacobini, Claudio 108
Inoue, Miyako 43
Institut National de la Langue Française 12

Jack, Frances 131
Janssen, Nils 168, 170
Jescheniak, Jörg D. 170, 180
Johnson, Mark 9
Jospin, Lionel 11–12

Karatsareas, Petros 118n
Keil, Frank C. 72
Kelly, Michael H. 72–73, 75
Khosroshashi, Fatemah 30
Kibrik, Aleksandr E. 107, 110
Kimball, Geoffrey 47, 57
King, Ruth 12
Kirton, Jean 50–51
Klein, Jared 93
Kölligan, Daniel 93n
Krifka, Manfred 10
Kroskrity, Paul V. 46
Kulick, Don 17

La Heij, Wido 169, 194, 202
Labov, William 40, 47
Lakoff, George 115
Leger, Rudolf 122
LeMaster, Barbara 49
Lemhöfer, Kristin 180
Lemieux, Anthony F. 83
Levelt, Willem J.M. 169, 193, 202
Levy, Roger 73, 76, 83
Lewis, Laurie L. 79
Lieberson, Stanley 75
Lindström, Eva 119–121
Livia, Anna 14–15, 17, 24
Lounsbury, Floyd 142
Lunau, K. 41n
Luthin, Herbert 47

Maass, Anne 83–84
McConnell-Ginet, Sally 6, 27, 31, 40, 71, 79, 84
McDonald, Janet L. 72–73, 76, 83
McQueen, Grant 77, 83
Major, Brenda 77

Author index

Malkiel, Yakov 69–71, 74–78, 83–84
Matasović, Ranko 87–88
Mathiot, Madeline 26
Matossian, Lou Ann 30
Mel'čuk, Igor 92
Mervis, Carolyn B. 72
Meyer, Antje S. 169, 202
Mikelson, Kelly S. 75
Mikos, Victoria A. 44
Miozzo, Michele 162, 169, 178
Mithun, Marianne 4, 47, 83, 121, 145
Modi, Bharati 115
Mollin, Sandra 69, 73–74, 76, 83
Motschenbacher, Heiko 42, 56
Mous, Maarten 191–192, 195
Muchnik, Malka 36
Muysken, Pieter 60

Naito, Maho 53
Neuberg, Steven L. 77
Nevalainen, Terttu 3
Newman, Michael 30
Noël, Georgine 14–16
Norton, F. J. 123–124

Ochs, Elinor 47
O'Donovan, Veronica 18
Orkaydo, Ongaye Oda 193–195, 203
Orne, Martin 76

Palancar, Enrique 123–124
Pandharipande, Rajeshwari 47
Parker, E. M. 114
Parry, Sir William Edward 44
Pastre, Geneviève 17, 26
Pechmann, Thomas 193–194
Pinker, Steven 72–73, 83
Plaster, Keith 113, 115–116
Polinsky, Maria 113, 115–116, 118
Pollard, Carl 9
Potter, Simeon 74
Pratto, Felicia 79

Queen, Robin 26

Raumolin-Runberg, Helena 3
Ribeiro, Eduardo 62

Roberts, Marjorie 26
Rochefort, Charles de 39, 58
Rodina, Yulia 118n
Roelofs, Ardi 169, 202
Rosch, Eleanor 9, 72
Rose, Françoise 60
Ross, John Robert 69–73, 75–78, 84
Roudy, Yvette 12
Rovai, Francesca 121n
Rudes, Blair A. 26
Russo, Aurore 83

Sag, Ivan 9
Sans, Pierric 60
Sapir, Edward 47
Saville-Troike, Muriel 47, 57
Schapper, Antoinette 124
Scheffler, Harold W. 41
Schiller, Niels O. 104, 168–169, 173, 176, 179–180, 194, 205, 207
Schriefers, Herbert 161, 163–164, 169–170, 173–174, 176–177, 179–180, 193–194, 205–207
Seifart, Frank 105–106
Sen, Sukamara 41
Sharoni, Lee'at J. 75
Sherzer, Joel 40
Simpson, Adrian P. 44
Skorik, Piotr Ja. 40
Southwood, Helen 83
Spivak, Michael 25
Stein, David E. S. 121n
Stolz, Christel 121
Suitner, Catarine 84

Taylor, Allan R. 56
Taylor, D. 58
Terrill, Angela 99, 121, 123
Thornton, Anna M. 108, 110, 118, 121
Treichler, Paula, A. 33
Tryon, Darrell T. 52
Twain, Mark 4

Vallejos Yopán, Rosa 58–59
Verdonschot, Rinus G. 180
Visser, Willem 121

Wagner, Gunter 41
Watson, Nila 77
Wechsler, Sara 118n
Wegener, Claudia 123
Whissell, Cynthia 75
Whitehead, Neil L. 58
Whittaker, G. 47

Wickler, W. 41n
Wright, Saundra 75–78, 81, 83

Yokoyama, Olga 41

Zaliznjak, Andrej A. 90, 92

Language index

Afar (Qafar) 114–115, 118
Alagwa 194
Algonquian languages 111, 124
Alutor 54–55
Arabic 119n
Arawak 58
Archi 98–99, 107–108
Austro-Asiatic languages 111
Austronesian languages 124
Awetí 45, 61–62

Bagwalal 110–111, 114, 116
Batsbi 91, 95–96
Bayso 191–194
Bengali 41
Bésɨro (Chiquitano) 60
Biblical Hebrew 121n
Bininj Gun-wok 112, 122
Boni 194
Burmeso 101–104
Burunge 194

Cappadocian Greek 118n
Catalan 162, 178
Cayuga 142–143
Central Pomo 131
Cherokee 141–142
Chiquitano 60
Chukchi 1, 39, 43–46, 54–56
Chukotko-Kamchatkan languages 54
Classical Armenian 92–94, 96
Croatian 163–164, 168, 173, 176, 178–179
Cushitic languages 2, 191–194

Dirayta 194
Diyari 111
Dravidian languages 111, 125
Dutch 104–105, 161–163, 169–180, 193–194
Dyirbal 113, 115–116

Emegul 47
Emesal 47
English 1, 5–11, 20–37, 69–86, 180

Five Nations languages 142–143
French 5–6, 9, 11–12, 14–17, 26, 91, 95–96, 115, 162, 178

German 4–6, 9–10, 161–170, 173, 176, 178–180
Germanic languages 125, 178
Gros Ventre 45, 56
Gujarati 115
Guugu Yimidhirr 100–101, 104

Hebrew 36
Hijra Boli 19
Hindi 17–20
Huron 141–142

Indo-European languages 4, 8, 116, 119n
Iraqw 192, 194
Irish Sign Language 43, 45–46, 48–49, 63
Iroquoian languages 1, 121, 141–143
Island Carib 46, 57–58
Italian 97–98, 108–109, 121, 162, 173, 176, 178, 203

Japanese 3, 43

Kala Lagaw Ya 111
Kalmyk 50
Kannada 111
Karajá 62–63
Kerek 54
Khoisan 111
Koasati 45, 47, 57
Kokama-Kokamilla 45–46, 58–59
Konso 2, 191–208
Koryak 54
Kuot 118–121
Kupto 122–123
Kurux 45, 49–50
Kushi 123

Latin 108–109, 121n
Lavukaleve 99–100, 121, 123

Macedonian 108
Maltese 121
Mawng 123
Maybrat 101
Mele-Fila 101
Mian 105, 112, 123
Miraña 105–106
Mohawk 1, 4, 83, 131–160

Ngan'gityemerri 105
Niger Congo languages 111, 124
Northern Iroquoian 141–143

Oceanic languages 53
Old English 22
Old Nubian 96–97
Oneida 142
Onodaga 142

Palana Koryak 55
Papuan languages 121, 123–124
Parji 111
Pidgin Carib 58
Pirahã 44–46, 59–60
Portuguese 62
Prakrit 47
Proto-Five-Nations 142
Proto-Iroquoian 141–142
Proto-Northern-Iroquoian 142
Proto-Oceanic 53

Qafar 114–115, 118

Rendille 194
Retuarã 105

Romanian 91, 93–96
Russian 55–56, 89–91, 113, 116–119

Sanskrit 47
Savosavo 123
Seneca 142–143
Sesotho 118n
Southern Bole-Tangale languages 122
Southern Iroquoian 141–142
Spanish 123, 162, 178
Sumerian 47
Swedish 25

Tamil 1, 111
Tangoan 45–46, 52–54, 63
Tariana 105
Thai 43
Tidore 105
Ts'amakko 194
Tsez 122
Tsova Tush 91
Tuscarora 141, 143
Tutuba 52–53

Walman 123
Wendat 141–142
West Frisian 121
Wyandot 142

Yana 47
Yanyuwa 45–46, 50–52
Yawuru 123
Yuchi 41
Yup'ik 54, 131

Subject index

accusative case 93
adjectives 108–109
age and gender assignment 10
agency 77
agents 143–144
agreement
 – feminine forms 146–158
 – gender systems 132–133
 – and referential pressures 8–11
agreement classes 90–91, 96, 102–104
Agreement Hierarchy 9
agreement targets 3–4, 6
anaphora 8
androcentrism and word order 70–71
animals 134–135
animate first rule 72–73
anyone 29–30
areal variation 52
assumptions, about gender 27–28
avoidance language 50
awareness of gender 1

bare noun naming 169, 180, 198–203, 206
behavioral effects of Det NP production 180
binomial phrases
 – androcentrism 70–71
 – change over time 74
 – effects of stereotyping 78–80
 – empirical studies 72–74
 – flexibility 73–74
 – frequency of occurrence 73
 – name order 74–78
 – phonology 72–76, 81–82
 – proximity 75
 – semantics 72–73, 76–78, 80
 – situation-specific 74
 – word order preferences 69–71
birdsong 41n
boys' use of female dialect 60
British National Corpus 73

ceremonial speech 135, 150
children's acquisition of rules 118n
class markers 106

classification, gender as 89
classifiers 105–106
cognitive associations 27–28
combined case system 101, 104
combined gender system 104
conceptual baggage 27–28, 79
conservatism, origins of gender dialects 46
correlates of gender 47
cross-expressing 17
culture and language 131

definite nouns, Konso experiments 203–206
deictic reference 8–10
demonstrative pronouns 8
determiner competition hypothesis 178
dialect merger 46
dialect, use of term 40
dialect variation *see* gender dialects
Differential Object Marking 124
Differential Subject Marking 124
diversification, origins of gender dialects 46
division of labor, and gender assignment 11–13, 36
double-gender 12, 36
drift, origins of gender dialects 46

E/e 25
em/eir/eirs/eirself 25
enforced gendering 21–25
epicene forms, neologisms 24–25
epicene nouns 5, 11
euphemism 45–50
everyone 29
expressive usage 13–20, 26–27
Ey/ey 25

false generics 34–35
familiarity and name order 78
feminine alternatives 36
feminine forms 136–143, 146–158
feminine generics, enforced gendering 31–33
feminine-indefinite form 137–138, 142–145
feminine-zoic form 137–140, 142

Subject index

feminism 11–13, 35
feminization 12–13, 36
feminizing affixes 35
formal assignment 113–125
formant frequency 44
France, linguistic politics 11–13
French literature, minority identities 14–17
frequency (hz) 44
frequency of occurrence
– and name order 74–76
– and word order 73
frozen binomials 69–71

Garifuna people 39
gay men 17, 26
gender
– correlates of 47
– derivation of term 89
– use of term 3
gender and number 191–196
gender assignment 4–5, 9–10
– biological and social 40–42
– and characteristics 5–6
– and division of labor 11–13, 36
– formal assignment 113–125
– human beings 8
– loanwords 121
– morphological assignment 116–121
– phonological assignment 114–116
– recategorization 121–124
– semantic assignment 110–113
gender attribution, avoiding 22
gender congruency effect 161–164, 193–194
– discussion of experiments 177–181
– indefinite determiner NPs experiment, Dutch 169–174
– indefinite determiner NPs experiment, German 164–169
– Konso experiments 196–208
– possessive adjective NP production experiment, Dutch 174–177
– stimulus materials 184–189
gender dialects 30
– acquisition 43
– areal variation 46
– bidialectalism 43
– categorical 40

– derivation 45
– distribution map 48
– documentation 40
– lexical differences 45
– morphological differences 45
– origins 46
– structural typology 44–45
– typology 42–43
– usage 42–43
gender disagreement 9–10
gender equity 36–37
gender feature competition hypothesis 164, 168–169, 174, 177
gender feature selection hypothesis 205–206
gender ideologies 30
gender-incongruence 62
gender marking 19, 35
gender-neutrality 22–25, 36
gender separation 63
gender stereotypes 27–28, 32, 77–80
gender systems
– agreement 132–133
– Cushitic 191–193
– distribution 124–125
– grammatical vs. natural 3–8
– interactions with sex and sexuality 6
– reform strategies 35–37
– see also gender typology
gender typology
– analysis problem 89–90
– assignment 110
– distinction across lexemes 106–110
– distribution 124–125
– evidence for 90–91
– formal assignment 113–125
– morphological assignment 116–121
– phonological assignment 114–116
– recategorization 121–124
– semantic assignment 110–113
– unique distinction 97–100
– word classes 100–106
– see also gender systems
gender variation, phonetic expression 44
genderlect 41–42
– see also gender dialect
generics 13, 31–33, 105, 136

genus alternans 94
grammatical categories, development 131
grammatical gender 4–6, 21
grammatical gender systems, vs. natural 3–8
greetings cards, name order 77
Gricean pragmatics 76

he generic use 29, 71
hen 25
heterosexuality, presumptions of 28
hijras 17–20
Histoire naturelle et morale des Iles Antilles 39
hit neuter pronoun 22
human beings 8
humanity, as male 34–35
hybrid nouns 9–10

ideologies 30
inanimates 134–135
indefinite determiner NPs experiment, Dutch 169–174, 177
– stimulus materials 187–189
indefinite determiner NPs experiment, German 164–169, 177
– stimulus materials 184–186
indefinite forms, extension 143–145
Independent Network (IN) model 202
inflection classes 102, 117–118, 120
inflectional morphology 89
inquorate gender values 96
interference effects 169–170, 193–194, 202–203
internal change, origins of gender dialects 46
internal evidence, feminine-indefinite form 143–145
internet, name order 77
intersexualism 16–17
it in reference to humans 22–23

job titles 11
Journal of a second voyage for the discovery of a north-west passage from the Atlantic to the Pacific (Parry) 44

kinship terms 41, 143–146

labeling 17, 36
ladies and gentlemen, word order 74–75
language
– and culture 131
– and social status 47
– written 47
language ideologies 30
lesbians 17, 26
lexical differences, gender dialects 45
liminal identity 14, 17–18
linguistic politics 11–13, 25
linguistic processing, effects of grammatical gender 161–162
linguistic strategies 35
loanwords 55–56, 62, 87, 121

Mädchen gender agreement 10
male-first hypothesis 70
male humanity, as humanity 34–35
-man suffix, masculinity 36
maps
– distribution of gender dialects 48
– Konso 208
markedness 73
masculine forms 133–134
masculine generics 29–30
me-first principle 70–71, 77–78
minority identities
– gay men 17
– hijras 17–20
– intersexualism 16–17
– lesbians 17
– transsexuals 14–16
morphological assignment 116–121
morphological differences 157
– gender dialects 45

name order
– effects of stereotyping 78–80
– phonology and frequency 74–76
– and popularity 81–82
names
– form of 143
– as gendered 22
– number of syllables 75, 81

- phonological characteristics and popularity 82
- statistical differences 75
- structure, and word order 81

natural gender
- in English 20–21
- as myth 18–19

natural gender systems
- as potentially misleading 7–8
- vs. grammatical 3–8

neologisms, gender-neutral 24–25
neuter forms 134
non-autonomous values 96–97
notional gender systems 3, 5–7, 21, 79
noun classifiers 105–106
noun phrase (NP)
- *any/every* 29
- pronoun choice 21

nouns, assignment of gender 1, 4–5
number 122, 134–135, 151
number and gender 191–196

parent, gender assignment 32
patients 143–144
personal pronouns 8
phonetic expression, gender variation 44
phonological assignment 114–116
phonological factors, sex identification 44–45
phonology
- name order 74–76
- word order 72–73, 81–82

physical separation of genders 63
picture-word interference paradigm 163
plural masculine forms, as generic 13
portraits 83–84
possessive adjective NP production experiment, Dutch 174–177
- stimulus materials 187–189

power source first rule 77
prescriptive grammar, pronoun choice 5
prestige in gender dialects 47, 53
presumptive leaps 27–29
pronoun choice 5, 6–9, 21
pronoun switching 26–27
prototypical first rule 71–72, 78
proximity and word order 75

psycholinguistics 2
- behavioral effects of Det NP production 180
- discussion of experiments 177–181
- further research 206
- gender congruency effect 161–164
- indefinite determiner NPs experiment, Dutch 169–174
- indefinite determiner NPs experiment, German 164–169
- neurocognitive effects in gender classification task 180
- possessive adjective NP production experiment, Dutch 174–177
- stimulus materials 184–189

quantifiers 29–31

recategorization 121–124
referential pressures and agreement 8–11
referentially linked pronouns 5
reform strategies 35–37

selection mechanisms 180
selection of grammatical features 181
selection of lexical nodes 181
self-attribution 13–17, 20
semantic assignment 110–113
semantics, word order 72–73, 76–78, 83
separation of genders 63
sex
- as permanent personal characteristic 23
- use of term 3

sex-differentiability, threshold 122–123
sex identification, phonological factors 44–45
sex reassignment 14
sexually mixed groups, gender assignment 13
shamanism 55
she 20–21
significance of gender divisions 3
singular feminine generics 31–33
situation-specificity, word order 74
social status, and language 47
sociocultural gender 3, 8–11

sociolinguistic variables, stigmatized and prestige 47
Spivak pronouns 25
stereotypes 27–28, 77
suffixes 35–36
syllables, number and word order 72, 75, 81

taboos 50, 55
"The Awful German Language" (Twain) 4
they 22, 29–31
third sex, hijras 17–20
transsexuals 14–16, 23

United States, promotion of gender-neutrality 36
unknown sex 29

variable gender agreement 9
variations in gender assignment 5
verb forms, gender-marked endings 19
visibility, males and females 34

WEAVER++ model 202–203
wifman 22
word order 75
– androcentrism 70–71
– change over time 74
– effects of stereotyping 78–80
– empirical studies 72–74
– flexibility 73–74
– and frequency of occurrence 73
– frozen binomials 69–70
– names 74–78
– phonology 72–76, 81–82
– preferences 69–71
– proximity 75
– semantics 72–73, 76–78, 83
– situation-specific 74
– and word popularity 81–82
World Atlas of Language Structures (WALS) 124
written language 47

ze/zir/zirs/zirself 25

www.ingramcontent.com/pod-product-compliance
Lightning Source LLC
Chambersburg PA
CBHW021353300426
44114CB00012B/1212